When I was on the TARTAR

BLACK CAT SEA STORIES

AS TOLD BY JACK

MICHAEL PAYNE

Royal Naval MUSEUM PUBLICATIONS

SUTTON PUBLISHING

First published in the United Kingdom in 1999 by
Sutton Publishing Limited · Phoenix Mill
Thrupp · Stroud · Gloucestershire · GL5 2BU
in association with The Royal Naval Museum, Portsmouth

British Library Cataloguing in Publication Data
A catalogue record for this book is available from the British Library

ISBN 0 7509 2286 9

Whether a sailor says 'in' or 'on' a Royal Navy ship will depend on if he
or she is an officer or a rating. An officer will tend to say 'in', a rating
'on'. As this book has been written by a former rating about life on the
lower deck, we have opted for the title *When I Was on the* Tartar to reflect
this variation.

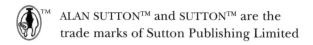 ᵀᴹ ALAN SUTTON™ and SUTTON™ are the
trade marks of Sutton Publishing Limited

Typeset in 10/13pt New Baskerville.
Typesetting and origination by
Sutton Publishing Limited.
Printed in Great Britain by
Biddles, Guildford, Surrey.

This is dedicated to my wife Jan, my Mum and my (now passed away) Dad. Without the second and third I would never have been in a position to write it – without the first I would never have bothered!
I further apologize to my wife for all the Saturday afternoons and other evenings I have spent writing this, when I could, according to her, have been helping her in the garden! Mind you, I do cook Sunday lunch . . .
I also dedicate it to the memory of a great inspiration to me – Mr Alan Chalker who I met only briefly before he died, suddenly. He took great delight in showing me the book he was researching, on the military careers of his ancestors.
They say there is a book inside everyone, waiting to get out. I regard Alan as my catalyst. Perhaps he really was the trigger I had been waiting for, and I thank him for that.

Contents

Contents

Foreword

In his Dedication, the author reminds us that it has been said 'There is a book inside everyone . . .'. For most of us that is where it stays, inside, but Michael Payne has fulfilled a desire to tell his story – the story of twelve years spent in the Senior Service: The Royal Navy. Enlisting at sixteen, the period covers his transition from boyhood to manhood, although it would seem the Navy makes no allowances for youth, and also disregards age in its demands and expectations.

The story is postwar, so there are no epic battles relived here. On the contrary, there is much about having a good time: visits to foreign places, much drinking, joking, teasing, and testing the limits of tolerance – sometimes of comrades, sometimes of those in command. Camaraderie was the essence of life ashore and no doubt an essential ingredient in the cramped conditions of a small metal ship subjected to the rigours of sailing in storm force conditions.

Some readers may find the language offensive – the slang terms, the swearing and the obscenities – but anyone who has served in the forces will know the author is portraying life as it really is in those spheres. An expurgated version would placate the sensitive mind, but would also be unreal.

For ex-matelots this book will revive memories of their own experiences and escapades. Others will find it enlightening and the racy style makes it an enjoyable read.

Admiral Sir (John) Jeremy Black GBE, KCB, DSO
Commander-in-Chief, Naval Home Command, 1989–91

Acknowledgements

The acknowledgements for this book are made to many thousands of people – to those I went ashore with, and those I met while ashore, to those I drank with, ate with, swore at, played cards with, learned from, taught seamanlike skills to, taught antisocial things to, trained with, lent money to, borrowed money from, sang with, did favours for, swam with, saw things with, 'subbed' for, did rare, stupid and often dangerous things with, turned to with, did basin trials with, threatened, tied bends with, tied bends on, went on benders with, learned things from, taught un-seamanlike skills to, tied hitches with, tied hitches on, laughed at, laughed with, cried with, performed with, got frustrated with, played uckers with and more often than not beat, threw uckers tables at if I lost, threw wobblies at, threw spikes and chipping hammers at, did innumerable other, various, assorted, unmentionable, and best forgotten things with and, if I've omitted anyone above – all those who remember serving alongside me. I probably wouldn't recognize you nowadays if I ran over you, however, I still think about you, good or bad, and about the times we were forced to share.

I have, though, deliberately omitted you from the above list if you either accidentally or deliberately gave me the ache, as I also refused to accept you into my life at the time. I hope you have subsequently had a bad life, because on the form you had when I knew you, you very much deserved it. There is a simple rule – if I went ashore with you, or spoke to you ashore, you were probably classed as a 'good hand'. If I spoke to you onboard, voluntarily, you were probably a good hand, but I never got around to proving it. Otherwise . . .

However, and notwithstanding the previous disclaimer, I acknowledge, and above all happily wish well, all those people who gave me their friendship and trust, as I, in return, gave mine, and I thank all those very same people who gave me that trust and friendship during my naval days. If you ever met me, you will know who you are.

I will remember you for the rest of my life, especially if you served between 1969 and 1980, on the *Achilles, Active, Aisne, Ajax, Albion, Antrim,*

Acknowledgements

Apollo, Arethusa, Argonaut, Ark Shark, *Ashanti, Blake, Bristol,* Bagshanty, *Bellerophon, Bulwark, Cavalier,* Cherry-B, *Chichester, Beachampton, Brighton,* 'The Britt', *Bulwark,* Cleo, *Coventry, Dainty, Danae, Devonshire,* Didlo, *Dundas, Eagle, Eastbourne, Eskimo,* Kepple, *Euryalus, Exmouth, Grenville, Minerva, Falmouth, Fearless, Exmouth, Mohawk,* Glamorous-Organ, Tigger, *Llandaff, Salisbury,* Raving-J (*Juno*), *Gurkha, Hardy,* Herpes, Hermi-One, *Naiad, Intrepid, Lowestoft, Penelope, Scarborough, Phoebe, Rothesay, Rhyl,* Torquack, *Scylla, Sirius, Triumph, Ulster, London, Kent, Yarmouth, Nubian, Norfolk, Whitby,* Unwanted or *Tenby,* or RASed with me from *Olmeda, Olna, Olwen,* Tiddlypoo, *Tidespring, Blue Rover,* or any other RFA during that time.

Also, anyone who served ashore (remember shore drafts?) in *Cochrane, Rooke, Dolphin, Osprey, Raleigh, Dryad, Drake, Excellent, Vernon, Sultan, Collingwood, Mercury, Malabar, Victory, President, Tamar, St Angelo, Terror* and *Nelson.* I mention these as I either visited, exercised with, tied up alongside, got 'called round', or saw you in the distance somewhere!

I will also never forget you if you were on any of the ships sunk by the Argies, just after I was discharged. I cried for days whenever I watched that on the television. I had mates on the *Sheffield,* the *Coventry* and the *Amazon,* and I still can't watch it when they show it, even now.

But my thanks and memories go most especially to those who were with me on the *Zulu* (1970–2), *Tartar* (1973–6), *Plymouth* (1977–8), *Londonderry* (1979–80), or *Raleigh, Dryad,* or *Osprey* while I was there. Good luck fellas!!

I would also like to acknowledge my thanks to Chris Howard Bailey and Alastair Wilson and the trustees and staff of the Royal Naval Museum and Sutton Publishing, as well as Admiral J.J. Black.

My final acknowledgement goes to my Uncle Cyril (my mum's sister's husband), who did me the great honour of reading this book while it was very much in its infancy. He was in the RN for a very short period, but is one of the reasons I pressed on with the project. He – and my aunt – are both quite religious, you see, and it was with great trepidation that I asked him to read the rough (as in 'flowery', not 'jagged') copy of this. I had thought that if he didn't appreciate the stories and the swearing – then nobody would. When I next saw him, he laughed out loud, and pointed out that without the rawness, it wouldn't really portray 'Life in a Blue Suit'! After some discussion, we decided to keep it in that intentional 'flowery' style.

Introduction

I'll explain now – my *Tartar* was a sleek, shiny, grey-painted, Type 81 frigate built in the early 1960s, bristling with guns and missiles, radars and matey-ness, two funnels, and a pennant number of F133. It was not her more famous predecessor of the line, which took part in the Second World War. Though, coincidentally, that one had Sir Ludovic Kennedy as their 'gunner', and I met him when he came aboard us one fine day. I was on watch in the gloom room, and he chatted with us for a while. See, only the first paragraph of the introduction, and the first sea stories have made an appearance.

I served on many ships and shore bases, but my *Tartar* was the best ship I was ever drafted to, and it is where most of my better memories originate. I often wonder whether she ended up merely as a target, or if she had a more dignified end.

My story, then, is one of growing up in the Navy of the 1970s, and, as it is totally about my own experiences of sealife, everything is first hand. There was never a time when I stood and thought 'What am I doing this for?', although many was the time I thought 'I don't want to be doing this'. The difference being between wanting to be out of the Navy doing something else with my life right now, and wanting to be in my chariot. Most of the time I spent entirely committed to serving my country in the Navy was absolutely brilliant, a 4,000-day adventure, with memories I will treasure, and with deeds being plotted/perpetrated and exploits being snatched in the moment, that I will remember forever, even if I would prefer to forget some of them . . .

The maxim of my day was, 'If you can't take a joke – you shouldn't have joined'. That was so, so true. As was 'Not so jolly now – are we, Jack!' in times of stress, guaranteed to get an instant reaction. Or a smacking if you didn't get away fast enough, or duck whatever sharp or heavy (or both) object was thrown at you.

The title is based on the naval tradition of telling sea stories, generally starting with 'When I was on the . . .'. These stories would get wilder as they were told, finishing with the words 'Black cat that then', with someone else coming in with an even better story being told, followed by others, all trying to outdo, or 'black cat' each other. The 'stopper' to all these was 'Listen sonny, I was in Baghdad before you were in your Dad's bag'. Or we would make swishing noises while pretending to swing an oil lamp around to embarrass the storyteller into silence, which would normally be followed by indignant cries of 'I'm tellin' yer I did', or 'Ask so-and-so, he saw it too'.

Every sailor past or present, any time, anywhere will have a large repertoire of 'black cats' or sea stories, most of which will be mostly true, though they must sometimes be taken with a pinch of salt as 'narrator's licence' occasionally creeps in. This book, then, is full of perfectly true black cats, related exactly as I remember them.

I was in the Royal Navy between 1969 and 1980, during a surprisingly peaceful era – we could always create our own trouble, without any help from politicians – but I was extremely proud to have been part of such a professional band of men.

They say 'Join the Navy and see the World'. Well, I did, and I did. And it really made a man of me. Well that's my opinion, and I should know – I did the time, I did the runs, I did it all, in ten-and-a-half very short years. And yes, I do say 'Been there' and 'Seen that' and 'Did that' – ask my wife and children!

The Royal Navy was, if anything, a 'quiet' service. After basic training there was none of this shouting and screaming of orders '1–2–1–2getyour bleedinaircutsonny' business. Of course, if it was on the fo'c's'le in a force six, or in the middle of nowhere you'd have to shout, or while carrying out guard duties or something similar. But normally, you quietly asked/told someone to do something, and they got on and did it. You knew how long you'd be confined to the same small area of grey space for, and knew how either side could make life more difficult, so orders were obeyed, immediately, and mostly instinctively. Unless you felt like annoying someone . . .

'Disobeying A Direct Order' was just about therefore the most serious crime you could commit, and one you could expect to get liberally lashed up for. So, while the book apparently describes the life of Riley we normally enjoyed, we were ALWAYS aware just how close to the wind we could sail, and still get away with it. Mind you, the threat of being '. . . down on your head like a ton of shit, Jack' was enough to forestall most direct conflicts between us and our 'superiors'.

'Baiting', or 'winding-up', was a popular pastime, enjoyed by everyone. This is where you deliberately sit goading or needling someone, even if it's your best run ashore oppo, by talking about various things you know annoy them. Like their crap footy team, or the ugliness of, or previous sexual experience you had with, his current party, or the fact that he still can't backsplice, until you got him to flash up. You would then dance round singing 'you bit, you bit', or be off running up the Burma Road with him behind you carrying a marling spike, or worse.

It was always more fun with civvies, as half the time we considered them to be too dumb to realize what you were doing, especially if they were 'dockies', and dockies were definitely in a league of their own. Nevertheless, baiting was something we did easily – unthinkingly, and continuously. If nothing else, it passed the more monotonous off-watch times at sea. Clearly, the bigger and better the bite, the more we enjoyed it, and the higher the authority of the person we targeted, again – the more we would enjoy the response. I wonder what trick-cyclists would have made of us – probably they'd have put it down to an attention-seeking disorder.

Some days it would backfire, and we'd get the shitty end of the pineapple. We'd then look at the person baiting us, and snarl 'You don't have the brains to wind me up . . .', and continue what we were doing, absolutely seething inside, ready to tear his head off. Or sometimes, (through pure stress, you understand), we'd knock the daylights out of him anyway. Nothing too severe, just enough to serve as a warning to others. Whoever started it would then ask 'Got a shitty on then, Jack'? We just couldn't leave it alone.

So, you'll find that a lot of the escapades described here, were 'wind-ups', done to annoy someone, done to get a reaction. Like doing a 'Zulu Warrior' in a hotel full of civvies, or singing filthy songs to them about lobsters, or steam-powered willies, or whatever else it required to goad this totally unsuspecting 'audience'. I sincerely hope today's 'tars' are still permitted to continue with this tradition, as it would be a great shame to think this particular sociable and very matey aspect of naval life has evaporated.

At sea during 'roughers' it was bad. I spent many hours attempting to balance in the middle of a Mid-Atlantic force ten, coming off watch after four hours scanning a swaying radar screen, dog tired and irritable as hell. Hungry, I would struggle to carry my scran on a tray to a table, while using my other two hands to brace myself against anything available as the ship both pitched and yawed simultaneously while in passage with the swell off the bow. Or trying to remain coherent and report radar contacts to the bridge while 3,000 tons of grey painted ship slammed into the next milestone, smashing me and my mates yet again into the unforgiving steel of the bulkheads or, on occasions, deckheads. Or when I (frequently) physically strapped myself into my pit while the blunt end corkscrewed around trying (and sometimes succeeding) to eject me from it, as – after yet another sleepless night – I waited for the 0345 'shake' for the morning watch. And these are just some of the easier bits.

Of course, just to help me rest more easily in these conditions I could be fortunate enough to sleep in the aft messdeck, and have the phosphor-bronze screws right beneath me, which would race and vibrate the entire ship whenever the arse end lifted out of the water, giving me another unnecessary awakening from my already light doze. Or if I slept amidships, the machinery powering the stabilizers (when they worked) below me would be fighting noisily to keep the ship on a (more) even keel. Or the gash-nasher (garbage disposal unit) could scream away above my head, trying to digest some dopey sod's knife. No wonder whenever we cleared a storm, we (from the Skipper, right down to his steward, and below to the ship's cementhead) all slept at standeasy instead of continuing with our usual pratting around. Of course, we quickly recovered as soon as we heard the pipe 'Secure – shore leave for port watch and first starboard will commence at . . .'.

Along with my shipmates, I visited well over a hundred different ports around the world, many of them more than once, and most of them were tremendously enjoyable and memorable, for one reason or another. I also went on numerous inland visits to see many more places clearly inaccessible by sea. I feel very fortunate to have done what I did, and to have been where I went, and to have seen what I saw, as since my days the RN has been shrunk to such an extent that it would be difficult for today's sailors to visit so many different places in such a relatively short period of time.

In between bouts of creating or receiving trouble, one thing most matelots did a vast amount of, while relaxing both at sea or if in harbour on duty, was read. If you were reading, it was generally assumed you did not want to talk to anyone. If you stuck your cassette player headphones on AND read, to disturb you could be like prodding a rattlesnake – the reaction would be instantaneous, vehement and directed four-square at you. We had little lights on the 'buggery boards' that separated our adjacent pits and were designed to prevent mutual interference, and many was the night someone's light would still be on while everyone else slept.

Personally, I could rush through a standard paperback in a little over an hour. Books on ships were like currency, we'd always be raiding other messdecks to swap books, and would never read the same book twice. Good books were at a premium, but we would wade through 'shitkickers' to sci-fi, historic novels to 'Confessions of a . . .', Russian authors with unpronounceable names to James Herbert, *Mayfair* to Commando comics, even seamanship manuals took a beating – anything to pass the off-watch hours. Occasionally, we'd find a really good read and the rest used to be given 'the float test' – down the gash chute which was permanently rigged off the blunt end of the ship. In one book – I don't remember where I read it – I came across a 'naval curse':

> Oh Lord Above,
> Send down a Dove,
> With Wings as sharp as Razors
> To cut the Throats,
> Of them there Blokes,
> Wot sells Bad Beer to Sailors.

I remember that even now and often, while ashore, I wished it to be true. But most of the other books I read made little immediate impact, never mind a lasting impression.

I hope all my hard work doesn't end up as a floater, but whatever your point of view – ENJOY THE BOOK.

CHAPTER 1

Baby Sailors: My First Few Days

It was a normal morning for the rest of the population of Northampton as I stood on the southbound platform of Castle station in September 1969, and waved goodbye to my Dad. But the only thing signalled was the end of my childhood, and of my life up until that day, when I used my free ticket sent by the Navy and boarded the Euston train, en route to a place called Torpoint, with instructions to call on the vicar who christened me all those years ago.

What had started as a choice I had to make between joining the RAF as a pilot or the Navy as an anything (but under NO circumstances did I ever consider the Army) was made by me when I opted not to wait for my GCE results, but to go in the Navy anyway. An inspired decision as it turned out – I didn't pass enough exams at that time to get me flying in the RAF. Fortunate anyway, as I later found out the RAF (as the most junior service) is merely tolerated by all other servicemen, whereas the Royal Navy was not only the Senior Service – as the oldest established armed force – but clearly, far and away the best. This is not just my opinion – ask anyone who has ever drunk the Queen's shilling. We frequently met people who had transferred from the other services to us, but never met anyone deserting us for them.

During the previous months, I had taken and passed all the entrance tests at the Royal Navy and Royal Marine recruiting centre in Northampton, right opposite where I used to catch the bus home from school. I had gone to Derby for the entrance medical where I had my hearing and sight vigorously tested to determine my ability to distinguish between different sounds and pitches, and between ever so slightly different coloured pinpricks of light. It was apparent at this early stage that applicants were already being screened. Those who passed these tests but who didn't know what they wanted to do were being guided towards being sailors, especially radar operators or sonar operators.

I had proved my ability to cough properly while someone put their hand down my Y-fronts and tampered with my goolies, and finally was offered the role of Junior Seaman, which was odd, because up to then I

1

had actually thought I wanted to be a chef. Fortunately, after thinking how hot it would get cooking in an already scorching galley, while sailing around sweltering, tropical climates, common sense prevailed, and I accepted the offer the Navy made me. I was possibly also swayed by the monochrome booklets I had been sent, showing 'sailors' having a good time, while chefs and others looked like they were working.

Soon after, I was sent detailed travelling instructions and orders to join HMS *Raleigh*. Now finally, the train doors slammed and off I went. All I had was what I wore and toiletries. What was going to happen? Now I couldn't see familiar faces, great trepidation crept upon me. My Mum couldn't face seeing me off, that fell to my Dad, who was now on his way back to work, very likely via the railway canteen where he ate his dinner every day. Was my Mum as upset as Dad clearly was? I cannot remember now because my mind was full of my own worries and concerns.

I arrived at Euston station and for the first time navigated my way across London to Paddington station, boarding the large, maroon, grubby, diesel-hauled train travelling to Plymouth. Here there were more like me – nervous, spotty, beardless sixteen year olds – in a train that smelled like all the other trains, of cheap smoke and thousands of previous travellers. We talked, the kids in my part of the carriage, and especially myself and a lad called Arthur from a town in Essex I had never heard of. I was torn between chatting to him and gawping at the wonderful scenery on the South Devon coastal line. I had never been to that part of the world before, and as with many things since it did not seem relevant or possible that it would be weeks, months even, before I travelled it again. Nor how many times I'd travel the route after that. The changes that might be made to me between those future trips were not even being considered. The enormity of what we were about to do had still not yet sunk in.

We would never have dreamed of attempting to buy alcohol from the buffet on THAT train – didn't even know we could get away with it – so it was with dry mouths all round for more than one reason that we drew into Plymouth station. We were met by officious naval 'people' of unknown rank (to us at that time, so to be safe we addressed them all as 'Sir'), who ushered us into big blue coaches with 'RN' emblazoned on the side, for the trip to Torpoint. Nothing registered on that trip, except that as we got to the unexpected ferry, we all craned out of the windows to see the sea – like any tourists, really. Due to the appalling weather, we could not see the warships, but gossip assured us they were there, then all too soon we were across the Tamar and driving off the ferry. On reaching HMS *Raleigh*, we embarked on a life and existence I never expected – but something I still dream about even now.

I don't really know what I or my new-found 'oppos' expected. I'd seen the field gunners and the Royal Tournament, and perhaps I expected them to be greeting us, and I maybe also thought I would see frigates and destroyers gliding down the main road towards the vast parade ground. A naval base named after the greatest sea hero should have had more than a couple of silvery looking cannons and acres of grass, tarmac and wooden huts – shouldn't it? Okay, it had a sea view (when the tide was in on the muddy estuary we overlooked), and just a few sailors stamping about with round white hats on, but I was not impressed yet.

Maybe our bewildered reactions were transparent, for suddenly we were accosted by a short, black-uniformed (sleeves covered in red badges), red-faced shouting individual, demanding our attention. Perhaps that was the idea, him distracting us from our wool-gathering, forcing us to concentrate on our new lives. He indicated in Anglo-Saxon that we were here because we had chosen to remain, that here we were to be for the next sixteen weeks in some cases, and that if we were not prepared for it, we could get back on the bus and go home to mummy now. Or at least that's what it should have come across as. He was rather more graphic and succinct, even to my previously trained ears.

Those of us who stayed – for surprisingly few actually ran off – were herded together, fallen in 'one behind the other twice' – i.e., three deep, and 'tallest at the ends, shortest in the centre' – then 'marched' (gentle left wheel, right wheel) to the New Entry Block and shown our 'mess' where we were to sleep. We were then told what to do next, and when it would happen, and were suddenly left with a person we were told to call 'Peeyoh'. That was expanded by (there was always one, even then) the ex-sea scout. 'That is a petty officer' he explained, tiresomely. 'Known as a PO.'

I got talking to the kid in the bed above mine. Two things registered, one was that I was in a bunkbed, which I had got to make by myself with the supplied sheets, blankets etc., secondly I actually knew him! He had left my school some time before me and had actually left the area – but now here was Glen in the bunk above me. We became good friends over the next few weeks, and beyond.

Later that evening, after we'd been fed and while we were chattering, excitedly (still), came 'lights out', and amid people calling out 'whatever you're doing now – don't', and the resulting sniggering, and among the muffled sobbings, I suppose we eventually fell asleep. But then almost immediately, it seemed, we wondered what the hell the noise was. Milliseconds after, the messdeck door imploded and all the lights were thrown on, followed by the Duty PO, who stormed in, shouting at us to 'get your hands off your cocks, and on to your socks', and, conversationally, – 'get your fucking feet on the deck, two six'. That was bearable, and made us giggle nervously, like schoolgirls. The next surprise was the large metal ashtray (known throughout the Navy as a spitkid) being kicked down the mess ahead of the PO. This came to be accepted as a standard, though noisy, early morning alarm call, usually only moments after 'Call the Hands' was bugled on the tannoy around the camp.

Our first job of that and every following day, was that of making these beds up Navy fashion – nothing loose or saggy, no rough edges, taut counterpane, complete with right-way-up anchor design (that is – right way up and not inside out either) and smoothed out pillowcases. We washed and shaved off the overnight gathering of bumfluff, which was why everyone called everyone else 'Skin', as we were to find out. We then gathered together (soon to be 'mustered') outside the Nissen hut we were to call 'home' for the next week, before being 'marched' to breakfast, where we queued, but due to the sheer numbers serving behind the counter we quickly reached the front. We chose and ate whatever we wanted, providing we could bolt it down in three minutes flat, a precedent set that day which became a habit I have tried for years to break. I remember there being a vast spread all along this huge cafeteria-type counter, with cereal, fried acres of sausages, bacon, greasy eggs, fried bread, mushrooms, baked beans (for breakfast?) and vast tanks of tea. And milk. And toast. After several minutes luxuriating in this, we were marched back and told to make ourselves ready for the Joining Routine.

We started the Joining Routine later that morning, with a talk by the Captain Weir RN of HMS 'Raaahlly' (not Rally as we all read it), during which he explained what we had volunteered for, commended us on our commitment, warned us things would get tougher, smiled and left. So, we drew our oilskins and had our teeth inspected, then waited for the next event.

It had not occurred to me up until that time how different people were, although all were ostensibly British. There were short, fat, tall, thin, odd, quiet, noisy, chatty, sullen, ugly, mouthy, clever, thick, kids there, all of my own age, but because we couldn't understand each others' accents, we thought we were all foreign. We originated from places as far afield as Scotland, Devon, Berwick, Hull, Chichester, Essex, Derby – as I said, up until then it had not even registered that other people lived in faraway places in the country, much less that they would all congregate on Torpoint. I had hardly heard of some of their home towns, except to know some were north of me – they had perhaps previously been a note in a school geography exercise book or a small flag on a map. I know that we all lead fairly insular lives, but to be thrown in among all these faces, accents and attitudes at the tender age of sixteen was like being smacked in the mouth with a brick. I wasn't naïve, but I could see we all had a lot of catching up and growing up to do in a short period of time. Having said that, once we got over the initial surprises and began to settle down, we quickly formed cliques within the classes we were assigned to. We were introduced to divisional POs, divisional chief petty officers, and then to our divisional officers (we had to stand up straight – they were lieutenants or sub-lieutenants, and consequently very, very important).

'Colours' was probably the first thing stamped indelibly on us. Every morning, the Navy has Colours, where the ensign is ceremonially raised up the mast on the quarterdeck. The quarterdeck is normally the blunt end on ships, but is where the mainmast is on shore establishments. Colours (and 'Sunset', where the reverse happens) means that anyone on the upper deck (or in our case, out in the open) has to 'Face the mainmast and salute'. They stand there at attention, saluting, until the flag is completely raised, at which time the 'carry-on' is sounded, and you continue about your business. God help you then, if you continue to walk round, gob-off, or do anything except stand and salute. This, and walking (instead of doubling) over the parade ground, entitled you to be sworn at loudly and at length by anyone who happened to notice you breaking this first set of rules. And what a prat you feel, having someone, his face inches from yours, questioning your ability to hear/see/have a father. You only did it the once, even accidentally.

We were now marched everywhere, and on the next occasion, it was to the barbers, past other, obviously older, more experienced hands, who had arrived the previous week or month, and who jeered at our newness wherever we went, and there we were shorn of our dead trendy hair. We went from there to the tailor to be measured for our suits – one blue serge, the other the very proper tar one – thence to the stores, where the only analogy is 'like Christmas'. We were given, YES GIVEN, the following: three sets of Y-fronts (referred to as 'dung-hampers'), vests, gloves, (both of which we pointedly refused to wear on the grounds that only little girls wore gloves and only little boys wore vests), blue shirts and trousers, several pairs of woollen socks, a pair of shoes, two pairs of boots (one studded, one not), a gas mask, sheets, pillowcases, striped pyjamas (worryingly referred to as 'brown hatters' overalls' – but not explained, at that time), mugs, sports gear, including plimsolls, two gleamingly white hats (sorry – caps), a belt with a built in, buttonable, adjustable money-pouch, several white towels, a huge macintosh – called a Burberry (very warm), two thick, blue (and extremely itchy) 'seaman's jerseys' (otherwise known as 'woolly pullies'), a zippered, nylon anorak type thing said to keep out wind and rain, polish, soap, bits of white string called lanyards, mysterious sheets of silk, called silks, strange T-shirt things with very fetching bits of blue round the square neck called white-fronts, shoe/boot cleaning gear, a wooden scrubbing brush, and the most oddly shaped blue-jean things, known as collars. Oh yes, and a housewife (bag full of sewing kit, scissors, needles etc.) and a large offensive weapon, initially known as a clasp knife, subsequently called a 'Pusser's dirk'. A large brown canvas kitbag, and a large, strong, green suitcase were provided to carry all of this in. These items were valued then, at around £50 – a fortune compared to the £7 we were to be paid per fortnight – the going rate in those days, when the men were made of steel, and ships were made of wood, as the expression was relayed to us.

We were also given two cap-tallies (black bands with the ship's name picked out in gold thread) to tie round our caps, so while ashore we could be identified to a ship. The bow to secure these 'tallies' must be the hardest one ever devised by man, similar to that used to secure bow-ties, only ours had to be totally symmetrical before we finished it off with the scissors, or it was forcibly removed for another attempt. By the time it was secure, it was tatty – you had to buy a new one to replace it, or come up with some pretty creative ironing. Luckily we had the ex-sea scout, so we got all ours done after only ten or so lessons.

We each had a wooden 'block' made up – letters joined together to form our name on it, and told what would happen if we EVER lost this, or what would happen if we were EVER found with an item of someone else's gear (or kit), with their name 'blocked' on it. The block had to be dipped into paint, and the paint applied to the item of uniform. You obviously used black paint to mark light clothing, and white paint for dark clothing. Then we were told afterwards (or were we too excited to listen in the first place) to stamp ONLY where it would not be seen. You should have seen the gear ruined that day, with the name stamped on the outside of brand new collars, on the outside of even caps, halfway up whitefronts, and clearly to be seen on trousers and shirts. The only cure was replacement, so it was a very costly mistake to make. All these tasks were overseen by an old boy who was hated in much the same way as traffic wardens are. He was, as far as we were concerned, neither civvy nor jack, but seemed to exert enough influence and wield enough power for us to obey him. I think we referred to him as 'Cap'n Pugwash'. He was – to us – a little shit of a man.

We were now expected to wear all our new kit, which we did, self-consciously at first, but getting more used to it day by day, especially those funny little round caps. These acquired dirty fingermarks as easily as shit stuck on a blanket, and then refused to be removed, even though we scrubbed them with our little brushes, drenched in washing powder ('dhobey dust' to the older hands). We also discovered – the hard way – that it was extremely silly to 'blanco' the hats clean, as the first drop of rain dumped diluted blanco all over your suit and collar, precipitating an expensive trip to the dry-cleaner to remove all the very fetching white tramlines from your collar down to your shoes.

All our civvy gear was then wrapped in brown paper, and sent home to mum. Except that not everyone complied with this. I can still visualize one mate dressed in bell-bottoms, highly charged black shoes and a lemon-coloured shirt, pretending to be a civvy in Plymouth, not knowing he looked a bigger plonker than all the rest of us, and had less chance of pulling in Plymouth anyway, than a broken tug.

So we all got on with readying our gear, washing it, starching it, ironing it, and now here was our first uniform, the blue serge one. 'This, lads, is your Number Two uniform', Explained the resident PO. 'Not to be worn on ceremonial occasions because it only has a red wool badge, but to be worn on duty. The blue shirt/trousers is Number Eights, and when you get your best uniform, it is your Number Ones, complete with gold wire badge.' And more, 'Eights are worn during the day, unless you are on duty, in which case you wear Twos. With or without collars. Or without a top – known as half-blues.' He continued, 'to make life easy, ALL ships and establishments issue "DAILY ORDERS", telling you of such things as daily events, sunset/sunrise, Duty personnel, Duty part of the watch, special events, but especially DRESS OF THE DAY. This takes away your decision of 'what to wear today'. It IS Eights during daytime. You have two sets. If one set is in use the other set is in wash. You will change your Eights on Monday or Thursday, or if they are grubby from use. You may buy further sets. Your silks must be folded EXACTLY like this. The strings are called lanyards and must NEVER be any colour but snow-white, the collars must be folded like this, but, of course, the creases MUST be razor sharp. Your Number Two trousers MUST have either 7 or 9 completely parallel creases, but NOT 6 or 8, and they are to be ironed concertina fashion like this, to facilitate easy stowage, but NOT ironed "fore and aft", as the RN irons their uniform trousers across the leg [which made sense considering to size of our lockers].'

We had to sew cotton name strips on our Eights, and branch badges – little pictures of shackles – a fetching blue colour on a white background. These badges first had to be cut to shape to prevent them becoming unstitched, then folded round the edges before being sewed on the outside of the right sleeve of our shiny Number Eight shirts, NOT the inside, NOR the rear. 'Homeward bounders' (bloody big stitches) were NOT to be used, just small, neat stitching. We were sixteen years old and here we were sewing! Mind you, we quickly learned not to mess the job up – as with everything else, if it was not Pusser fashion, it came off rather faster than it went on, assisted by 'our' PO, and you did it repeatedly until it was right.

Unfortunately, we also now had to do what thousands of other trainees had done for countless generations and years before us – spit 'n' polish our boots. You started with the hot spoon to remove the dimples, then the laborious build up of polish and gob with the filthy rag moving monotonously round in small circles, until – suddenly – the glimmer of a reflection appears. This is followed by more reflective bits until, miraculously, the whole toe of the boot shines blackly, and what a sense of achievement that is. We used to spend hours bulling them back after we'd stuffed them up on the assault course, for example. Strangely, you are either one of those who can put a mirror on the toecap or you sit there for more endless hours, getting nothing but a sore arm.

Did the tea really have bromide in it? It came in huge steaming urns and was supposedly treated to suppress our urges. What was bromide anyway – did it taste anything like iodine? Is that why the tea was always so brown? And anyway, before we could drink it we had to get a china mug, which involved waiting in a queue until someone else had finished with one. Perhaps that was why the Naafi sold plastic mugs, either half-pint or pint-sized, orange or bright blue. We quickly invested in our new drinking vessels – preferring to pay then, rather than waste valuable 'off' time lining up for a china one. Once bought, we decorated our trophies with our name, in paint, with indelible ink or even with a bit of plaster with our names inked on. We could soon spot our mug from a distance, which made no difference whatsoever, as they regularly were stolen or left behind somewhere. There must be shops in Plymouth, Portsmouth and every other Navy town selling used plastic mugs. Whichever ship or unit you then served on there would always be the shop where you could buy mugs, or you'd buy your own from some foreign shore, and use it until it got smashed, nicked or lost. Occasionally, we'd have an official issue of Pusser's mugs, but they'd all get smashed in the first spot of rough weather and back we'd go to the plastic.

The food was good that first Navy week – it had to be to sustain us through all the new things hitting us hourly. The important thing was that we had hope. That following Monday we would move in as 'The New Intake'. No longer the new, new entries – we had moved up the heap. No one could laugh at our shiny trousers and dull boots any more – we were here to stay, matey-bubbles – we were Jack! We could now laugh at the new boys. We still had the alarm calls, complete with spitkid kicking, but when told 'feet on the deck', we knew we could get a few extra, precious seconds in our beds by swinging our legs out, while keeping our bodies in and under the warm covers. We could now call the new boys 'Skin', and talk knowledgeably about things 'giving us the shits' and tell them to 'stop gobbing off while I'm talking', watching them return the same blank looks we gave just last week.

One of the significant occurrences of these first few days was when we all gathered (sorry, mustered) in the common room at the top Nissen hut of the block and were read the Official Secrets Act. We had to sign this and the contract of service between the Navy and ourselves. As if any of us understood it at sixteen. We signed though, but not before a repetition of the 'if you have any misgivings, we will put you on the train home to mummy now' routine. Following the crying we had heard coming from various beds in our messdeck over the preceding days, we were not surprised when several kids got up and left, obviously preferring their mothers' warm and tender company to ours.

We had our photos taken for our ID cards, with the lecture about how we would be instantly executed (or something) if it ever fell into enemy hands, and were presented with a paybook. This was a green covered book, supposed to record all data about ourselves, what we had been issued with, brief rules and regulations about 'Navy life', and now we had signed our lives away, the bits in invisible ink. The bits that now became visible revealed that now they had our signatures, they could stick needles in us to guard against various unheard of and undiscovered tropical diseases. Oh yes, and the bit that said everything anyone said to us from now on was definitely not preceded with 'Please . . .', but with any shouted word/profanity/order! Fortunately, paybooks were exactly the same size widthways as the distance between the creases on our trousers. Imagine how helpful that was! At this stage I was also given my official number. I remember this even now.

We had our photographs taken, this time for our passports. Most of us had never seen a passport before, so we were indeed quite pleased when we got received royal blue permits. Then we found that not only would we never need them in any port we entered, but that they were also a receptacle for certificated detailing injections against the above mentioned diseases.

One day a WRNS officer questioned us about our home lives, educational backgrounds and inclinations, presumably because the Navy wanted to find out as much as they could about us. We also continued to learn more Navy slang. Whenever we talked while supposed to be listening, we would immediately be told 'Shi' ni', later expanded to 'Shit in it', (SHUT UP NOW!). Everyone said it, and for all I know they still do. Talking instead of listening was called 'transmitting instead of receiving', which could quickly get you slapped or bollocked.

CHAPTER 2

The Next Few Weeks

We marched from the new entry block to another dull, black Nissen hut on the other side of the camp, carrying everything we couldn't wear. At *Raleigh*, weather did not exist – if it rained, we just got on with it. We mustered for diversions (divisions) every day except for the days I remember it really being too foul to go ahead. In which case we used to hear it first from 'the beano man'. The broadcast used to crackle into life, followed by 'D' Y' hear there – there will be no divisions this morning'. But that was on exceptional days. Otherwise we had divisions in the shed at the far end (for us) of the parade ground, having first doubled across or around the parade ground, so as to not get too wet.

We were assigned to PO Robinson and were messed into Revenge Block, class Collingwood 37 for six weeks' basic training. Our daily routine was: breakfast 0610, 'clean ship' until 0830, then divisions, prayers and instruction. Dinner was at 1210, training from 1330 to 1610, then tea, then sport until 1815, which was generally rugby, trying to beat the crap out of anyone stupid enough to play against us – normally the 'tiffies' from the other training base right across the road from us. Supper was at 1835, with 'free periods' (mending, repairing, cleaning, washing, ironing, showering) until 2200. On Saturdays, training finished at 1200. On Sundays no training, but divisions then church. Church was an oddity, with the irreligious being advised to go anyway right from the start, as non-compliance resulted in extra duties! As a lapsed Methodist, I thought I might get away with it, but was lumped in with 'the rest' every Sunday. Except for the day I escaped, claiming I had been invited to attend a service with the minister who had christened me. I can only recall tea and the evening service before hurrying to meet my mates later on in the pub.

During this time, except when on duty, leave could be taken up until 2245, nightly. Aggie Weston's and The Seamen's Mission were the places recommended to us, but we rapidly swerved past them and headed for 'The Strip'. The former were both explained away as being there for the more God-fearing of us. So despite the Navy's best intentions, and the fact that these places were there for our entertainment, we avoided them.

We were allowed to go into the Naafi (at standeasies or in the evening), which, as it was quickly explained stood for 'Navy, Army, Air Force Institute', and most definitely not 'No Ambition And Fuck-all Interest'. The food in there was interesting – milk, coca-cola, pies, cakes and nutty. As was the jukebox and snooker table (if you got there early enough), but none was as tantalizing as the beer, served to older ratings. As a junior seaman aged sixteen and a bit – the beer was definitely off limits. As were the Wrens' quarters allegedly up the hill, patrolled by armed guards, accessible only over a wooden bridge, which rattled and shook, over which we had to break step as we marched. Mind you, the bromide took care of thoughts of girls. Didn't it?

Standeasy was a naval tradition. Where anyone else would have a break, a cuppa, or whatever, we'd have standeasy. What happened at *Raleigh* was that all standeasies were ushered in by a bugle (on a tape) playing the standeasy tune. It came across as 'dee-da-didlediddledi-da-dee', which we always gleefully mocked as 'If ya wannoo have a shit, go now'. Which we'd do, unless we were near the Naafi, at which point we would slope off and have a fag or three, or a very quick cuppa.

We learned seamanship skills which involved absolutely every aspect of anything to do with the word sea, starting with tying bends and hitches, but not knots. Boy scouts could call them knots but we were much more sophisticated, and could (honestly) tie anything, within seconds, in front of us, or behind our backs, with or without our eyes shut. We had to – we were told that 'one day your life could depend on it'. We believed that – and therefore learned the bend thoroughly. Every time we entered the seamanship training room, we first had to go through these hitches and bends until the PO was satisfied, and that could take several attempts.

The first time we entered one particular room containing the absolutely complete, scale models of ship fo'c'sles was a wonderful experience. We were shown the principles of mooring, anchoring, replenishing, with all the miniaturized moving and working parts. We were allowed to play with these giant toys, and learned an enormous amount about blocks (not pulleys), derricks (not cranes), real life-jacket drills (in that cold pool) and real-life raft embarkation, having first been taught how to jump off the top board, wearing a life-jacket, without breaking your neck as you hit the water. We were also introduced to Naval General Knowledge – who fought who, and where, why the Russians had the hump after the Bay of Pigs, how the aircraft carrier had dominated recent naval battles, etc. And the fun bits. We carried out damage control in a semi-live environment, being aware that if you didn't stop the water coming in pretty handsomely (we soon picked these nautical phrases up!), you would get a belt off the live wires left dangling precariously near the rapidly rising floodwater.

Engaging in the practical boatwork at Jupiter Point was eagerly looked forward to. It was terrific fun – a release valve as well as being educational. We would drive there in the back of a Pusser's lorry with its canvas roof, and were allowed to charge round the River Tamar in 27-ft whalers, either under power (with engines which had to be convinced to start before propelling us very slowly through the water), or pulling (under oars). I had (and since have) always loved boats, and was in my element here. Even when we were literally thrown into Mirror class dinghies after minimal instruction, and drifted miles downtide after the wind dropped, totally, it was me that regarded this as an adventure. And when we got rounded up and towed back, all one behind the other, all fastened to the powered whaler, it was me that couldn't wait for the next visit.

The firefighting course was the most impressive. A large pan of oil was ignited and left to catch, fiercely. The instructor showed us what not to do, which was to hit the fire with water. The memory of the immediate and enormous eruption of fire when he did this has stayed with me for years. We were given foam extinguishers and shown how to use them properly, off the wall behind the fire so the foam drifted back over it, smothering it. Piece of piss when you know how. We came back from this training totally black from the 'fires' extinguished. It took days to get the soot out of our skin and hair, those of us who had hair left – some had singed bits of eyebrows and hair remaining which took several weeks to grow back. There was actually quite a bit of instruction based on the 'Don't do it like this, because this is what will happen if you do' principle. You tended to learn much more quickly by this method, and it avoided expensive and time-wasting mistakes.

We learned that bell-bottoms were designed the way they were because it made them easy to roll up to scrub decks, and that the silks were originally to tie around your head to mop up the sweat, and that the lanyard was to fire the cannon, and that the three stripes on the collar represented three great naval battles, and the idea of the collar was to keep oiled pigtails off one's uniform. One useful piece of information – if we fell overboard, we could remove our bells, tie the bottoms, and then trap air in the resultant bags, to float with . . . Oh Yeah? Not that we cared – we looked brilliant in our bezzy (best) 'ones' when we dressed with silks, collars, white-fronts and lanyards for the first time, and we all paraded excitedly in front of the mirrors for ages.

We spent endless hours at parade training and drill, learning how to throw around an SLR (Self Loading Rifle) with easy familiarity, and how to about turn, and right turn, and move to the left in threes, which all became progressively easier. Naval drill insists on 'dwelling a pause of two marching paces' between each movement. We would therefore 'move to the right in threes – Riiiight Turn', at which point we would swivel on the heel of the right foot and ball of the left, count 'two three', then complete the movement by bringing our left foot up 'smartly' against the right. Everything was done with a pause of '2–3'. With us being made to shout it if we didn't immediately get it right, which was quite frequent. Or having to 'hold' a movement like 'changing arms while at the attention', which involved changing the SLR from right arm to left. Pausing in the middle meant you now held several pounds of rifle at arms length, (very, very painful after several seconds) until the DI (drill instructor) got bored, and shouted 'TWO-THREE', at which point (if your arms hadn't locked up or fallen off) you would gratefully complete the drill. You tended not to mess about when doing that particular drill, just in case. Of course we were dragged out periodically and made to run round the parade ground with the SLR held above the head, or even worse at the aforementioned arm's length, for the very slightest infraction, but we even got used to that. 'Bags of swank' was the maxim we learned to good effect. Chests out, stomachs in, heads up, eyes front, shoulders back, push back the arms, bring them forward until parallel to the deck, fingers clenched at first and second knuckle, bang those feet down, thumbs in line with the seam of the trousers, feet at a 45° angle. And so on and on . . . and the pride in ourselves, and what we were doing, and what we were starting to accomplish grew by the minute. We were beginning to become part of that team called the Royal Navy, starting to become men.

We learned many things over those few first weeks. Straight away we were told how to wriggle our toes while standing at attention to prevent fainting, rather than sway in the breeze and receive the inevitable earbending from the DI. Or worse – pass out. 'Don't you fuckin' DARE help him' we were told as they dropped to the unforgiving tarmac of the parade ground on the odd hot Sunday in immaculate Number Ones, as the Marine band played while the armed guard was inspected by the captain, and as we stood motionless for hours (it seemed) at a time. Eventually, though, the 'first-aid' party who had been up until then on 'stand-by' by the side of the parade ground, would trot over, complete with stretcher on to which they'd load their human cargo, before trotting back to sick bay with the failure. Personally, I used to hum along to the band to try to keep alert, though that was dangerous. If you got too involved in the humming, you would be 'at-ease', while everyone else was 'Ho'd, then you would get another bollocking from the DIs who constantly prowled the parade ground with their yardsticks or swagger canes during these ceremonial divisions. As the tallest in the class, I was always 'marker', against whom everyone else fell in and dressed. I was consequently never out of position. If I moved – the others had to dress up against me. No one ever caught on to me doing that.

The tunes the band played used to have me sniggering at times, especially when they played the 'Sousa March' (the *Monty Python* theme tune). I will confess that 'A Life On The Ocean Wave' is very stirring for a sixteen year old trying to stand still. Except for my toes. We were actually told, that if we felt faint, we were to go down on one knee. That seemed even more ignominious – more attention seeking!

We fell in, and fell out again, we put our caps on, took them off again, saluted (front, left and right, and stand from under, if you were stupid enough to salute to the left with your left arm), and had ticktocking pointed out to us. This is normally when marching a co-ordinated person's right arm/left leg go forwards then backwards together. Except the ticktocker. He goes same leg, same arm, and looks totally hilarious. Even now, I can't watch people marching without scanning for the ticktocker. And when I do see one, I am reduced to uncontrollable laughter. We were taught nautical phrases, like 'Son of a Gun', and 'Between the devil and the deep blue sea', and were educated about their origins.

We learned the hard way that if we were caught ambling around with our hands in our pockets, that we would soon be sitting with our 'housewives', sewing up those same pockets.

We assembled, disassembled and fired the SLR (Self-Loading Rifle). We all looked forward to a day on the firing range – on one occasion I got twenty-two hits on my target, with only eighteen rounds, and received a well-coveted 'divisional strip' for it. No one ever questioned that one. At some point we were given bayonets to play with, and discovered they were not only sharp – they were very pointed, and hurt if you accidentally stuck yourself with them.

We were given the SMG (Sub Machine Gun) to play with, and were told to put it on single, not automatic. We all duly fired off round after round, and then put it on auto. We then discovered how just a quick squeeze of the trigger sent three rounds off, no matter how quick your squeeze was. You could, if you kept it pointed low enough, see the rounds driving into the ground, and as you adjusted your aim, the rounds gradually crept towards the desired aiming point. Once we mastered that, we were allowed to fire off the rest all at once, if we liked. There were many rules on the firing range – keep it pointed down range AT ALL TIMES was just one. But, when you squeezed the SMG trigger, the weapon jumped upwards and to starboard – and there was not a thing you could do to prevent it. This was why you only squeezed three off at a time – you knew they'd get to whatever it was you aimed at. Of course, we were also told that if we DID use it in anger, just to point it and hold the trigger until the weapon was empty, then change the magazine and repeat until all the mags were empty. Then you grabbed the hot end and used the weapon as a club until there were too many in opposition, at which time you threw the useless weapon at whoever was coming towards you, and ran in the opposite direction, screaming loudly.

All these weapons were kept in the armoury, and we would queue for a weapon, check it was empty before accepting it, use it all day without ammunition, take it back where it would again be checked for emptiness – and all we did was swing them around on the parade ground, usually. The checks still had to be made. Just for added effect, we were shown the film about the squaddies playing with an unchecked weapon. The scene where the rifle discharges, and the round goes through the pongo holding the barrel, is unforgettable, and one which made us vow to always, always check our weapon. We didn't talk much on the way back from the cinema that day once we'd seen what a 7.62 mm round does to a human. I know it was only pretend, but it still shocked.

We underwent the ritualized attempted drowning where we were forced to swim for several lengths, fully dressed, in order to prove we could do it. It was actually a 'back-classing' offence to not be able to swim. Fortunately, I swam well, and got another 'strip' for my ability to do this and rescue various irrelevant items from the bottom of the pool – I also passed a couple of lifesaving awards for doing this. What did surprise me, however, was the number of entrants that could not swim, or who swam badly. I would think that a prerequisite of joining the Navy would be a desire to float under one's own power

We did physical training – we marched up the hill over THAT bridge, past the Wrens' quarters, did our exercise in the extremely and impressively well-equipped gymnasium, and marched back down again. I don't remember seeing anything female. Or any Wrens. We covered the assault course, where in any weather we descended into muddy and, on occasions, water-filled holes, clambered across ropeways over ditches, climbed walls, got filthy, and enjoyed ourselves immensely. I was very pleased with myself the day I traversed a rope bridge on my stomach, one leg hooked – the other dangling. Even the people at the far end shaking the rope didn't manage to put me off, despite throwing the inevitable thunderflashes at me. To be truthful, we all actually got extremely fit during our time at *Raleigh*, we doubled everywhere, we undertook assault courses, swam, played rugby – you name it, we rarely stopped moving. We also learned teamwork, something which was to stay with us for very many years, and then some!

We had only been there three or four weeks when the First Sea Lord came especially to see me . . . and all my mates. Well, the whole of *Raleigh* I suppose. Admiral Sir Michael Le Fanu GCB, DSC. I clearly remember all us baby sailors lining up and forming the word 'RALEIGH' for him to see, standing to complete attention in several inches of very sloppy mud off the bottom of the parade ground. Immensely proud we were that day, especially when he addressed us all. Until afterwards, when we had to scrape the mud and crud off our boots, then polish them again ready for the inevitable daily divisions in our immaculate Eights the following morning. But we had at least seen a real admiral.

Oh yes, and the kit inspections. There was a magical place called 'slops', wherein we could buy extras, such as replacements for kit that had gone walkabout from the communal drying rooms or had been ripped/wrecked on that assault course. Although on £7 per fortnight it was difficult enough to survive let alone buy extra kit. So, if you had extra cash, and were sensible you bought extra gear, washed and ironed it to the highest standard, then kept it for kit inspections. The rest of us merely pissed it up against the walls of Guzz's pubs. If the kit inspector found something annoying, he would take exception to the point of throwing all your gear round the room for a rescrub later. This exception could be an unaligned collar, or uncoiled lanyard, or a skidder on your hampers, or a hole in a sock. We learned that in the final week of Part One training we would have not only kit musters but full exams, which if not passed would immediately entitle us to at least one further week's training in Part One, among those pointed out to us like lepers, as 'the backclassed'. These people didn't feature in social lives, they were clearly lowlife – and we were scared witless in case we ended up like that. So we made sure our kit was good. The one very good thing about 'slops' was that it was where you collected your ciggy ration in return for stamps. You were entitled to 300 cigarettes a month at that time, costing about ten bob. They made you cough after you'd smoked them all, but you got better when you ran out and went back to proper ones, like the 'Number 6' which was all we could afford. These 'Blue Liners' were allegedly sweepings up, along with the rat hairs etc. Still, at ten bob, who was going to complain. And you could always illegally scrounge or trade a few more stamps, especially from the non-smokers, to supplement your ration.

We also had to attend school, where we did what I thought was the most basic in maths and English, striving towards the NAMET (Naval Maths/English Test) where the highest attainment you could get was a zero-zero. On the first try I scored a 2/1, but then received my GCE result which automatically gave me a zero-one (or was it one-zero), at which time, despite thinking I wouldn't need to do another test, I discovered I had to anyway because all the rest of the class had to.

At this time there were constant dental visits, plus the odd jab to keep you on your feet. Also a strange film that explained to us how to diagnose tertiary syphilis – said to turn the strongest stomach. There was also a film about the dangers of drug-taking, especially LSD, where the anti-hero let down all his mates. We looked forward to these films, and took special interest in those showing damaged warships, or how to replenish.

Each afternoon was still spent doing sport, usually rugby or cross-country and sometimes as a treat deck-hockey. This kept our minds off most things really, which was fortunate, as the food was never that terrific now. You generally needed to line up for many minutes in order to be at the front of the interminable queue, to guarantee first digs at a decent meal. If you left it too long, the best scran would go, you'd be left with the scratchings and scrapings, or even nothing but toast and beans. If that happened, you were within your 'rights' to demand a meal. But it was not in your interests to make that kind of a fuss – better to ask, please, for a couple of eggs to go on the toast, then scarper quickly to the Naafi to top up. Strangely, each suppertime, an officer would cruise the dining hall, asking in a loud voice, 'Has anyone any complaints about the food tonight', to be met with stony silence. We weren't that daft.

We had evening rounds daily, regardless, where, on top of everything else we did, we had to clean up for the Officer of the Day (OOD) to come and see how immaculate we could get the room. Or not, in the case of the ignominious rescrub, and cancellation of the snooker game. The Saturday morning rounds were made by 'someone important' – the Training Commander for example, who (it was said) wore white gloves, and went over every square inch. The mess considered to be the cleanest, or which clearly had had the most effort put into it, or was the best improved since last time, won a sponge cake, iced all over and lovingly baked by the chefs. I mock, but it was actually a terrific feeling to win it – it made you extremely proud to know that your efforts had been recognized.

One of the most degrading jobs was that of 'skirmishing'. This entailed going round the outside of the mess and block, picking up anything unnatural. Grass, buildings and roads were considered 'natural', everything else had to be picked up: dog-ends, matches, nutty-wrappers. Skirmishing was the last resort – if you hadn't got anything better to do, or if you finished your previously allotted task early, 'Go and skirmish round the parade ground' was the order we all dreaded to hear. So we prolonged the chore. It didn't matter that it wasn't you who dropped it, or that you knew who it was, someone, soon, would end up picking it up. We were even set targets, 'Pick up ten bits of garbage each, then report back to me'. Where the hell were we expected to find ten bits of crud, each, in a class of thirty? Fortunately we knew how to raid rubbish bins, and we could always go back to the spitkid in the mess for a few dog-ends. Not that we ever used to do things like that. . .

To get the messdeck up to the expected extremely high naval standard, the class leader would detail us off for various tasks, from the heads or bathrooms, or the beams (holding the roof up/on), or the buffer (the polishing machine – a large vacuum cleaner type beast, with a revolving head covered with a large soft pad) or whatever other jobs needed doing. All this gear was kept in a communal cleaning gear store, which was shared with all the other classes/messes within the block. Due to this shared option, it meant if you didn't get the gear out early, you had to wait until everyone else had finished with it before you got your crack. You would then spend hours hanging around someone else's mess, so he didn't shit on you, and give the gear to another mess, ahead of your turn.

Smells are very evocative, for example, the smell of the first pub you ever went in, the smell of school dinners, but the all-prevailing smell during this entire period was that of the wax polish, which we applied by hand, before buffing it up to a high gloss with that damned machine. The polish came out of a large tin, was coloured orange and stained your fingers as you applied it with a clean cloth. It was therefore in one's interest to make sure the class leader was your mate, so you polished the ashtrays rather than the toilet seats. Our class leader was a fearsome chap of seventeen, who had come from HMS *Ganges* – where they trained 'boy sailors' below sixteen years of age – who was supposed to have 'leadership qualities' and knew all the wrinkles. Except the one which eventually got him backclassed. We would spend hours each getting the mess up to full brilliance in time for superman to find some minuscule fault. All cat and mouse, however, the week we won the cake for the best one we were absolutely over the moon, going ashore full of wind and piss. And cake.

After spending days and evenings putting it all together, we would unwind by raiding other messes and classes, which involved huge pillow fights, often degenerating into real fights as stakes were raised. Then we would run back in triumph, waiting to see if we would be raided in retaliation. Or we'd hold impromptu wrestling contests in the corridors. One thing, of course, that we were not allowed to do was take out the crabby bastards who had lower personal hygiene standards than others. We were warned not to do this, and we therefore never took them to the bathroom for an enforced bath, and were told the rumours were not true that dirty people were scrubbed with yardbrooms and hard soap, dressed or undressed. Finally, we were told, the large, open tanks of water scattered round the base were specifically not for throwing these crabby people into. They were deep and therefore dangerous, which is why they were fenced off. Their scratches soon healed though, as did the atmosphere.

It wasn't all relaxation(!), we were divided into watches, either PORT or STARBOARD watch. Then into First and Second Part of the Watch. Meaning that every fourth day we had extra duties to perform. Like staying in the mess and cleaning while our mates stuffed themselves with cakes and lemonade at the Naafi.

We learned about Naval traditions like watches, and that clearly The Last Dog ran from 1800–2000, and that the Middle ran from 2359 (not 0001) to 0400. A strange thing is that 0000 does not exist as a time in the RN. Only 2359 or 0001. Nor do you say 2330 *hours* like the rest of the idiots and Army and Air Force do – we understood 2330, and didn't need to be told or reminded that time was measured in hours. It annoys me terribly even today when people add the word 'hours' after saying a time. What is the point of saying 'It is 22 hundred *hours*'?

We were taught one day that the phrase 'No Red Port Left' contained all the ingredients we needed: to tell left from right – sorry, port from starboard – and what colour lights were on which side of the ship. Therefore, we were told – starboard was right and had green lights! We also learned various 'calls' and 'pipes' on our bosun's calls – peculiarly shaped whistles which you held in a particular manner, and, depending whether you had your hand open, or cupped over the hole, the call could be made to issue a range of notes, therefore tunes. Again, either you could do this or you couldn't; plenty couldn't. Following this, a tradition at *Raleigh* was to pipe (on the bosun's call) the tune for 'hands to dinner', and I remember being picked as one of the piping party when it was the turn of our class to do it. We proudly marched to the Quartermaster's lobby, from where all tannoy broadcasts were made, stood in front of the open microphone and blew a note-perfect rendition – to no applause, just an 'off you go for lunch now lads'. I was very disappointed.

A strange description, but 'catching the liberty boat' was a euphemism for going ashore. Not easy, you would think to catch a boat from the main gate to the bus stop. However, the Navy knew best. Catching the liberty boat, meant suffering first at the washer/iron, then getting into full blues, best hat and lanyard, then trying to get past the Duty PO at the gate, who, it was said, would send you back to your mess with no leave if your dress, bearing and demeanour didn't come up to his standard. To get by him, you had to all fall in three deep, for him to inspect you, and boy did you get hauled over. If you were caught with more than the twenty-five Blue Liners allowed per night, you'd be sent back, but not before being 'trooped' for the privilege. On the bright side, if you made it, you'd march nicely through the gate, then whoop and run to the bus stop to get the bus to the ferry. While on the Torpoint ferry you'd always be looking for warships tied-up (not berthed – liners berth, not warships), then you'd catch another bus or the walk into Plymouth. This became standard. However, what I hadn't anticipated was the reception we got when I first took shore leave, splendidly turned out. My friends and I were ruffy-tuffy sailors on our first shore leave, we were smart cookies resplendent in our Number Ones (with seven razor-like creases alternately facing front and back), best collar (with three razor-like creases, one inverted, in the middle, one either side between the middle and the outside going the other way), best white front (with a crease starched so stiffly, you could cut steak with it), best silk (with no burn marks from having the iron too hot), best hat (well nearly, we kept a special 'going ashore' cap, with specially created 'bow-waves' in it to show off with), high-gloss shoes – the absolute shining example. But we were met with – well, nothing. The people of Plymouth had seen it on countless thousands of occasions before (and have it to come for many years yet), and they clearly weren't about to empty the town to come and look at a just another bunch of new recruits. Oh yes, and we stank of cheap soap, and tins and tins of starch – we didn't wear aftershave, we couldn't afford to, and anyway only poofs wore that stuff. Apart from that, we didn't even shave properly (though it was coming along nicely), so it would have been totally pointless. We settled for just a good deodorant!

You must understand though, that we were generally downhearted by the reaction of the population of Plymouth to our sudden emergence. Again, it wasn't that we expected massed bands, ticker-tape parades and the local female population ripping their clothes off for us as we walked by (although we lived in hope), but thus far we had been 'gee'd up' by trainers and to some extent by ourselves, and at that time we were full of the most incredible pride. Pride in ourselves for getting accepted and trained by the RN. Pride in the RN. But mostly, pride in our incredible new appearance. We had been transformed from scruffy, shambling, semi-upright, part-lucid teenagers with stoops, to broad-backed, broad-shouldered, upright, forward-facing, healthy, literate servicemen, dressed immaculately in the best uniforms Pusser could provide, all in a matter of weeks. And nobody in Plymouth gave a flying shit.

It occurred to us later that Plymouth (and Portsmouth and Chatham and Rosyth) was, after all, a naval base, and was full to the brim with sailors. Baby sailors, experienced sailors, old sailors, all dressed alike, and we were the only ones who knew we were fresh out of the factory, and therefore needed a welcoming committee. But it was too late – I still remember the feeling of rejection. It hurt us all for a long while. Well, actually, until the next day, when we were allowed ashore again to gallivant round. We soon got over most things, because we had just recently learned how to be extremely resilient, but above all we got over it – because we were Jack!

It was good to get my first pint of Courage (so called, allegedly because you need courage to drink it), then to stamp around the Hoe and the town, feed greedily on burgers and milkshakes at the bowling alley, then repair to the Rooftop (I think) to finish off the job, sucking in large quantities of brown ale, and rum 'n' black. Bearing in mind we got paid £7 every second week, we used to make a large hole in it at that place at 1s 8d for a pint of beer. It was then a game to see if we could time it right to get the bus, to connect with the ferry, to buy an oggy at the greasy spoon, to give us enough time to catch the bus back to HMS *Raleigh* before we were declared adrift at 2245. At this time, you collected your station card, a device to check whether you were on board. If you left the ship, you left your card behind and when you returned you collected it. If your card was still there past the allotted time, you were adrift.

Believe it – if you weren't back by the correct time there were no excuses good enough nor were there any places to hide in front of the Captain at his table. Once again you were in your Number Ones, but much improved on the night out, and were lectured on how everyone in the camp got back in time except you, and how the Navy would under no circumstances tolerate lateness in any fashion, and when we went to sea, and the liberty boat left us ashore because we were adrift for it, how would we get back to the ship? Therefore, it was impressed upon you that you would be back on time on the next occasion, and to remind you of the importance of that, you would have your leave stopped for several weeks at a time. This must be rhetorical – I was never in all my naval career late! Sorry, adrift.

One evening, I forget who it was, but a colleague came back off shore a bit worse for wear (or 'shiters' as we used to say), then woke us all up barging about, and banging and smashing around. When he fell asleep, we held a hurried blacked-out messdeck meeting, and when he awoke in the morning, he didn't realize his bed had been elevated one level up above someone else's. He swung his legs out, passed his centre of gravity, and pitched on to our highly polished deck several feet further below. Not that we laughed. For very long. Or very loudly. After that, everyone woke up cautiously, and first felt with their toes for the deck before swinging out, so we had to find a new game. Another night, somebody else did it, and was amazed to find someone had removed the roof from his mess during the night. Or was it that we'd carried him and his bed outside on to the roadway while he snored noisily in his drunken stupor.

We visited a ship in the dockyard one fine morning, passing the massive bulk of HMS *Ark Royal* on our way, then in dry dock in the middle of a lengthy refit, surrounded by scaffolding, canvas dodgers and covered with different shades of grey and red paint. Not what we had come to expect. Subsequently, rumours were spread that it would be going back to sea fairly soon, and that it would require large numbers of junior ratings. Us, in other words. Until then, I had never seen so much metal in one place at the same time, and I marvelled at the organized chaos of men and 'dockyard mateys', as they were known, all carrying different items from here to there, or wearing welding masks, or toting drums of paint, all travelling on small trucks dashing around the dockyard with their drivers perched precariously at the front. These seemed to be the official mode of transport, along with the official Pusser's bike, never left unguarded under any circumstances.

The ship we finally reached was a Cat class frigate, covered with radar, funnels and guns, and it was with awe that I, at least, spent as long as I could clambering round it. My first footing on a real warship, even though the crew sneered at us as we squealed excitedly at each new bit of kit.

Robbo, our PO, was in the habit of requesting babysitters, so he and his wife could go out. We would have to wait our turn, but volunteering meant Robbo collected us (me and my friend Glen from the main gate (still in our Number Ones), and took us to his house on the married patch. Once there we could go to half blues, watch his telly, drink the bottled beer and eat the sarnies – both extremely thoughtfully provided – and while away the hours until they returned. Then we'd have a ride back to the main gates. It didn't matter if we were late, in fact, I think we had special dispensation to be so. We all volunteered when we found out about this, not everyone got used, not everyone got a go, so we considered ourselves fortunate and took full advantage of the extra night out.

We spent one weekend on Dartmoor, where we yomped for miles, passing various checkpoints until our boots became too tight. These were the boots that on the previous day we had polished to a high shine for divisions and which were now caked in mud. This 'exped' finished on Sunday afternoon at an inn on the moor, and the incentive to get back in time was that it would still be serving beer! I clearly remember me and my team batting down the hillside, reaching the inn with seconds to spare, and gulping down Courage before bussing back to Torpoint. Even then there was no peace – we of course had to clean and repair before divisions the following morning.

On another occasion we had the much dreaded 'gas-mask test', which consisted of waiting outside a building, with just the one exit/entrance door. We then masked up and entered a smoke-filled room. After several circuits, we were told to remove the mask, and head for the door. Not me. I wasn't that stupid. I did not see why I should have to inhale tear gas deliberately. So I headed for the door hidden, I thought, among the rest. As I neared the door, and just as I thought I had got away with it, my mask was removed for me, in one swift yank, followed by a 'light' tap to the abdomen – just enough to make me breathe in sharply. If you ever get the chance to taste tear gas, don't. It tastes vile. The whole class stood coughing and retching. That was one 'test' everyone passed. It took hours for our eyes to stop smarting and for our noses to stop running.

The next weeks were a blur of more training, less parade training but more seamanship training. This became more involved and interesting though, as we learned how to climb safety nets, lower bosun's chairs, make up and lower paint stages, and lower and raise seaboats (from the derricks, known as davits, with the ropes on them known as 'falls', on the parade ground, in the full knowledge that if we fouled that one up, there would be a heap of highly painted but very smashed up wood at the base of the 'falls'). We learned how to distinguish between clinker-built and carvel-built boats, and how to repair them, and, most importantly, how to preserve the metal the ship was made of, to 'prevent' it from suddenly decomposing in the middle of the ocean and sinking. This is achieved by a top secret method – something called 'painting'. But you have to know how to paint, properly. We, therefore, first had to learn how to prepare the surface to be painted. This overall procedure is known as 'ship-husbandry' and was to be how I would spend a large proportion of my time in the RN until I finally got promoted, at which point I could detail off and watch, while others 'did'. We learned how to use paint remover, not just the chemicals that burned your fingers if you weren't careful, but chipping hammers, sandpaper – all sorts of interesting ways legally to deface paint and metal. We were then taught how to paint it again, layer by layer – primer, undercoat and topcoat. Holidays were explained (otherwise known as 'you've missed a bit there – were you on holiday then?'), as were sagging and other technical terms.

We also learned how to RAS or Replenish At Sea, where the movies were fascinating. Who would have thought two ships stamping along at many knots could transfer people and stores between them by using bits of rope. Not just any rope, mind you, but special manilla, of a certain thickness and predefined length, in accordance with the official Manual of Seamanship. To be precise 80 fathoms of 4 in. This required twenty or so sailors to hold this jackstay taut as this took place. As part of our training for this, we learned to abseil down one side of the parade ground, a drop of almost ten feet.

Among other nautical lessons, we learned how to tie even more varied and technical bends and hitches, what various coloured buoys signified, how to perform lookout duties, how to clean the gleaming paintwork once we'd applied it, how to weigh anchor, and a thousand and one different nautical terms, all to be memorized ready for the final exams.

One weekend, we went on an 'exped' to Pier Cellars – a small man-made harbour, once used to handle torpedoes, left over from the bygone age of war, we were told, around the coast from *Raleigh*. We slung hammocks in cold, bricked caves, then practised what we had been taught up until then. We undertook various seamanship evolutions, such as jackstay transfers over and across the harbour, and went on the death slide. That was an experience to have – the high end was some hundred feet up the cliffside, with nothing below until you reached the bottom. In this very atmospheric setting the weekend was fantastic. We were introduced to the delights of 'potmess'. Potmess is everything from everyone's individually issued survival rations which we ate every time we went on any kind of trip. Whether it was steak and kidney pud, bacon, sausage and beans, curry, peaches, soup, and/or biscuits, it was all thrown into one cooking pot tastefully named a 'fanny', heated, then eaten with more of the biscuits (tack) provided and washed down with several crates of Courage, thoughtfully provided by our PO. We did more evolutions, more games, clambered up and down the cliffs, explored every inch of the place, and finally returned to *Raleigh* on the Sunday afternoon, tired but happy.

A further exped found us once again up on the moors. We ate more potmess, and tried to keep ourselves dry in the interminable, horizontal, driving rain and snow. We attempted to sleep in the tents, but were too cold to, so we dozed fitfully during prolonged shivering bouts until being plunged back into the rain early the following morning. We again walked miles and miles over the moors. One fortunate thing we discovered about eating your rations in this way was that it took away the necessity to use toilets. You went away on the Friday night, started on 'the compo', ate it all weekend, returned on the Sunday, then, finally, your bowels exploded on the Monday, if you were lucky.

Throughout all the weeks at *Raleigh*, we were continually appraised and tested, whether by test papers or by head-to-heads with officers. We must have done well for ourselves, I cannot recall anyone being backclassed from the seamanship training.

CHAPTER 3

Our First Days on the Ocean Wave . . .

Towards the end of the year, we were taken for real sea training for a week, on the old Second World War frigate HMS *Ulster*, which had a bad reputation, because of her having had several accidents in her time. We were terrified as we boarded the first time, making sure we saluted the ensign on the quarterdeck as we did, but we had a wonderful week on her. She was then probably the fastest ship the RN had, and one day to prove it we did a full power trial on her. I seem to recall 45 knots being the speed we attained – with a wake out of the blunt end you couldn't see over! Or was it that we had a race with the *Cavalier*, or the Rapid, which herself turned out to be the swiftest. Whatever – it was still a bloody big wake we created, just astern of a very noisily vibrating grey metal box!!

We kipped in the aftermess in hammocks, and collected our food in fannies from the galley. It took every bit of strength to hold on to that pitching, rolling ship and the food, enveloped by the exhaust fumes from the funnel. We did a mortar shoot one day, although Arthur and I weren't aware what or where the mortars were, nor that they were about to fire until someone screamed at us to 'get out of the fucking way'. As we moved away, and only seconds later, the dull, triple thump made the ship recoil and vibrate as the huge depth-charge mortars were fired – right through where we had just been standing. We had got out of the way sharpish, below decks, and expressed surprise when someone came looking for us. That was my first 'near death'. We cruised Portland, standing deck watches, crewed the seaboat, watched the radar – in fact did everything we could. I even used a 'maul' (large sledgehammer) to knock the slip off the cable to drop the anchor, although it took me two swings to do it! It was related at the time that the buffer of a ship once had trouble slipping an anchor, and had screamed at the inexperienced bosun's mate on the bridge to 'Fetch a maul up'. The BM heard that as 'Fetch 'em all up', and instead of providing the large hammer as requested, actually piped 'Clear lower deck – all hands muster on the fo'c's'le'.

The seaboat one was scary but was something we all had to do – the Navy way of putting a seaboat out is to whack the ship through the sea as fast as necessary while lowering the seaboat halfway to the waterline, slow to around six knots, then drop the boat on the crest of a wave (to prevent its back breaking in a trough). The seaboat coxswain then throws the tiller hard over towards the ship, the seaboat veers to starboard and moves sharpishly away from the ship. At some point, the boatrope towing the whaler at this stage is slipped and the seaboat makes off.

To recover it, there is a piece of equipment called the Robinson's Disengaging Gear. We had to play with this bit of kit until we could rebuild it, again with our eyes shut and behind our backs. This gear is extremely critical for hoisting, and if it isn't made up correctly, the boat will be hauled halfway up the falls, then crash back into the sea, probably drowning everyone who used to be in what was left of the boat. There is, therefore, enormous pressure to get it right first time. So when the boat comes back alongside, the bowrope is secured, then the front fall put on (hopefully correctly made up) then the after fall. Then the boat is raised – to a sigh of relief if it was made up correctly. During all this chaotic activity, you had to make sure all the boat's fenders were brought inboard as you got above deck level, but the 'Jimmy' would always be there anyway, dancing around, screaming 'FENDERS – FUCKINFENDERS'. When we went alongside one day, Glen and me shot off into Weymouth, where we next caught a train to Poole (where he lived) for the day, swaggered into his old local pubs in rig and got served. That made a wonderful break while we were supposed to be watching some boring sporting event.

Of course, being (extremely) naïve baby sailors, fresh out of our cardboard box, we didn't have much idea about anything, other than what had been drummed into us, so it was left to our PO, as well as the *Ulster*'s crew, to teach us the immediate rudimentary lessons, and this one is THE most important lesson you can ever learn in the 'Mob'. If the sea state is 'bouncy', and you feel a 'yak' (sickness) coming on, you have two choices. First, get below, quickly, to the heads where you can hide and cuddle the bowl. This is nice and safe, and no-one can see you. You feel fine after a few minutes – until the next time. The alternative would be to find a spot on the upper deck where no one can see you, and throw up over the leeward side. This is also quite safe, as long as you hold on to something. Except, as babies, we were not accomplished enough to tell the difference between the leeward (no wind) side, or the windward (very windy) side. If you chunder over the windward side, it falls several feet, gets caught in the strong wind, comes back, and redecorates you from head to toe, in your hair, clothes, boots, ears – everywhere. You can, therefore, easily tell when this has happened to someone – and it is a long time before anyone allows you to forget it. People will stand behind you making retching noises and sniggering. I stress I was only ever seasick the once, and it wasn't aboard the *Ulster*. But I took the piss out of plenty who were! This was a fantastic lesson not to pass on to others later in one's career. Talking of which, the ultimate 'collapse laughing', is watching someone closed up in full anti-flash and respirator, already feeling ill, trying to keep breakfast down and failing. The look of surprise in their eyes as their gas mask fills up from bottom to top with fresh puke is something else. Panic is one word I'd use, as they try to rip the mask off before hurtling to a safe place to clean up, with the rest of the worlds' laughing ringing in their ears!

Amazingly, we survived everything the *Ulster* and Portland could throw at us that week, and could add a bit more swank when we got back to *Raleigh*, as we had been to sea, and we were Jack.

Eventually our final passing out divisions were held one fine day, where we were 'guard class'. We had rehearsed and trained for this, and were to be inspected in front of our families by the Captain. I looked forward to that, as we all did, and I can still remember the bitter disappointment on discovering that my mum and dad hadn't come down to see my passing out parade. I scanned the onlookers, then scanned them again for a familiar face, but nothing. I (and my mates) had spent many hours getting our kit absolutely shining for those divisions, but I completed the parade with a heavy, heavy heart.

Actually, there was no reason for me to expect them, but I still lived in hope. I can, though, remember every drill we did, stamping our feet down hard, to create maximum noise and impression. We even had pennies in the otherwise empty magazines of our SLRs so they rattled noisily, emphasizing each swing and drill manoeuvre.

We got to late December 1969 and were by then suffering from the traditional naval 'RDP' (Run Down Period) leading up to Christmas leave, until that day arrived and we were to go 'home' for two weeks. We all got buses to the ferry and to the station, then on the fast train to London. We attempted to buy beer, but the buffet man demanded proof of age. So we slunk off and stayed sober instead. We sat on our kitbags – there was no room on that train for seating. During the journey, we passed the time looking for a lad classed as a 'nause', as in a person likely to 'cause nause'. He had a habit of poking his face into yours and calling you 'sunshine'. We were out gunning for him, and you may rightly assume he was not a popular kiddy. I think the word went out, because we didn't find him until just before Waterloo station – by which time he had got himself locked in the guard's compartment. I still don't know whether he or the guard had done it (or even if someone else had). We all split up, and headed for our next stations, then home, and never saw 'Sunshine' again, even when back at *Raleigh*. He really knew how and when to keep a low profile.

We travelled home in our Number One uniforms. Gold badges, lanyards – best hat – the works. And while all this went unnoticed in Plymouth and on that train, I felt the urge to (as our PO told us, repeatedly) 'give it stacks of swank and swagger'. So back went the shoulders as I virtually marched in my studded boots across the underground to Euston, stamped noisily down the platform to my train under the gaze of whoever would look in my direction, and thence on to Northampton.

I got a taxi to my home, which hadn't changed a bit in the fourteen weeks I had been away, but it was nice to be there for Christmas. I was now sixteen, going on twenty.

CHAPTER 4

Farewell to Plymouth –
Hello to Dryad

My first leave was over in a blur, and once again I left Northampton to return to Plymouth. I completed my last week of baby sailor training and was then drafted. As I was detailed now to be a radar operator – clearly the best job going, you never, ever met a stupid RP, – that meant moving to HMS *Dryad*, just outside Pompey. This was reached after a long journey, eventually arriving at our destination of Portsmouth and Southsea station. We (Arthur, Geoff, Stevie and me) then caught a Navy 'tilly (utility vehicle) to the small village of Southwick, on the outskirts of Portsmouth.

We collected our bedding and cap tallies, having first dumped our gear off in the tattiest huts I have ever seen. These Nissen huts, collectively known as Anson Block, were to be our home for the next six weeks. Our training there began with the traditional divisions, followed by the course PO (PRI) (Plot Radar Instructor) explaining what we were to learn over the next six weeks of our basic radar operator's course.

This introductory radar course consisted of learning all the technical specifications, bandwidths and operating frequencies of every radar in use by the Navy, and being word perfect on them every time you were tested, which was daily. We learned at what range we could expect to locate an aircraft on the air radar, or what range to spot the difference between a tin-can and a submarine periscope on the navigation set, and where we could locate other ships on the surface search. Also, we became familiar with the principles of IFF (Identification Friend or Foe) just so we could be sure we wouldn't unnecessarily engage friendly aircraft. We were given extensive training on how to talk to other ships, aircraft etc. over UHF radios, learned how to use HF radio, which made your voice sound like you were on heavy helium, and how to annoy everyone else by repeatedly saying 'coco pops' into the 'radio' whenever you got bored.

We learned about attenuation and super refraction, both being meteorological effects on radar. We were also taken into 'models', where we were able to put the lessons into practice by creating as near to live situations as possible without getting seasick. *Dryad*'s 'models' were mock-ups of various ships' operation rooms, complete with radar fed from a control room. Any kind of situation could be modelled, any kind of war game could be developed. We were thrown into the models alongside experienced ratings, going either for their 'twos', 'ones', or 'I' (second class, first class or Instructors) qualifications. That is, they were being trained as senior, more useful operators. Us? – we were firmly at the bottom of the heap, but still learning fast. It is amazing how quickly you do something once you've been smashed round the ears with the heavy metal rolling ruler normally used to plot 'dead-reckoning' lines. We also became aware that standing in front of live, transmitting radar aerials was not conducive to your health. In fact, we were told, it would cook you from the inside out. A great opportunity missed by someone there, in the light of microwave ovens!

There were many Duty watches with us doing the crap jobs no one else wanted, with a Naafi we could go into, but where we still could not buy beer – we had to go into Portsmouth to do that. At that time, as juniors, we still had to wear 'rig' to go ashore. Though as it was a thirty minute bus ride to Portsmouth, and as we weren't allowed (due to our tender ages) in 'the Beast', we contented ourselves with the shared TV rooms, the football tables and the badminton.

There were, though, more fascinating machines in a special room just outside the Naafi, called 'the automat'. This, as we soon learned, was where everyone gathered after the Naafi shut, to feed up for the night. The automat consisted of three or four machines full of various foods, one hot, one cold, one nutty and cakes, one drinks, where you put money in the top, pressed the button on the visible selection and hoped that the correct door opened to feed you. Except that when you were three sheets to the wind, they refused to work unless you kicked the shit out of the machine, which was why they always had a Duty automat rating in there, and which was also why we used to gather there most evenings.

Apart from this very visible entertainment, other events there were mostly initiated by a very old (it seemed, though he was probably no older than twenty-five) able seaman, called Jed. Jed could play guitar and sing. And eat, and drink – all seemingly at the same time. Accompanied by a Wren called Blodwyn. That's what she was known as – being Welsh. I don't think they were 'together', but they may have been, it didn't occur to us to ask! Everybody at *Dryad* at that time knew (of) Blodders, even now, if I find someone who admits to being there at the time, I will ask 'Do you remember Blodwyn?' If they say 'No', then either they didn't 'mix' well, or they're fibbing to me about when they were there.

We were introduced to TV rooms here – there were two rooms with tellies in, one showed BBC, the other ITV – remember those days of only two channels? By consensus, the channel could be changed, unless someone wanted to watch something else, otherwise you changed rooms. Fights broke out in TV rooms. They always stank of smoke, were normally full of cans and nutty wrappers, and always had the spitkids full. It was a Duty watch job to clean them out at 'lights out' – a job to be avoided, at all costs. All shore bases had these TV rooms. It was where you ended up, either after you'd pissed all your pay up against the wall, or were Duty watch but were not detailed for anything special, or if you were just a git, who didn't mix with the rest of 'the lads'.

Towards the end of the radar course, and after our final exams, we were given our 'drafts', and mindful of the fact that the *Ark Royal* was being stocked with boxes of new baby sailors, it was with extreme relief that I received my draft to join HMS *Zulu* – once again along with Arthur, Geoff and Stevie. My relief was tempered though by two pieces of news. Firstly, it was in refit and secondly, it was in Rosyth, wherever on earth that was!

At the end of our course, and while we were waiting for our draft, I was assigned to the 'Buffer's party', which meant being attached to a group of real sailors, who walked around *Dryad* most of the day doing such tasks as cleaning-up type things. This meant you could go anywhere in the vast grounds of *Dryad*, virtually without restriction, provided you either carried a naval issue stiff broom, or pushed the (garbage) 'truck', at that time christened 'Thunderbird Three'. As the grounds were enormous, it was possible to disappear for hours on end without question while exploring the estate. I found out one day, that what was the officers' wardroom was in fact Southwick House – where the D-Day invasion had apparently been co-ordinated. There was also a commemorative D-Day tapestry, although I never saw it despite many visits there.

The Buffer, so called because he was a buffer between the Jimmy (or First Lieutenant to give him his correct title) and 'the lads', was a seaman branch chief or petty officer, occasionally a leading seaman, who always knew more than was good for him. He commanded authority, was generally an expert on most things and could usually be relied upon to organize anything, anywhere. If you were told to report to the Buffer, you did so immediately, or later at your peril.

There was a joke going round at the time, about a young sailor, Junior Seaman Smith, being assigned to the Buffer's party, and being detailed off by the Buffer to go out and sweep up with the rest of the sweepers. Most importantly, whoever saw the Admiral first (he was due to arrive later that afternoon) was to tell the Buffer immediately. JS Smith vanished with his broom, and was desultorily sweeping the gutters, when a large black car, complete with Admiral's pennant pulled up alongside him. The Admiral leaned out, and asked who he was addressing. 'Junior Seaman Smith', was the reply. 'Why – who wants to know?' 'I am the Admiral' said the Admiral. 'Well I'd make myself scarce if I were you . . .' said JS Smith, '. . .'cos the Buffer's after you'.

To be assigned to the Buffer's party was like getting a crash course in naval life. I learned much while in the 'party', most importantly that at standeasy, the Buffer's store became a sudden tea shop, complete with strong cheese and thick onion in crusty rolls – something I still enjoy hugely – or ham if you preferred. Amazingly, one member of the Buffer's party was permanently assigned to creating these rolls and to wetting the tea for those standeasies. This was all sold, very cheaply, presumably with the profits going to the welfare fund. It was staggering the amount of people who could cram in there among the brooms and buckets and mops and cleaning fluids and ropes at any one time. So too, was the number of people who would just 'drop in' for a cuppa, a fag and a chat. I acquired a vast amount of knowledge based on gossip, and sea stories, getting more wild as the standeasies went on, a game forever played then – 'black-cat'-ing. This game went on ashore, onboard, during work, out of work – every sailor past or present, any time, anywhere will have a large repertoire of 'black-cats'. I did, though, learn how to sweep roads, on top of my other skills!

The Buffer's store had a telephone, which would periodically ring if someone was looking for anyone. We wondered at the old hands who would answer the phone with 'War Office – wanna fight?', or 'Stonehenge – Duty Druid', or 'Netley Hospital – Duty Loony', or any one of a number drawn from the large repertoire based on previous performances. We also learned not to give our own name away when answering, and, when asked if 'so and so' was there, we could answer either, 'In the bathroom doing basin trials' or 'Gone down the bakers for a loaf' or 'He went mad, so we shot him', or 'In the fridge, getting hard'.

These guaranteed instant crack-up locally and a great deal of yelling on the other end. We were quick to hang up, and to make ourselves immediately scarce. The Buffer's store was, somewhere to lurk, and thus had comfortable, handy, 'rabbited' (knocked off) tatty red leatherette armchairs scattered around. This was no mean feat considering the size of the place, but the best seats would always be taken by the same old faces, and if you happened to be reclining when you should have been (respectfully) leaving – heaven help you!

One thing literally burned into my memory was the day we went to the fire-training school, near Portsea, where we spent another day learning how to put fires out. In this 'simulator' (which was a mock-up of a section of a ship), we were taken round, up and down all the ladders, in and out of the compartments, shown where the fires were to be lit, and again instructed how to put them out. These were oil fires, so they burned, fiercely. We were then shown how to get into 'Fearnought' suits (fire retarding) over our ovies and how to don and switch on the breathing gear. That seemed easy enough. But as always we looked for the 'catch'.

We swiftly found it. The ICBA gear we had so carefully checked was swapped for facemasks that were blacked out. Totally. We were essentially blind. The fire pan was ignited and in we went, dragging the hose with the water jet switched to spray, in order to form a protective water wall to shield us from the intense heat, while the other one was linked back to the foam can, pumping foul-smelling bubbles everywhere.

Having ascended the external ladders, we progressed slowly. We entered the hatch at the top (doing all this by memory and by feel), and painstakingly worked our way through the simulator towards the seat of the fire, carefully slapping the back of our hand on the bulkheads. This, we were told, was the safest way to feel the heat. If we did it with our fingertips there was an excellent chance they would weld on to the steel with the heat, whereas we would not miss the skin off the backs of our hands. We checked deck after deck, descending all the time, and compartment after compartment, eventually deciding this was where the fire was, as we could see a dim glow through the face masks. It was also extremely hot, even with our water wall. We therefore called up the foam team and then threw the foam everywhere, dousing the fire.

Scared? 'Course not, we couldn't see anything to be scared of. We were more worried about the PO Stoker who continually prodded us in the ribs with his spanner, insisting we keep going further and further into the unseen blaze. Mind you, had we been able to see, we'd have been shitting clump blocks, I'm sure.

A further skill learned rapidly was that of armed security guard. One weekday morning, a mate and I were detailed off to accompany the Pay Officer to the bank in the minibus. I don't remember the bank we went to but we were heavily armed on that run. With helves (pickaxe handles), and boots and gaiters. I am not sure how much money we collected, but with several hundred sailors of all rates being paid the following day, there must have been a small fortune there, even in those days.

Queuing up for your pay was traditional then. You had to fall in, get to the front of the queue, salute, announce your name and official number, and hold out your opened paybook and station card in your upturned cap for the Pay Officer to give you your dosh. At that time, the Regulators or Master-at-Arms (who liked to think they were the RN equivalent of police, which made them not only hated personally but made them the most loathed branch in the 'Mob') would deliver a swingeing attack on the length of your hair, saying that you would have to report to them next day with your hair cut. As a reminder, he would swiftly remove your station card, meaning you couldn't get ashore. As such, you dreaded going to get paid, and would find any excuse to avoid pay parade. You thus rapidly got your ears lowered either ashore – where you'd stand a chance of getting a decent cut – or at the base barber, who'd shear most of your locks off, and reported back to the 'joss' to reclaim your station card. You also learned to 'lose' a station card, and apply for another one to use as a spare, though if you were caught doing that, you were in deep trouble.

The other role of the security guard was that of 'security foot patrol', whereby you patrolled the whole grounds and perimeter of the vast *Dryad* estate during non-working hours. This got you into all sorts of darkened corners, accompanied only by a 'stornophone' (short-range, two-way radio), a helve and a Pusser's torch. You did this or the building patrols, where, even though all the 'secure' buildings – models, trainers etc. were locked, you still had to creep round making sure there was no one there or that they were in fact locked. We also checked all the safes, and God help the keeper of any safe found open or any door unsecured.

Although the security patrol had to sleep fully dressed in the same room, behind the QM's lobby, ready to react and muster with helves, boots, gaiters, torches and windy burbs within seconds, and even though they had to get up to do two-hour patrols during the course of their duty, at least that was preferable to being detailed for the fire-cart. This cart contained fire-fighting gear, hoses, hydrants, ladders, and was kept by the MT (motor transport) garage at one end of *Dryad*. If there was a fire exercise, or indeed a real fire, the fire-cart crew had to leg it from wherever they were to the cart, wait for everyone else, then haul it to wherever the fire (or exercise) was. It was not a light cart. One person was responsible for the hydrant key, and in due course the stand pipe would be fitted, the hydrant and hose connected and the water turned on. Afterwards it all had to be stowed away and returned to the garage. Absolutely knackering. It was therefore critical that the broadcast worked throughout the camp and especially in the Naafi, where most of the Duty watch seemed to muster after supper. As long as you were sober enough to do your job, no one seemed to mind too much. At that time, *Dryad* used to have an old, blue, single-decker bus, converted into a greasy spoon, known as 'Dot's'. 'Dot's' seemed to be open all day, every day, for what I still remember as the best SRE and BRE (Sausage, Runny Egg and Bacon, Runny Egg) sarnies ever made by human hand. Also for strong tea and coffee, excellent for waking and sobering up from the previous evening's Naafi run. It was always a difficult decision between there or the Buffer's store for breakfast, assuming you hadn't got up in time for your real breakfast or were, indeed, still hungry anyway.

CHAPTER 5

HMS Zulu, in Rosyth, in Dry Dock

It was soon time to move on, so once again we packed all our gear into the obligatory kitbag and suitcase, but by then we had also proudly acquired a Pusser's holdall. As its name implied, this carried everything and anything and was made from heavy duty brown canvas, with a ropey zip, usually replaced quickly with 'eyes' and rope. One's name could be emblazoned on it, along with the ship(s) served on. Grips (as they were known) were the RN equivalent of the Ford Capri – customizable and unique to you. Once correctly packed, they could, in emergencies, be used as pillows, seats or even footballs.

We boarded the train to Waterloo, crossed to King's Cross and travelled to Edinburgh. There we found the train for Inverkeithing where we were finally met by the 'tilly for transport to the *Zulu*. One feeling I remember, not only on joining the *Zulu* but joining any ship, whether for a course, two-year draft, whatever, was the feeling of elation and expectation, coupled with unease and fears of the unknown. What would it be like there? What would my new mates be like? Would there be anyone there I already knew? Where would we go? What would the runs ashore be like? What would the senior rates and officers look like? How long would it take to settle in? To find my way round? Would my 'pit' be comfortable? What would they think of me where I was going? These and hundreds more worries and fears would tumble through my head each time I approached new territory. I assume my comrades also felt them.

Of course, you knew, deep down, that wherever you went there would always be a good bunch of mates you would team up with, initially to go ashore with but eventually to form absolute bonds of friendship with – people you would fight with and alongside of to the complete exclusion of everything else. If you were matey with someone, you would always go ashore with them, play cards, uckers, doms and crib with them. Sometimes with others, but usually with them. You got to know their moods and behaviour patterns – and they knew yours. These were very much man-to-man relationships. From this bonding you soon accepted others into your group, until there was a whole gang always doing everything together. This wasn't safety in numbers, as we didn't need gang mentality or behaviour, but it was a group of men doing what 'civvies' would love to do, but found it to be not really acceptable. We disregarded those conventions and went round together anyway. So that took care of the question of mates. And we didn't entertain poofs.

If you met up with someone you knew from a previous draft, you'd clearly be matey with them, if that was what you were before, otherwise you let the Navy take its course and began building friendships again. After that, the rest of the worries eased and evaporated quickly. Once you'd settled in for that first sleepless night, and listened as that first 'Call The Hands' went, you knew the only way forward was to 'fit in'. If not, you'd have a very lonely future ahead of you. That first morning of any new draft, then, was the one to get past as it contained all the surprises. After that – dead easy!

I recall being absolutely and completely overawed by my first sight of the Forth Road Bridge, nearly as much as the sight of the rail bridge we found ourselves actually crossing, noisily. I also remember the first sighting of the dockyard at Rosyth, thinking we'd soon be boarding our first ship, wondering where it would be carrying us. We hadn't been told much at that stage, just that it was a Type 81 Tribal Class, General Purpose Frigate, with loads of different radars and well armed with missiles and guns and all sorts of things. And obviously painted grey. I still get a thrill whenever I go across those bridges and unconsciously look over to the dockyard for the *Zulu*.

We boarded the 'tilly and sped off towards the dockyard, gabbling excitedly all the way, taking in all the scenery as we travelled. We were somewhat annoyed, then, to note that we turned off the road before the dockyard, into HMS *Cochrane*. Surely some mistake, we thought, as we disembarked the bus. Not so, we were told, the '*Zulu* is currently in dry dock being refitted. She is over halfway through a two-year refit. She'll be afloat in summer, and . . .'. At which point our little Junior Seamen (Radar Plotter (Basic)) hearts plummeted. We had expected to at last go on a real ship and to sail off into the dawn. That was not to be. Not tonight anyway, as we unhappily unpacked our gear into the very smart (after the low standard we'd endured so far in our short naval careers) accommodation. We were in together with other *Zulu* ratings. They gave us the run down: it was in refit, it would be afloat in a couple of months, but as yet it was a mystery where we would be deployed.

Throughout our time at *Raleigh* and *Dryad*, we had been exposed to lots of abbreviations, JS meant Junior Seaman, ME, Marine Engineer, OEM, electrician. We found a new one, one that worried me. What was an MNE? A Bootneck, we were informed. What do they do? Not a lot apart from what they are told. And weren't marines put on board in the old days to keep sailors in check? Yes, but not this lot – marines are very keen and eager, and when not cleaning their weapons, they would be assigned to parts of the ship with us. Oh yes, they were also riot squad, and landing party. More to worry about – what the hell were they? You'll soon find out if you get assigned to them, we were assured.

We got on with our first real Joining Routine, which included acquiring the anti-flash hoods and gloves we wore at Action Stations (to protect us against explosions, fires, that sort of thing), as well as locating the Naafi, returning to the mess, unpacking, going for supper. Go to the Naafi. In civvies. Buy a pint. Yippee! – no one cared how old we were and we got served. And then to the obligatory automat, as we didn't (then) go out off base unless we had to. The nearest 'town' was Inverkeithing, a taxi or bus ride away. Or Rosyth, which was full of 'married patches' and consequently of no interest to us.

Joining Routine is a naval tradition whereby every time you join a ship, even if it is only for a few days, you have to go through this procedure. It means registering your presence, being added to the Watch and Station Bill (which records the watch, action station, defence station, day job, emergency station and liferaft station of everyone on board), which we took extremely seriously, and obtaining a new cap tally to tie. It meant getting blankets, pillows, mattress – all of which had to be carefully carried to your pit along with your other kit items. If you put it down, it would grow a set of legs by the time you got back and disappear. That is one thing about sailors: if it isn't nailed down, it will either walk or vanish into thin air, as if it had never existed. Theft from an oppo, or theft of personal property, however, is not tolerated.

The down side of the Joining Routine was the leaving routine – the reverse, but this time you'd have to return everything you signed for when you joined. If you didn't have enough blankets then, officially, they would be stopped from your pay. So you always made sure you had enough, to take back exactly what you drew – even if you had to 'find' it elsewhere.

When we bedded down that night, in our PJs, we suddenly discovered that nobody else ever wore them. Now we found out why they were insultingly called 'brown hatters' overalls' – it was assumed only brown hatters (homosexuals) wore them in bed. They were therefore their overalls. Simple – but it ensured many laughs when 'new boys' joined the ship(s) and wore them. Nobody ever lasted above one night with them on (except Stevie, who was slower on the uptake), and we quickly swapped into the much more acceptable boxer shorts and T-shirt, as worn by the rest of the Navy.

Next morning, we were all mustered outside the 'block' and marched through the base and dockyard, round the dry docks, eventually coming to a halt against a red and grey blob sitting half covered with tarpaulins. It was situated at the bottom of an extremely large dry dock, surrounded and dwarfed by huge, grey cranes on railway lines, swinging seemingly impossible loads around. I was not in the least bit impressed – I had really expected more, at least a real grey thing. We scrambled down the gangway to the quarterdeck, saluted and waited to be told what to do next. I will point out now it wasn't just us who had been marched down, it was the whole ship's company. We marched back to *Cochrane* for lunch (and a pint or two), and back afterwards. This was your routine unless you were 'cooks', in which case you cleaned up the accommodation until 0900, then walked down to the ship unescorted, via 'Bernards' (Naval Jailers (tailors)) if it was open.

By the time we arrived on that first morning, it was within seconds of 0805, or BWH (Both Watches of the Hands) – in naval terms time to start work. We had already been assigned to our 'Parts Of Ship', and were fell in by the POS (Part Of Ship) Petty Officer. The PO reported to the Buffer, who then reported to the Jimmy, who then told the Buffer to carry on, who then told the PO to carry on, who then ushered us away to start work. If the Jimmy wanted to say something special, he'd have his few words, as would the Buffer. We were also introduced to 'Father' Tribe. Very old (compared to us), with three (long service/good conduct) 'badges', and a great deal of experience, he was the LHOM (Leading Hand of the Mess). He looked after us and the rest of the radar plot department. We had our own PRI, but it was Father who virtually ran everything else. He quickly assigned our daily work detail, which was either a) cleaning a part of the ship where a dockyard matey had just made a mess, or b) painting over where a dockyard matey had just finished with a welding torch, or c) removing paint from another expanse of metal, ready for it to be rewelded. We used to get through gallons of red lead primer and even more gallons of ship's side grey, as well as more paintbrushes than you could ever imagine, due to our indolence in cleaning them after use. Why should we? Pusser was rich and could afford the new ones. We also had a 'painter' – a rating assigned to issue paint, of whatever colour, in 'kettles' with thick-bristled brushes of a type determined by what you intended to use it for. No good issuing a varnish brush to paint with. Nor a paint brush to varnish with. He'd also recover the brushes just before 'secure' at 1600, at which point he'd clean all the brushes, hang them all up to dry, empty all the kettles back into the drums, clean them, then run like hell to join the rest of the RAs in their dash to get ashore. However, it was not the done thing to wind the RAs up, so the paint would have to be returned by 1530 (or thereabouts, or earlier if possible, say before lunch).

One of the perks of being painter, was that he had to keep the 'crests' in good condition. Crests were shields, each with arms or heraldry on, representing the ship or its battle honours. For the *Zulu*, we had a Zulu warrior's shield and assegai on a blue/white wavy background, surrounded by a gold 'rope' design. It was the job of the painter to not only keep all the crests gleaming, but to be able to create new crests. We sailors would also be on the earwig for crests, as they were handy little souvenirs to get off the ship unnoticed, and could be traded for beer and other goodies ashore. So the painter would be leaned upon to make these, unless you were the QM or BM, and had the keys to the paintshop at night, or were bored, or could paint with a steady hand, or knew where the plaster of Paris was, or could find the right moulds.

RA stood for ration allowance, otherwise known as 'living ashore', with their families. They were allowed leave slightly before us, and would set records changing out of Eights and into civvies, before chucking all their 'gizzits' into their grip and hurtling down the gangway to get home. It was not acceptable to get in the way of an RA under full power. We had one who, after the afternoon standeasy, would put his civvies on, then put his Eights over the top. He then only had to rip off trousers and shirt, and change boots before getting away ahead of the herd. How we respected him! Gizzits means exactly what it sounds like. If someone was emptying out his locker, or had superfluous gear, he would say 'Anyone want any gizzits?', we would crowd round to see what he had. Or we would see someone doing this, and muster there, asking 'Got any gizzits?'

We had only been with the ship for one day, when I was invited to go and find a stoker, 'Nutty' Slack, a large, red-faced, fender-bellied chappy who, it was said, had a pair of overalls for me. I searched for him for hours, from one end of the ship to the other, and never did get my ovies – he later told me it was a wind up. Not that I ever, ever fell for any more. Though my mate spent a while in the Buffer's store, where he had been sent for a long weight (wait). Apparently the junior electricians would be sent all round the dockyard for red or green oil for the port or starboard navigation lights, or even for replacement filaments for light bulbs, and other people would be sent in gangs to find a 10-ton shackle, only to find you could actually put it round your finger. Oh it was fun. The really gormless ones actually went looking for the good old bucket of steam.

What we did get, though, was an upgrade to our 'Pusser's dirk'. The dirk had been carried by us, tied to a lanyard, then secured around our waists, since day one at *Raleigh*, and God help you if your dirk was rusty or your lanyard any other colour but pure white. So we marched down to the ship on that first day, and found no self-respecting tar wore a dirk. What they wore instead was a rigging set. This was drawn from stores, and comprised a leather pouch, leather belt, marling spike (or 'fid') and a large sharp knife with a wooden handle.

With the fid, splicing became dead easy, and I can still put a splice in any kind of rope, within minutes. Not that that helps me in any way, it is just one of those things you never forget. What we didn't bargain for was that the 'older the hand' you were, the more personalized your rigging set became. We could extemporize the pouch, enlarging it, then find (smaller) sailmaker's knives, small spikes and anything else to weigh the pouch down. Essentially then, the longer you served, the more crap you would load into the ever-growing pouch.

One chap I knew used to cart a hand-axe round with him, which he would throw in your direction if riled. Others would 'borrow' mole grips, pliers, small saws. You needed to guard these items zealously, in case any unscrupulous gits liked them more than you. The original dirk, then, was never used again. I still have my original one with my name stamped on it. We'd also sit for hours, with a whetstone, sharpening our dirks and knives until we were able to shave with them. Literally. We knew that, one day our life could depend on our knives and that if the time came when a piece of unruly rope wound itself round our foot, then we could instantly cut ourselves free, while we screamed and headed towards the ship's side. Actually, the most common use of a fid was to puncture goffa cans and beer cans!

Another article most prized was a green Pusser's torch, which was avidly guarded. You could even nick the batteries that went in them once they ran down, and throw the old spent ones at anything that moved. Shite-hawks, for example. The other piece of equipment consigned to the bottom of the lockers was our Seamanship Manual – our book of knowledge. We knew it intimately, and could reel off information from any page about any subject.

We discovered scranbags at this time. If you lost any gear, and it was found by someone else, the scranbag was where it would end up. The scranbag would be 'opened' monthly for people to claim gear back, at a price; any money realized went into the welfare fund. Oddly, gear would repose there for months and never be claimed. Conversely, if you lost anything useful or valuable the chances are it would never reappear. After months of non-movement, the scranbag would be consigned to the paintshop and anything in it would be used as rags. Alternatively, 'Scranbag' was what you were called if you looked a mess before you went ashore, or if your Eights looked like you'd slept in them. 'Scranbag', along with 'Shit-tip' and 'Gro-bag', were, then, terms of endearment. If though anyone hinted that you looked like a scranbag, it was a good cue to smarten yourself up.

The welfare committee, responsible for the welfare fund, comprised a group of ratings, presided over by the Jimmy, who would allocate outgoing funds against income, making sure the one never exceeded the other. Money went in there from a variety of sources, mostly external to the ship, and was allocated to, for example, ship's company dances, subsidizing ship's crested lighters, ties, etc. It was a very useful committee, and one everybody tried to get on to. Ship's company dances were organized infrequently during a commission. Generally held in home port, they could be held abroad too. Unfortunately, I only ever got to one during my entire career, as I was Duty for every one ever held on every ship I ever served in. The one I went to was held at HMS *Victory* (as the Navy base in Pompey was named in the old days), and I was Duty shore patrol for that too.

We were educated into 'dhobey bags', and 'dhobey dust'. The bags were where we kept all our personal wash kit. We also hung variously coloured towels on our lockers to dry, as by now we'd got shut of our white Pusser's issue ones. Our bags held soap, shampoo, razor and shaving cream, toothbrush, toothpaste, deodorant and foo-foo (talcum powder). If you grabbed your dhobey bag and towel, it was a pretty good bet you'd be off to do your own basin trials in the bathroom, for the traditional naval 'shit, shave, shampoo and shower'. The 'dust' was washing powder, for although we'd gladly give all our other gear to the laundry crew, we'd never dream of letting them have our 'nix and sox'! We'd therefore carry that day's shorts and socks and crash them out vigorously in the metal sink before rinsing them out, wringing them dry before moving to the shower. Incidentally, we would run with just two pairs of black or navy socks, and two pairs of shorts. We would wear one set, while the other was 'in the wash'. It was the height of luxury to have three or more pairs of each!

Shower over, we'd then drop our wet gear off in the drying room before proceeding back to the mess for the final rite – spreading the foo-foo about. Finally, we'd get redressed. All this would normally take place just after 'secure', and last between fifteen minutes and half an hour, depending on how sociable you felt, or whether you were in a dash to get ashore. It usually took place well before supper, except if you were Duty watch, in which case you'd do the fire exercise first, then eat supper, then dhobey.

It was, though, dangerous to leave your dhobey bag anywhere else but in your secured locker. It was recognized that if you came offshore and found a bag lurking, it wasn't unknown, that when you cleaned your teeth, you might be tempted to borrow someone else's toothbrush, and to put it in places it wasn't designed to go. And then watch as the following day, you saw the owner putting it innocently into his mouth.

These basin trials were a constant source of amusement, obviously, as the bathrooms were tiny and cramped, and would be full of people, butt-naked or wrapped in only a towel ('dress of the day' for basin trials), all trying to get ashore. Space was at a premium, with queues developing for a basin, then for a shower. The air was always full of water and ribald comments about other people's anatomy, about the placement of various tattoos, whatever – we had to let off steam somehow, and it was accepted this was one of those places. Rank and seniority didn't exist. Comments like 'I've dropped my soap – everyone stand still', or 'If you wash it more than twice you must be wanking' would be the more repeatable. You can see, it didn't pay to be shy or retiring – you had to join in, or be thought of as . . . well, you decide.

If I make this sound like a 'brown hatter's tea-party', that is most definitely not my intention – the Navy is not like that at all. I will say now, that whatever anyone thinks about sailors, the incidence of queers aboard

Navy ships was non-existent. I only met one during my entire career, and he was very successfully working his ticket, so we were never 100 per cent sure about him. Nevertheless, it was common practice to pretend to be, to wind other people up, and I heard phrases like 'I joined the Navy for rum, bum, and baccy, I've had me rum, I've had me baccy – come 'ere boy', or 'Fetch I another cabin boy – I've split this 'un'. Or you'd be in the heads (or a toilet ashore) in a pistil next to someone you might not know, look over at what he had in his hand, and innocently ask, 'New shoes, Pal?'.

On a daily basis, we learned new slang, insults and greetings. It was common to walk into the mess – at standeasy, say – and shout 'Morning men' and the response would come back 'Starboard Ten'. Or we'd shriek 'Morning chaps – oh, and you Poison' (or whoever), just for the reply, which I'm sure you can guess.

As the ship was on shoreside power, and you were obviously not allowed to use the ship's 'heads' or bathrooms, you had to climb up the gangway off the ship, across to the nearest shoreside ones in order to relieve or clean yourself. Bearing in mind we joined the *Zulu* in Scotland during winter, we quickly learned to do everything in a hurry, just in order to keep warm. We used to dress in our Number Eights, with a sweater, and our foul weather jackets, and put on the odd T-shirt (until that was banned). What we were issued with though was foul-weather jackets and steaming bats (boots). The jackets were thick, waterproof (to a point), windproof and extremely warm, with a padded bit that fitted round your face when the hood was put up. The bats were to be worn as dress of the day, to save wear and tear on our shiny boots and shoes. What a godsend they were – I don't think a day went by when you didn't spill paint or oil on them, or catch them against something. The best bit was, when they wore out, you replaced them with a free new pair!

We found our way all round the ship in no time, and explored every inch of it, from the magazines to the mast head, from the bridge to the radar office, from stem to stern, learning each compartment and its location. Each compartment, passage and flat on a ship has its own identity. Normally, this identity accords to a marking, which (from memory) comprises the first number corresponding to the deck above or below the main deck, the next letter gives the compartment from 'A' the most for'ard then progressively aft, then which side of the centreline, then a final number. This makes it easy for fire and emergency crews to locate the compartment containing the crisis. However, to make life even easier, some are individually named. For example, 'the bridge flat' is the one behind the bridge, while 'the tiller flat' is the most aft place you could go below decks and where the steering gear is located. It gets hot in there, and can be the scene of major panics if an emergency arises.

We were also assigned by then to our 'watches', taking as usual one Duty every fourth day, with two long weekends per month. One snag with long weekends was the train fare. At the time, we were still paid £7 per fortnight, and still had to queue up and salute, and this clearly wasn't enough to get us home. However, shortly after we joined the *Zulu*, we had a massive pay rise to almost £25, which gave us money to burn. In those days we didn't even have to pay for food or accommodation while living ashore.

What we did get in our pay were two things. One was KUA (Kit Upkeep Allowance). This was a set amount of money paid directly to us that went towards replacement kit, except that it was such an insignificant amount, we just spent it along with all our other dosh, then bought replacement kit only when our gear started to fall from our bodies. The other item was what some far-seeing admiral included and became known as the 'X factor'. This was allocated into all future pay reviews and rises, and meant that when the extremely mean-fisted civil servants had finished haggling over our rises, the admirals could then say 'Ah yes – but what about the X factor?', and add a few more per cent to our rises. Unsurprisingly, the X factor was highly popular, as was the person who introduced it, whoever he was.

By now, we had been 'exposed' to the rest of the ship's company, especially to our own division, and therefore to the more able sailors who were to guide us over the coming months, and who took to letting us accompany them into the 'Central' in Inverkeithing. We felt we had 'arrived', sitting with the rest of the old hands in our division, sucking down pints of heavy, chasing it with 'wee ones'. Then calling at the chippy for a 'black man's dick' (haggis) supper before returning by shared fast black (taxi) to *Cochrane*. We had a leading seaman – Mac he was, or 'Foul-Bowels' as he was known. We fell in for BWH one cold, crisp morning, with snow on the deck. I give him his due, he warned us he was going to, but we were not prepared for the result. I kid you not – he cleared the open quarterdeck. We hung over the guard-rails, gagging and gasping for breath. I have never inhaled anything so disgusting, not even the tear gas. Mac? – he just cracked up laughing, and kept sniggering for the rest of the day.

Fast blacks were always the preferred mode of travel, we would not usually walk through the dockyard to get ashore, relying instead on a quick shore call to the taxi rank outside the gate. They would nearly always be there in minutes, at which point we'd all scramble over the gangway to ensure we didn't have to ride shotgun. Shotgun was next to the driver, from which there was no escape from paying. We liked it in the back!

The only time we ever fell over getting the fast black, was Friday secure (1600), when we started long weekend leave, or Saturday lunchtime, the start of a short weekend. In most ports it wasn't such a problem, having to wait for a taxi to get off on weekend, as the trains were at least twice hourly. But from Rosyth, we'd either have to get to 'Inverqueerthing' for a connection for the 'every other hour' train, or get a taxi direct to Waverly in Edinburgh. The latter clearly cost more, but got you on to an earlier train.

As RPs we used to muster in the Ops Room occasionally, for briefings and debriefings, and one day we were told we would be going for a weeks training at *Dryad* – called a PCT (Pre-Commissioning Training). The plus side of this was that we would get a weekend leave at either end of it, the down side was that we would have to stay at HMS *Victory*, commuting from there up to *Dryad* daily.

CHAPTER 6

Our First 'Run' in Pompey

We packed 'steaming kit', the minimum required to get us to Portsmouth, do our course and get back, with enough room for our civvies. At this time, 'going ashore rig' had to be good, clean civvies. So you could tell 'Jack' a mile off – sta-prest trousers, open necked shirt, and jacket, as well as steaming bats. Or a 'thousand-miler' (similar to a 'polo' shirt), so called because of the distance between washes. By the time they had been packed, there was precious little room left for the two sets of 'Eights'.

We all met up at Waterloo on the Sunday evening for the specific train (to ensure we all turned up together) to Portsmouth, and bundled into *Victory*, going through the Joining Routine and on to the mess we were to use. This was on the second floor of an old building, heated by a stove in the centre of the room, surrounded by bunks and kit-lockers. Except that they didn't lock and during that week things vanished mysteriously during the day while we weren't there.

On the first morning, we mustered, boarded the bus, all twenty or so of us, and went to *Dryad*, complete with 'attitude', as we were now Jack weren't we? We were proudly part of the ship's company of HMS *Zulu*, and now here we were with our HMS *Zulu* cap tallies, among all the *Dryad*s. In among the trainees, who obviously envied us as we strutted and swaggered into the Naafi at lunchtime for our beers with the lads, we enjoyed that week of training. We went into the Tribal model, and took up the roles we had been given back in Rosyth. We operated the radar, made all the correct reactions, didn't get sunk too frequently and learned what the officers looked like who were to rule our lives over the coming months. We also noted how they reacted – who tended towards flat-out panic and who didn't.

We juniors learned much that week, but it was the after hours that was the most fun, and moulded our 'crew'. Each evening we returned to *Victory*, checked to see what else had gone missing, changed, ate in the massive dining hall and then vanished in among the hundreds of like-minded matelots on to 'The Strip'. We were taken round the old pubs – I don't even remember most of their names apart from the Albany, but I can remember some of the inhabitants and recall that at least some of the inns had sawdust on the floor (to aid in the sweeping up of multi-flavoured, many textured psychedelic yawns). One of the more memorable characters was 'Landslide Face', so called because one side of his face had dropped, dragging his eye with it. This, and the resultant stalactites from his mouth, were alleged to have been caused by his habit of keeping the money from the newspapers he sold, in his mouth. Guess where we didn't buy newspapers. And then there were the brown hatters, hair dyed and bouffanted, something I always found totally repulsive. Brown hatters could be wound up easily by ignoring them, or by showing them a traditional naval 'curse' – putting ones thumb-tip between the index and second fingers, wiggling the said thumbtip, and saying 'Sssssss' at them. This, for some strange and unknown reason, would irritate and annoy them intensely.

We drank 'blood' at 1s 9d a pint (scrumpy from the wood, blackcurrant top), and the local Courage, and more rum than we knew what to do with. All this was in the days, I'm sorry to say, when you could get out of your tree for a quid, including fish and chips on the way back. By the time we left after those few short days in Pompey, we could navigate our way not only through 'models', but also up and down 'The Strip', back via the chippy to *Victory*. We were, of course, still the lowlife juniors, but gradually we came to be accepted by our elders and peers. I also clearly remember my first Chinese meal, washed down with large amounts of Mateus Rosé. I even remember that I ate all my prawn curry and that it was extremely tasty. Whatever we ate, we'd always remember to bring back a pint of milk, ready to ease the hangover guaranteed to strike the next morning. Oh yes, and eventually we were actually properly introduced to 'Dot's', the gathering point for us now, running up the steps shouting 'SRE and a tea please'. We then played the one-armed-bandit at a tanner a go to try to recoup some of our spendings from the previous night's run, while we also attempted vainly to sober up.

CHAPTER 7

Back to Reality in Rosyth

All too soon it was time to return to Rosyth, with the promised long weekend en route. We got back in time for job changes and I was moved from Top part of ship to Bosun's Mate. That meant being the 'gopher' for the Quartermaster and standing on the gangway of the ship. The gangway was a piece of wood/metal, with sides, connecting the ship to the shore, providing a secondary way (after swinging across wires) of getting between the two. Gangways came in all shapes and sizes, from rudimentary to elaborate and ornate. We even carried our own, which was pressed into service if the port we were visiting didn't own one. It was also there in case we went alongside another ship. Gangways were where the ship's routine was run from while alongside, by means of the Quartermaster (QM) and Bosun's Mate (BM) making various 'pipes' (relaying various orders) over the ship's main broadcast. Everyone would obey these pipes, or risk serious trouble. It was embarrassing to make your first pipe which you knew everybody would hear, so you built up to it gradually. The most difficult to pipe was 'D'You hear there', then add a message. But you had to do it eventually, so you practised quietly to yourself beforehand.

Eventually, all aboard would have to cross the gangway, so we got to know the entire crew by sight within a short space of time. It also meant we could differentiate between miserable gits (for whom we had no spare time) and 'good hands' who we would make coffee/kye (chocolate) for, if pressed. Especially if they bought us suppers back from ashore. Duty people would be mustered there, shore telephone calls would be received and any Duty person knew they could come and chew the fat there. From the Duty clanky (who would always have hot water available) to the Duty PO, who would come up for a natter, or the OOD who would relax there between his rounds, if he wanted to – everyone except the Duty electrician, but greenies always were different to everyone else.

The QM and BM ran the daily routine by making pipes informing the ship's company of mundane things like 'turning to', 'standeasy', and – best of all – 'secure'. We had the best supply of books, magazines on a range of subject matters, and pens, also torches, batteries, expertise – you name it, it all lived on the gangway. If anyone wanted virtually anything on board, they would, nine times out of ten, ring up, or visit us to ask us. It was a thankless job, but it did have its benefits.

If anyone wanted to 'find' anyone, we would pipe 'Able Seaman Smith – Gangway'. If anyone better than the OOD wanted him, 'At the rush' would be added. If the words 'Lay Aft' were included, you were already in deep trouble, the only question was, how deep was it! Officers were '. . . requested to come to the gangway', unless the Jimmy or the Skipper wanted them, in which case they were (as before) already in the shit for not being available, and we'd pipe 'Officer of the Day (or Lieutenant So-and-So) Gangway – NOW', and wait for them to bitch about missing the 'request' bit off. At which time we'd indicate the Jimmy or the Skipper standing round the corner, waiting, fuming.

Through all this we had to be on our guard (not that we'd ever skylark), so if we were asked to pipe for example a 'PO(ME) Granite . . .'. Or we'd wait until we knew who was indisposed, then pipe him to the gangway for a shore telephone call. He'd appear dripping wet, pick up the phone, say hello, then throw it down. We'd say 'Must have been a wrong number/must have hung up', and watch him go back down below dripping. We'd maybe then wait several more minutes before repeating the procedure.

If someone was adrift at night, we could thoughtfully remove their station card from the box, hiding it from the Duty PO and OOD. The hapless rating would though have to stand where he could see, but not be seen, until the DPO/OOD went below, before they could hurtle up the gangway, unseen – except by us. They would then owe us big favours. You see, it didn't pay to mess with, or be 'anti' towards the gangway crew. Ever.

We used to work Dogs, Middle and Forenoon one day, then 24 off, then Afternoon, First and Morning. The Dogs were fine, except that you were coming on, as everyone else was going home. We stood there four hours on, four off, for the twenty-four hours, then got '24 off', with a double shift at the weekend, unless you were weekend off. 'Ginge' Harwood was my QM – a Leading Seaman, a gunnery expert and very wise. The Duty watch – who slept on board even though in dry dock, of which we as QM and BM were part, had supper and 9-o-clockers brought down to us nightly, and it was usually still warm when it arrived. We could make up for it if we did the First, by sliding over to the dockyard canteen for a haggis supper. Every Dogs, though, the Duty watch used to exercise fire and emergency, and muster wherever the OOD used to want a pretend incident. When the OOD rang us to announce where the fire was to be, we would scream over the tannoy: 'FOREXERCISEFOREXERCISE FOREXERCISEFIREFIREFIREFIREINTHETILLERFLAT', or wherever we were told, then we'd sit back while everybody else on board ran round in a flat spin, or until the OOD was happy. If he was displeased, he would make everyone put all the gear away, then throw another exercise, much later. That used to pass thirty minutes.

When we came off the Dogs, the 'watchkeepers', as we were known, had their own mess. As the ship, and therefore the mess, was still unheated except for small electric fires, we used to crash out on much-used mattresses and pillows, still dressed in our Eights, with our watchcoats on. Just as you dozed off, the BM doing the First would shake you for the Middle. You then sat there for four hours, listening to the radio and roaming the ship on 'rounds', making sure it was still there. We'd nose about and pry into everywhere unlocked, until we knew every place to go on the ship. With luck, you could make rounds last anything up to half an hour, at which time you'd come back, and sign your name to confirm you'd completed them and that nothing was amiss. Rounds were interspersed with endless cups of kye or coffee made by me for Ginge, unless he felt extremely irritable, in which case he'd make it. On board all ships, in the engine room, is something called a 'steam-drench'. This was a tap, out of which would pour superheated steam – hot enough to heat to boiling point any sized jug of cold water in seconds. You had to be very careful not to put your fingers anywhere near it. We'd drink the coffee with tinned milk and scrounged sugar from wherever to sweeten up an otherwise foul brew.

We'd forage for what was left of the suppers, usually stale bread, then attempt to toast it on the portable heater in the kaboosh. Mostly, we would sit on or close to the heater and talk. More accurately, he would talk, I would listen. We used to raid workshops for bolts and nuts, then attempt to shoot shite-hawks with a catapult we made. Or we'd put various delicacies on the quarterdeck for them. Things like yeast and curry sandwiches, or mustard rolls – enough to make them throw up shortly after they took off. Most times, we'd nick the nuts and bolts from the 'Engineers Workshop' or the MCR, the MCR being where the clankies run the engine and gearbox from while at sea, but also where the damage control state of the ship is handled.

Towards the end of the watch, we'd ascertain the ship's position, weather conditions – gleaned from the bridge anemometer and barometer, or visually ('Snowing', 'Raining', 'Clear'), as well as the 'sea-state' and the visibility, then record everything in that most important document – the ship's log. Actually, while at sea, every course, speed, position, BWH, sunset, important event, whatever, was recorded in the log for someone to read later back at 'The Admiralty'.

As gangway crew, we'd know the 'battle honours' – the board showing where previous ships of the name had fought, and when – and we'd be responsible for the ship's bell, which doubled as a font for onboard christenings. The bell and the battle honours were taken down whenever we sailed and put back up immediately we got back alongside, as would the huge nameplates bearing the ship's name which also had to be hung in position. It was also the job of the off-watch gangway crew to adorn the gangway with canvas dodgers, also bearing the ship's name. This was great for us – HMS *Zulu* was only seven letters and therefore very light, whereas ships like HMS *Londonderry* meant you'd be there all day, carrying heavier nameplates.

We would also spread a cargo net beneath the gangway, between the jetty and the ship's side, on the offchance that a lurching, legless matelot fell off the gangway. At least he would not get wet, even if it took him ages to sober up enough to make sense of, and extricate himself from, the cargo net. Not that anyone did that of course. We also used vaguely to monitor the dockyard mateys as they 'worked' the night shift, lagging engine-room pipes, spray painting etc. Only whenever we looked we'd find them asleep in one of the unfinished messdecks. It was little wonder that refits in Rosyth always ran over budget and way over time.

Eventually, the Middle used to end and we'd head for our pits, get warm and doze off, to be re-awakened by our opposite number to get up and do the Forenoon. That used to be a real soul-destroyer. Me as BM had to go and do Colours – this continued whether we were in refit or not. This consisted of the OOD, sometimes the Jimmy, the Duty Radio Operator (or flag-wagger) to haul up the ensign and me to pipe the still and carry-on with my bosun's call, still mainly asleep, and hungry having had no breakfast. The QM would ring the ship's bell vigorously, then broadcast 'Attention on the upper deck – face aft and salute' – which everyone silly enough to be on the upper scupper at the time had to do. After the ensign and jack had been hauled up, the QM would broadcast the carry on, followed by 'Both Watches . . .'. Occasionally, if he thought he could get away with it, the first broadcast could be 'Attention on the upper deck, chase arse in a blue suit'. Which sounded almost the same. Once we got through that, we were then 24 off. Ginge, an RA, used to head home, I used to expire in my pit at *Cochrane*. Occasionally, I even managed to sleep for a couple of hours, before heading ashore with the gang later.

On the opposite watch, we'd do the Afternoon, getting to the ship within minutes of midday. It was actually a point of honour in the Navy to 'relieve' each other at exactly five minutes to the hour, whatever watch you did, wherever you did it. If you were adrift even by seconds you would not believe the repercussions. The Afternoon usually passed quickly, then we'd relax off during the Dogs, fill up with food and do the First from 2000 to midnight. That would usually pass quickly too, and you'd generally be asleep shortly after midnight. Back up at 0400 for the morning, which would drag on, and on, and on. Nothing and nobody used to move in the yard until about 0700, then all hell was let loose. Once we moved onboard, one of the perks was that when the milkman arrived, with his churns of ice-cold, fresh milk, you could always skim off several pints before the Duty dining-hall ratings sleepily crossed the gangway, manhandling the huge churns down below.

During the Morning, it was traditional to write a short poem or verse, to be read out at 'Call the Hands', so at 0645 we'd pipe Call the Hands on the bosun's call, then launch into the poem. Normally, if bored, it would be (in a loud voice): 'CALLTHEHANDSCALLETHEHANDSCALLTHE HANDSWAKEYWAKEYRISEANDSHINEYOUVEHADYOURSLEEPIWANTMINE'. Or it might be: 'WAKEYWAKEYWAKEYWAKEYWAKEYWAKEYWAKEYWAKEYWAKEY WAKEYWAKEYWAKEYWAKEYHANDSOFFCOCKSHANDSONSOCKS'. Or perhaps: 'EAVOEAVOLASHUPANDSTOWTHESUNSBRIGHTENOUGHTOBURNYERFUCKIN EYESOUT'.

One of the jobs of the Morning watchmen was to 'shake' the early risers – the chefs (more later), the greenies, the bunting-tossers, men under pun(ishment) – anyone who had to get up earlier than the norm. We would shake them gently, if we wanted to, or violently if they had previously given us grief, or with the lights on/torch in the eyes otherwise. We had a 'shake book', which anyone wanting the shake had to sign his name against. It was therefore in our power that, once we got the signature, to slope off quietly to see if he went back to sleep again. He'd then be deep in the shit for not getting there, but we'd be clear –

we had the signature after all. It was in our (bacon sarnie) interests to ensure the Duty chef got up, so we'd go back several times, with coffee! Officers were shaken by us – we'd go once, knock on the cabin door, await the grunt, whisper the time and slink away again. We would NOT go back a second time, no matter which officer it was. We had enough to do to keep our mates out of the rattle, without guarding the interests of the wardroom as well.

If it was our 'relief' we were shaking, we'd talk to them, to make sure they weren't adrift to take over. We'd have a brew ready, wherever we where. As I said – we looked after our own! Sometimes, we'd wake someone else up (who hadn't asked for the shake) very gently, and whisper in his ear 'wanna buy a battleship, Jack', before creeping off. Oddly, if someone ever does this to you, you're immediately wide awake, thinking 'What was that? Why would I want to buy a battleship?' before you knew it, you'd be wide awake and unable to get off again. The not-so-good bit was entering a mess full of sleeping sailors at 0500 – the atmosphere would be full of the varied scents of thirty or so sailors, generally after a night ashore. Ripe is the word I use, unreservedly!

If the Captain went ashore, we'd have to keep an extremely good lookout for him coming back. If he ever got aboard without the OOD being on the gangway, he (OOD) would get his arse chewed off, followed by us getting ours bitten by him (OOD). To prevent this happening, we had a little code – whenever we saw the boss coming back, we'd immediately give two short pips on our bosun's call into the main broadcast, and sit back to see how long it took the OOD to get to the gangway. If the OOD had previously wound us up, we'd leave it till the last possible second until doing the 'pips', to ensure the OOD just missed him – but, of course, we'd be admonished – we'd fulfilled our bit!

We kept the keys to the Buffer's store, which was where we kept 'seamanshippy' things, such as ropes, blocks, various string, marline spikes, sailmaker's knives – all the pieces of equipment you could possibly need. And because, by then, Ginge had taught me how to splice, properly, and tie decorative knots, I made flattened out 'monkey's fists', which then looked like mats. These were made from thin nylon, and looked terrific when completed and washed. These were also cash valuable ashore, as were bell-ropes – highly ornate works of art.

One weekend, we embarked on a coach and disappeared up into the hills, alongside a loch somewhere, into log cabins, where we spent a pleasant couple of days washing in a stream, drinking ourselves silly and walking around the surrounding woods. We never did find out where the cabins were, but they were RN property, and gave us a break.

After several months, it was job-change time again, and I went back part-of-ship. By this time we were nearly out of the refit, and came the day the mateys tentatively opened up the sluices of the dry dock, letting the water rush in, around the ship. Imperceptibly, amidst mateys hunting for leaks, and not finding any, we began to float. Soon, we were high up in the dry dock, with the water level the same as the basin beyond the caisson. The caisson slid back, the tug came in and we were towed into the non-tidal basin. This meant more of the shore-heads routines, only this time we could (providing you didn't get caught) use the heads on board.

We juniors got the lousy jobs. We would always be the first to be volunteered to clean the 'flats', bathrooms and heads for the first hour every morning, generally under the most detested leading seaman on board; this was one of the 'perks' of being of his rank. He would make us clean the general areas thoroughly, and we yearned for the time when we weren't the shithouse sweepers any longer. Or we'd be volunteered for 'side party', sitting on a paint stage suspended over the ship's side, either scrubbing or painting. The one which really got to us was cleaning and degreasing and regreasing the 'slips' on the guard-rails all round the upper deck. That was a real pleasure on a cold day, when you weren't able to wear gloves.

After several weeks of practice, it became possible to distinguish new boys from old hands. The new boys would descend ladders between decks daintily, step by step – as you would when one over the eight. The real 'Herberts' would even go down backwards, facing the steps. But the easiest way was to jump the first two/three steps, grab the rails, swing your legs forward, then slide down with all your weight on your hands, and with your back to the steps. You needed to slow slightly towards the bottom or you would break your ankles with the shock of hitting the iron deckplate. I can still drop down a ladder like that now. We had a lieutenant aboard, Gregory, a nice chap, with a metal leg. He used to be a Fleet Air Arm pilot, and allegedly he left his real leg on a Buccaneer low-level strike bomber when he baled out. He could descend at an alarming rate with a loud thump as he landed, but wasn't quite so good on the ascent. This was a pain if you got stuck behind him while hurtling towards your action station. If he was on the ladder, you'd better find a different way, but at least you had an excuse for not being there when you should have been!

And he had a built-in alarm system, so we knew when he was coming to do evening or even night rounds. We'd hear his leg locking as he threw it forwards with each stride, followed by the clump as his 'foot' hit the deck.

Early in the summer life began to improve considerably. We started to warm up the ship, we did load trials, we did a main engine test. We tested the radar, we tracked aircraft. We moved out of the non-tidal basin to a jetty! Now we floated up and down on the tide, and had to either climb the gangway up to the jetty, or down to the jetty, depending on the state of the tide, which varied enormously in Rosyth. We exercised the guns (stopping short of firing) and tried out all the weapon systems. We stored ship, which was another major evolution – every available hand is detailed to form long supply chains from the jetty to the designated store room, and every item to be stored is transferred from person to person, hand to hand, until it is all stowed. It is the only time the stores ratings ever do any work, but is also the hardest work any 'tanky' or 'lockerman' does. Every item, from sides of beef and pork, to crates of beer, butter, brooms, batteries, sausages, eggs, fizzy drinks, nutty, soap, shaving foam, extremely large tins of fruit, bacon, tinned vegetables, fresh greens, sacks and sacks of spuds was brought aboard – everything required to make the ship totally independent of shoreside support. It is an amazing process to watch, heavily laden lorries would lurch along the jetty one after another and be stripped of their entire cargo within moments, empty lorries would then slink away, with absolutely no trace of their ever having been there. Just a lot of very tired sailors with aching arms and backs, and dry throats, all ready to be lubricated with 'heavy'.

We continued to visit the Central in Inverkeithing, punctuated by visits to Dunfermline. I distinctly remember going ashore one day, after coming off watch, and going shopping in Dumfs, for a pair of Adidas trainers, to wear with my Sta-prest trousers (at that time, jeans were not permitted to be worn ashore). I then proceeded to the pub, met some oppos, and there we sat for the rest of the lunchtime, imbibing. I can remember that I'd changed out of my old tatty shoes into the trainers, but had carefully put the shoes into the box, and the box back into the carrier. So, as I was walking towards the bus station, I felt the urge to sit down in a doorway. The next memory is of someone tugging at the carrier bag, of me letting go, and of someone running off. By the time I came to my senses, and realized what had happened, the only thing I could do was laugh. Imagine the startled look when my mugger feverishly opened the box to discover a pair of discarded old shoes. Serves him right.

Our own RP's mess – with our own locker and our own pit – was like a reversed 'L' in shape. The top was the quiet area, with the whole of the side of the 'L' being right on the ship's side and the bottom being the 'mess square'. In this area we drank tea, played card games and did our socializing. Bearing in mind there were probably twenty-four men in that mess, you can get a feel for how cramped it was. So the 'three high' pits were probably five deep. In each row of three pits, the top one tilted upwards out of the way, the bottom one was therefore available for seating, and the middle one, once secured properly, dropped backwards, so the sleeping part was pressed against the ship's side, with a cushion in front to act as a backrest. There would be boot lockers and blanket stowages beneath the bottom pit. If you were a junior, on the bottom bunk, you'd have to ensure your bed was made up properly, before sheathing it in its casing, before putting the seat cover on, so everyone could finally sit down. Now, if you wanted to go to bed early, tuff – if someone else in the mess square wanted to party, you'd have to wait till they were good and ready, before you could finally get your head down.

Each pit had its own small light, punkah louvre for some ventilation, and – importantly – a roll-bar, to 'prevent' you falling out of bed in rough weather. Each person also had his own kit locker on the front of which was a bar, to hang your wet towels and dhobey bag, while all uniforms were stored in a communal stowage, a large wardrobe, really. In this small amount of space you'd have to keep your uniforms, Burberrys, civvies, going ashore gear and anything else that could be crammed in. There were also tea lockers, table stowages, chair stowages, cubby holes and glory holes, all of which could hold gear of whatever description. All items had to be secured in these stowages ready for going to sea in rough weather.

Our mess was amidships, right over the stabilizers, and below the dining hall. Food was plentiful and remarkably good, especially if you were up early and could bribe a chef to knock you up a sarnie. The exchange on this was a cup of NATO standard (white, two sugars) coffee when you shook him to start cooking breakfast.

As the *Zulu* was relatively modern, we messed in the dining room, having queued up for our scran. We would then sit and eat cafeteria-fashion off metal plates. These were 14 in by perhaps 9 in, and had 3 compartments. One was for a soup bowl. We could have soup every lunchtime, if we wanted, and if it was on the menu. The second space was ostensibly for pudding. The last and biggest was for your main meal. The idea was to cram as much grub into each section as you could, then scoff the lot as fast as you could, so someone else could move in on your bench to eat his own. Having finished our food, we'd take the empty plates to the scullery, for the dining-hall party to wash up. Total luxury. Especially the toaster! This was an enormous device hanging from the scullery wall, and was essentially a box containing racks on chains on to which you put your bread, if you could find any. The chain revolved taking the rack and toast, disappearing for several minutes into the depths of the obviously hot machine. Eventually, it would drop out of the bottom on to a large tray, but if you didn't get there fast enough, someone else would RAS it, and you'd still be left waiting for yours or, at the very least, someone else's. If, however, you got caught having it away with someone else's toast – stand from under!

This was all very civilized and pleasant, unless you were detailed as 'dining-hall party', and thus had to clean everyone's plates and gobbling rods when they had finished with them. They had a dishwasher, and a 'gash-gnasher' to 'eat' the leftovers before chucking it out of the side of the ship. However, it wasn't unknown for the less observant to mistake 'food' for 'rods', and throw the lot into the whirling 'gnasher'. Very shortly there would be a terrible graunching noise as the choppers hit the knife or fork and the whole thing would literally grind to a halt. The machine would then be switched off while the Duty stoker/Duty greenie would, cursing violently all the time, stick his arm in to remove the rod, replace the fuse and start it up again. Of course, we would loudly jeer the idiot who was responsible for the error. Further, if the DHP didn't have any clean rods, and you had to wait for someone to finish eating before you could get a set, then the abuse really used to fly.

At about 1200 every day the RPs would knock off for eats. As of course would everyone else. But the 'pipe' made would be 'Seeeecure. Hands to Dinner' followed by the massed chorus from below decks, of 'RPs to lunch'. That never stopped us being among the first in line for anything and everything being handed out at any time. As RPs it was a point of honour to get to the bathroom early, get washed – using soap lumps squirreled away underneath sinks, between rounds – and be among the first in the queue for all mealtimes. We'd normally be beaten by the clankies, who we used to think had remained there since the end of breakfast.

We'd then gobble away, and be out of the dining hall rapidly to get back to the mess either for a lie down, or a sociable game of uckers, or crib, or just to listen to those sea stories. Whatever, the 'Out pipes – Hands carry on with your work' would always interrupt us, even if we did always query why it was that this German matelot called Hans was the only one on board who had to turn to again in the afternoons. It was a game, being the last one back after lunch, to get 'Father' after us, to see if he could find us, while pretending to have been turned to elsewhere.

We were given the 'promulgation' in the spring – to tell us where we would go during the commission, and when. It was relayed to us that we were going to the Fez (Far East Station). For a year. We were going to sail in January, returning the following December. That was better than I had ever hoped for. All the messdecks were suddenly a-buzz with chatter from those who'd been there before, that we would be going to 'Singers (Singapore) for a mini refit, then to 'The Fid' (Honky Fid – Hong Kong) for several weeks. En route via Beira patrol, Mombasa, four months in Bahrein as Gulf Guard Ship, then the Seychelles, South Africa – more than I could bear. Except that we were to keep it among family at this stage. All the married men griped and whined, all the single men could be heard cheering clear across Scotland, I should think. We couldn't wait. But first we had to complete weapon training, work-up and other nautical prerequisites before sailing around the world.

One of these was to muster at slops in *Cochrane*, for tropical kit issue – as if we didn't have enough gear to carry. This kit was only issued to ratings travelling to hot places, and you only got one issue, which had to stay with you whether you went there again or not. So we signed for two ice-cream suits, two pairs of cream shorts, two pairs of blue shorts, some white socks, thick, uncomfortable leather sandals and white canvas shoes. I said the shorts were cream – they were, so were the suits. Unfortunately they should have been white, so off they went to the dhobey wallahs until they were deemed white, at which point we were allowed to sew the blue badges on. Strangely, even though we dressed in these white suits, we still had to wear the black silks, blue collars and lanyards.

CHAPTER 8

A Farewell to a Part of Admiral Nelson

An extremely sad thing happened that year, one which depressed the entire Navy for quite some time – some nameless shitbag decided it was a 'good idea' to abandon Nelson's Blood, which had been served daily to all men 'of age' for decades. I had never before, and certainly never since, tasted anything quite like the tot. We juniors used to do anything for 'sippers' or 'gulpers', or 'halfers' right up to 'have the lot', which meant you got his tot. Since even swapping a duty only earned sippers, you can guess that the lot was only given in extreme circumstances. Juniors were classed as 'rumrats', which meant we'd lurk about at tot time on the off chance someone was too hung over to drink (or illegally bottle for a rainy day) his tot. The certificate produced at that time to mark that sad passing, featured a poem:

A MATELOT'S FAREWELL TO HIS TOT

You soothed my nerves and warmed my limbs
And cheered my dismal heart,
Procured my wants, obliged my whims –
And now it's time to part.
'Mid endless perils of the deep
And miseries untold,
You summoned sweet forgetful sleep,
Cocooned me from the cold

Ten years ago, the 'pound o' leaf'
That cast its fragrant smell
About the ship, expired in grief
And sadness of farewell.

Though guests might find the pantry bare
When e'er they choose to come,
Your hospitality was there,
A tot of Pussers rum.

Two hundred years and more you filled
The storm tossed sailors need.
Now you've been killed by spite distilled
From jealousy and greed.
And petty clerks with scrawny necks
Who never saw a wave,
Nor felt the spray nor heaving decks
Consign you to your grave.

Alas! However I protest
To save myself from hurt,
They tell me that it's for the best –
To keep us all alert.
And so the time has come, old friend
To take the final sup
Our tears are shed. This is the end
Goodbye, and bottoms up!

Although the beer allowance then went up from two cans a day to three, it was never any kind of consolation. There was a lot of bitterness felt and tears shed that day and afterwards.

We had, as all ships do, many characters in our mess. Dolly Gray, whose excuse for being adrift one day was that he had been run over by a train. Sid Saywell, known as PD (Poison Dwarf, on account of his lack of height, and the smell from his rear end after a night ashore). Jock Arthur who HAD been there, and seen it, and done it; he had more black cats than anyone else I have ever met and he was also my adopted 'sea daddy' – everyone has one, someone who teaches you 'the ropes'. 'Sugar' Kane, who eventually moved into submarines. 'April' Ashley – who knew more than was good for him. Jock Norrie, who had the biggest nose I have ever seen, MacNosh (from MacIntosh) whose run-ashore boots I used to borrow. And 'Charlie' Howe, whose party piece was to sing a song about a frog. We gradually got to know each other well enough to throw abuse at one another at the drop of a hat.

We soon learned lots of other tricks designed to get our own back. There was always someone, usually a poor RA, who could never afford his own fags and would pilfer yours. This we could get round by doing the 'Irish Fag Dance' – standing there patting all your own pockets to demonstrate their emptiness. Or we'd carry a dog end stuffed in our cap, and offer that. You learned to be more fly than they were. Or there were those who, every time you opened unwrapped nutty, or cracked a can of goffa, would say 'Giz a bit' or 'Giz a wet', and drain half the can. The antidote to this one – and remember, this was in the days when you had to make your own hole in the top to drink from – was to make a second drinking hole just below the first one. The RA would say his piece, you'd hand over the can and leg it away as he drank thirstily from the can, only to find it all poured out of the wrong hole, and dribbled down his chin, his Eights, his jacket . . .

The other trick was that at standeasy, when you'd have the tea wet, you'd industriously stir the cuppa with the shared teaspoon, 'borrowed' from the dining hall, while watching everyone else's concentration lapse. When they were distracted, you'd take the spoon out and, only for a fraction of a second, press the hot spoon on to the back of someone's hand. This would normally cause them sudden and intense pain, which actually only lasted for a few seconds before going away. Meanwhile, we'd all be on the deck, laughing – especially when the one you'd done it to would usually throw his tea down himself as well, giving us even more to giggle about. You were, then, always on the lookout for 'revenge' attacks!

One night, when Charlie and I were detailed to be QM and BM – I forget why, but the lads decided to throw a hooly in the mess. As it befell Charlie and me to stand the first on the gangway, we decided to take it in turns to visit the mess, for a can (or two) at a time. By the time 'pipe down' came, I was totally legless, and can remember being kicked awake by Charlie, having fallen asleep sitting on a locker on the opposite side of the ship to the gangway while I was supposed to be doing my turn! Good job it was him who found me and not the OOD or Duty PO, or I'd have been automatically given a ninety day break for being not only asleep on duty, but drunk on duty to boot.

We soon learned how to stretch out the grand 'staying in bed until the last possible moment' game. Call the Hands was 0645, and the Duty PO would be round shortly after, to ensure everyone was up. But if he wasn't too sharp, you'd stay there, listening to the hubbub of your mates as they shaved, farted, lit up, then clattered and chattered into life. Aware of the daily routine getting started the 'hands to breakfast' pipe being sounded, you would then rise, do the dhobey, make your bed up, drift greedily past the galley to see if you could swipe anything on the way past, and finally emerge on the upper deck five seconds before the pipe 'Both watches of the hands muster on the quarterdeck'.

CHAPTER 9

... and Off to Sea We Go ...

Eventually, 19 June 1970 arrived – Commissioning Day. We had worked hard for this – we had cleaned, painted, repainted, painted over rust and dust, scrubbed, swept and finally polished. The ship was dedicated by Commander W. Jenks, RN, and we held divisions in our Number Ones, cleared lower deck of all hands on to the gleaming quarterdeck for the reading of the commissioning warrant, ate the best meal I had ever seen at that time, then went ashore and got pissed.

RPs didn't stand deck watches like the rest of the seaman branches, but instead stayed snug in a warm Ops Room. Not for us the boredom of doing lifebuoy ghost (watching out for men overboard or ships coming up), or the cold of being bridge lookout – oh no, we stared, and stared, at the ever spinning trace on the varied displays hoping to spot the new contact first, or at least – before the OOW saw it, and demanded to know why we'd missed it. So, soon after the commissioning, we sailed for sea trials and shake-downs, which consisted of leaving Rosyth, sailing under the Forth Bridges and haring up and down the Forth at various speeds, doing various drills. We fired the mortars then dropped the seaboat, which came back loaded to the gunwales with fresh fish brought up by the deepwater explosions. These tasted good at suppertime.

Previously, we had always lowered and raised seaboats (at *Raleigh* and on the *Ulster*) by hand, with long lengths or ropes called 'falls' and a complicated series of blocks stretching down the waists, using the whole complement of seamen to raise it, but two or three very cautious ones to lower it. Consequently, everyone looked forward to seaboat drills with great trepidation: *Zulu* had electric hoists and wire falls. The operator merely released the gravity brake slowly, or engaged the drive later to recover it. Much easier.

We scampered down to Holy Island, and stayed out all night, which was THE big adventure. We conducted seamanship evolutions, and finally fired the guns. We did full power trials, steering-gear breakdowns, exercised fire, everywhere, but most importantly, we were let loose with the radar equipment. That was the most exciting thing we'd done so far, sitting up all night in the Ops Room, actually reporting 'contacts' as they appeared on the radar – being told to 'disregard' (too far away to worry about), 'watch' (if it does anything silly, report it again) or 'report' (keep telling me every 2–3 miles/2–3 minutes until I tell you otherwise). We learned that the reason the Naafi (onboard all naval vessels) opened at about 1930 (and at lunchtime, secure, and stand-easy), was so that the First and Middle watchmen could not only purchase soap and dhobey dust, but could also stock up with nutty and goffas, ready to take on watch with them. Whatever we bought before going on watch, and this could also include several tins of sausages in baked beans, it was a point of honour to have eaten all of it before you were relieved by the next watchkeepers, even if you had eaten both supper and 9 o'clockers AND scratched late suppers off the chefs. The nutty feast was traditional – as was not going for more than half an hour without having a (now duty free, as we were at sea) fag.

We launched and recovered the seaboat countless times. A dummy was kept on the quarterdeck, and the Jimmy would stamp down the arse-end and throw it over, to see how long it took the 'lifebuoy spook' to react. We reckoned to be able to recover 'a body' within minutes. The pipe would be 'Man overboard, prepare to recover by seaboat', followed by 'Away seaboats crew', which we would (being Scottish based) change to 'Away the noo the seaboats crew, Och, wait a minute – there's no fucker in it', and collapse giggling.

To relieve the tension, and expel some of our cooped-up energy, we were given a new game to play: 'scrubbing down' (the decks). This involved starting at the front end, throwing soapy water or even neat detergent everywhere, then following down with stiff brooms, scrubbing as we went. If we had wooden decking over the main metal, as Tribals had down both 'waists', we'd sometimes use a buffer similar to those used at *Raleigh* all those years ago, but these would be outdoor, waterproof versions, able to take much more stick. They also survived being hosed down, but were still unable to float once worn out or rusty, or even in the way at the wrong place at the wrong time. This was followed by the hosers, with the upper-deck fire hydrants and hoses being rigged to blast away all the resultant mess. This is why we started 'fore' and ended up 'aft', so we didn't finish and then have to clear up someone else's rubbish half an hour later. The 'hosers' were usually the ABs, whereas us juniors manned the brooms. We'd gladly prolong this for as long as possible, reasoning that we could at least have a laugh doing this – and (again) it beat the hell out of being shit-house sweepers. The older hands, though, would occasionally be inaccurate with the hoses, and we'd all end up soaked. Not a barrel of laughs on a cold day, but great fun while sailing in sunnier climes.

We quickly learned, too, that the detergent we used was mixable with salt water, quite necessarily really, as otherwise we'd use all the fresh water the clanks lovingly pushed through the small on-board desalination plant. We also noted that the best way to get water into the bucket was to turn on the hydrant, slowly, and fill it from there. The alternative (only tried the once), was to tie a length of rope round the bucket handle, chuck it over the side, and retrieve the full bucket. Easy when alongside, but try doing it at 20 knots. One of three things happens: you immediately get a sharp burning sensation on the palms of your hand as the rope rips through them; you try to hold on, and get dragged towards the stern of the ship until CDF prevails, and you scream 'fuck', and let go of it all, handsomely; you tie the other end of the rope to a handy stanchion or guard-rail, and watch as the stanchion bends, or the guard-rail breaks under the pressure of the entire North Sea being forced into that small bucket – or if you are lucky, someone with more CDF than you uses his extremely sharp rigging knife and cuts the rope before this happens. Surprisingly, the last two of these options cause you to stand mesmerized, in total disbelief.

Each part-of-ship had its own seamen assigned, and we had three parts of ship. 'Fo'c's'le' (FX) ratings obviously did the sharp end, 'Quarterdeck' (QD) did the blunt end and 'Top' did everything in between, including the radar masts and funnels. Each POS also had several 'below decks' compartments (heads, bathrooms, flats etc.) to clean twice daily. Considerable rivalry existed. Each POS had its own cleaning gear stowage containing the buffer, brooms, scrubbing brushes, detergent, ropes, heaving lines, bluebell (metal polish), squeegees (rubber blades mounted on broom handles, designed to sweep water in front of you – a quick way to get rid of surplus liquid), cloths and everything else necessary to keep the ship sparklingly clean and, well, shipshape and in Bristol fashion. Each POS had a 'lockerman' responsible for keeping gear safe. The lockers were places to go for a quick skive or for a quiet smoke. Lockerman was a valued job, as it meant not only could you legitimately draw new gear, but you could also slide round the ship RASing (stealing) gear from wherever it was left laying about, in order to build up your own stock. However you came across the gear, it was swiftly daubed with the paint coloured according to the POS you worked – in our case orange for Top, green for QD, red for FX – thereby authorizing only the relevant members to use that equipment. Woe betide you if you were found with someone else's gear. There was no excuse, not even 'I was just bringing it back'. You would thenceforth be known as a '. . . another fucking JUST rating'. There were plenty of them – 'I was just about to do that . . .' would normally result in a sudden pain in the backside from a well-directed, heavy, steel toecapped steaming bat.

One of the jobs of lockerman was to ensure a good supply of heaving lines, and other useful lengths of rope which you never knew would come in handy. Heaving lines were lengths of thin rope used to get the mooring wires and ropes across to the jetty. The idea was that the ship got manoeuvred to within throwing range, we'd bang out the heaving lines and, once a dockie had made contact, we'd tie the line to a wire rope. The dockie would haul that across and secure it and the ship would then be winched on to the jetty and made fast. So it was a point of honour to get the first heaving line across. The lockerman, on finding a spare coil of this rope, would then spend the next several days (although in truth it could be done in minutes) forming a complex, decorative knot called a 'monkey's fist' at one end of the rope, with an eye splice at the other end. However, the monkey's fist would not be considered heavy enough, so large nuts or lumps of heavy scrap metal would be found to tie the 'fist' around. Once that was completed, several layers of varnish could be soaked in, at which point a final topcoat of paint could be applied and left to further soak in order to make up the final weight. Eventually, the whole thing would be christened with several POS members taking it in turns to get the whole length of the rope out in a line. I used to do well at that, and could always be relied upon to get the first line over.

The problem lay in Rosyth and Portsmouth, where the dockies took exception to our lovingly crafted lines, and took pleasure in immediately cutting off the 'fist' before throwing it off the edge of the jetty. That would incense us, and the matey would be verbally abused over his parentage, or accused of having sex with himself. Or was it that we'd wait until he wasn't looking, and was offguard, before throwing the spare, bigger fist at him instead of near him. We always got our revenge, and we could always tie an even bigger 'fist' on (from the emergency supply!), to get him the next time. The mooring lines were stowed on each relevant POS, the headropes and foresprings were kept on the fo'c'sle, the stern rope and backsprings were stowed on the QD, and the breasts were kept on Top. At sea, they were all stored on their various drums or reels, and it was a difficult job to put them on.

Another naval tradition is that of 'piping' other ships. Generally, as you sail past another warship, whether it is tied up, or floating, the junior ship (that is to say, the one with the most junior skipper) pipes (the still) to the senior. The senior then pipes the still, waits a few seconds, then pipes the carry on. The junior then pipes the carry on, obscenities are exchanged, and both units proceed. While the stills are there, anyone (caught foolishly) on the upper scupper, has to face the other ship. So we became practised at spotting approaching ships and legging it to cover, or to the far side, so we wouldn't have to comply. Sometimes it was fun, like seeing another ship miles away from anywhere, sometimes it was poignant, like piping the war memorial on the beach at Southsea. Other times it was a pain in the arse, like piping FOSNI (Flag Office Scotland/Northern Ireland) in his house by the Forth Bridge, every time you went past.

Each time we went to sea, as soon as the last mooring rope was undone, we'd strike the jack and ensign, running up a second ensign on the main mast. We'd then lower the jackstaff, right in the bows, and the ensign staff, right aft, securing them tightly with heaving lines, until they were required again. The jack would remain stowed, but the second ensign would remain at the mast head until we returned to harbour, for all to see and recognize.

We also carried out 'Dipping the ensign'. If we went past a merchant ship, it was common practice for the merchantman to dip his ensign slightly, as a mark of respect. We would dip ours and immediately raise it, the merchantman then raised his. We'd then continue on our respective journeys. Obviously this didn't happen at night, only when we had ours raised, but we used to giggle, and watch intently through powerful binoculars as the merchantman suddenly remembered what he had to do. You'd then see his bridge door fly open and a figure would scuttle aft to his Red Duster, hurdling and dodging everything in his way, getting there just in time to dip it before we steamed past.

If we happened across a 'friendly' warship, or noticed aircraft 'squawking' on the IFF, we would be able to tell the type, country and exact unit. The aircraft were more difficult, but we could identify what it was and where it was from. We would also track airliners just for fun, and watch their squawks. We could interrogate them on our IFF to make their transponder automatically tell us who they were. It was all very good fun, for us, playing with all this technical stuff for real.

The contacts we tracked were all called 'skunks', that meant we didn't know what or who it was. It was therefore a 'skunk'. And we named them, from alpha to zulu, so we reported 'skunk alpha' – our first real radar contact to play with. We tracked that first contact until it disappeared off the edge of the table! If we ever got to handling more than twenty-six, we'd have been stuffed – it didn't occur to us to use numbers on the *Zulu*! It also didn't matter that the contact was identified, and that there was no real possibility of anything other than friendly ships or aircraft anywhere inside the 12-mile territorial waters – they were still called 'skunks'.

We did see the very occasional AGI (Russian 'fishing boats'), they were still skunks, but although we never took any official notice of them, we always stopped transmitting on all radars and sonars whenever we recognized what they were – probably too late. We'd also never transmit on the fire-control radar, nor would we ever under any circumstances train the guns on them, even for a laugh. We'd skirt them, they'd skirt us, and when we'd all finished filming and recording, we'd steam away from each other and get back on with what we were doing before we were interrupted. If we came upon a non-NATO ship, we'd frantically search through 'Janes' (*Fighting Ships*) to find something that matched the profile of the ship we could see. No matter that the ship would probably be at a strange angle, making all the silhouettes useless.

The *Zulu* actually had four radar sets for us to play with, the old 965 long-range air search, the 293 surface search, 978 navigation and the 944/954 IFF. All of which we were technically perfect on – our PRI Ray Antell had seen to that. It was still a wonderful experience though, actually to be standing behind the Local Plot, tracking real ships, working out real courses and speeds for real ships, and then calculating their closest point of approach, before telling the watch boss. He would then relay this data to the OOW on the bridge, who would then tell us either 'report' or 'watch'. Eventually, the OOW would tell us what kind of target or ship we were tracking, at which point we would scan the radar with great earnest, looking for more echoes to report.

The reporting procedure on the intercom went 'Bridge – Plot', the OOW on the bridge would say 'Bridge', at which point we would report the contact. Unless you had never spoken on an intercom before, in which case you would be told to speak clearly, or not to gabble, or whatever. I didn't have any such problems, and I took to it like a duck to water. Except when I attempted to copy the older hands who would, in the middle of the night, call 'BEE BOP' or 'PLIP PLOP' and the OOW would answer 'Bridge', as he would assume he had misheard. Anyway, I got caught out doing it, didn't I. And a right earwigging I got on the bridge that night. Mac, our leading hand of the watch, thought it hugely entertaining, but I learned a lesson, and was never caught again. I didn't say I didn't do it again, I said I never got CAUGHT again.

As the contacts were tracked, we used to record their progress on the plotting tables with chinagraph, a greasy pencil really, which shone highly when exposed to UV light. We also used small widgets, which were colour-coded shapes, green for friendly, red for hostile, orange for 'dunno', which we placed on the contact, so anyone looking at the table would see us, and everything around us, these also glowed under UV, which is what the Ops Room was continuously bathed in. Paradoxically, it also showed up our Eights – if they were clean, the UV would make them glow, but any grubby patches would not 'shine'. White fronts or white T-shirts were to be avoided, as they'd be completely dazzling to an onlooker. Otherwise, the room was in pitch dark, and known as the 'gloom room'. Gloomy or not, we always had an audience – from clanks (stokers) to greenies (electricians) to stewards – they would all come to see the radar. Or was it to scrounge a wet of coffee, which was always in plentiful supply for us official watchkeepers, even if we did have to descend two decks then walk half a ship length to get some hot water. Maybe it was purely because we were sociable people, or perhaps it was just warm in there with all that electrical apparatus running.

We would, while off-watch, and just for the mindless relief it offered, steer the ship. We had been trained to do this in the simulator at *Raleigh*, but now we could do it for real. We would go to the wheelhouse, and ask if we could have a go. Whoever was on the wheel would say 'Bridge – Wheelhouse' (or 'Fridge – Greenhouse'), and when answered, he would ask for 'Permission for Junior Seaman So-and-So to take the wheel'. If it was 'Yes Please', you would have to announce who you were, what course you were steering and what the telegraph and rev indicators were set at. You would be in trouble if you got that bit wrong. Then you had to steer the ship, following the compass. On the compass was a thing called the 'Lubbers Line' which was what you steered to, and God help you if you started to 'chase it', that is to say drift off course and apply the wrong and opposite wheel to get it back on course. You'd normally be instantly thrown off the wheel, and banished from the wheelhouse. It was, though, a point of honour to be able to steer the ship, continuously to within just one degree, especially if the weather was bouncy and the ship wanted to veer about. If you did well, the OOW would always praise your spell. Apparently, and allegedly, (according to the black cats) someone on another ship, unspecified, had actually taken the ship round in a full 360° turn one night, without the OOW noticing. Could this be true? Whatever, the first time you plucked up the courage to steer was scary, after that, after steering it for several thousand miles – it became much easier, and you learned how straightforward it was to predict which way it would try to drift next, and by how much, and thus how to move the wheel gently to stop it and to regain the original course. All on board eventually succumbed to driving the ship, even bone-idle greenies would come and steer it, and chefs seemed to prefer the pastime to making biscuits.

Slowly but surely we were shaken down and worked up gently to the big one. We sailed to Portland – an inhospitable area in summertime, but a nightmare to us whatever the time of year, whatever the weather conditions (normally a full gale as far as we were concerned).

As armament on that and all the other Tribals we had a 4.5 in gun fore and aft, Seacats (missiles) port and starboard, Oerlikons port and starboard, A/S mortars aft, and a helicopter. In addition we had many small arms and assorted machine-guns – light and heavy – in the magazines. All or some of these were exercised at various times, sometimes all at once at Action Stations.

With the ship at the highest state of readiness, we'd sometimes pretend there was a nuclear, biological or chemical (NBCD) threat, and rig 'pre-wetting' on the upper deck. This meant rigging hoses all round the ship, spraying water all over the superstructure, the theory being that if anything dangerous or radioactive or mind-altering wafted down on to us, the nice water would wash the nasty bits away, and that would clearly leave us quite, quite safe from harm, wouldn't it? So anyone going out on to the upper scupper would have to come back in through a decontamination shelter where a special shower would be rigged. In here, the person would be scrubbed to get rid of all contamination.

Action Stations meant everyone was closed up. Whether that meant the stewards manned the hoists in the mags, or the chefs manned the gun turret, passing the bricks and the cordite, or the stokers on the throttles, or the greenies ready to mend broken wires. Sometimes when we got bored we'd put our anti-flash on back to front to annoy someone, as they could not then tell who you were.

CHAPTER 10

And Now Portland

Portland, otherwise known as 'work-up' or 'shake-down', lasted in the region of six weeks, during which we sometimes got evening shore leave (if we needed to store, without RASing), but never got weekend leave, unless it was a short one, from Saturday lunchtime until Monday morning. We did, however, get grief, exercises, grief, more grief, more work and more exercises.

Portland meant anchoring out most nights, going alongside rarely, carrying out seamanship evolutions like RASing, towing, mooring, anchoring, coupled with exercise fires, damage control and pretend NBCD attacks. And being closed up at Action Stations before the rest of the world was awake, and sailing out of the harbour line astern with all the other ships down there, knowing quite well it would be you who first saw the tell-tale echo of the Buccaneer from not more than 5 miles away as it came in at sea level to 'bounce' you. By the time you reported it, it was upon you with a roar you could hear below decks. Or you would see just one trace, which could either be a tin-can or a submarine periscope. It was not in your interest to keep quiet, so you would scream now, rather than be screamed at for missing it. What would annoy us more was that this particular Portland visit was during peak holiday season, with all the tourists, all with their daughters – and here we were, sitting in a grey steel box, doing things we didn't want to do, while they were sleeping in their caravans snoring and dreaming about the sailor they met the previous night!

It was now we really found out about keeping everything to 'Zulu' time. All exercises started at 0730Z, or 1000Z, or 2030Z, and if we happened to get there at 0730A (Alpha; British Summer Time), or 1000A – we would therefore be an hour late. Or was it an hour early?

Portland was famous for 'FOST Funnies'. FOST was Flag Officer Sea Training, and his staff officers used to find it amusing to drop an exercise on you, any time day or night. For example, waking you up at 0300 to say there was a SUBMISS or SUBSMASH (Submarine missing/Submarine Smashed), gearing everyone up to sail, as far as singling up all the lines, then saying '. . . just an exercise'. Or calling a fire on you just as you were about to go ashore, so the whole ship's company were either involved in it, or became caught up in it.

At sea, we in the Ops Room would be conducting a CASEX (Combined Anti Sub Exercise), or ARREX (Air Raid Reporting Exercise) or Gun Firing Exercise, or whatever. Our job was clearly the most important on the ship. It was obvious really, if we didn't see 'the threat' coming in, we'd soon have large holes to repair. In the meantime, the rest of the ship's company would be rehearsing Damage Control exercises, power failures, chemical attacks. We would start at 0600 for the 'weekly war', sail out the harbour having got everyone up at 0500 to weigh anchor, close up the Ops Room crew before passing the breakwater, then we'd be hit. Then we'd have the DC exercise, then the NBCD attack, by which time we'd be sitting there in the gloom room in Eights, trousers tucked in non-nylon socks, anti-flash gear, gas masks – looking like a bunch of ultra-violet-lit pervies, all gazing at various displays and shouting various attack threats at the person who needed to know. Occasionally, the staffies used to either 'kill' the Ops Room officer, or the Captain, or some of us. Or they'd cut all the power. They used to think that was a brilliant move. So did we, but we never let on. It was always much more peaceful without radar to play with, except that it got hot without the fans going, and we'd lose pounds waiting for the FOST prats to get bored and allow us to go in peace.

Occasionally, when everyone from the Skipper down to us, started to get a bit ratty, 'the proceedings' would come to a natural break, and 'one-all-round' would be announced. Everyone would then gratefully light up, drawing the ciggy smoke deep down, to ease the tension. Once 'closed up' at Action Stations – you stayed closed up either until stood down or until you were reduced to defence watches (either the whole of the port watch, or the whole of the starboard watch), meaning half of you could stand down (and get turned to) while your mates remained closed up (and sat down), and in the warm.

Some exercises required running silent – we'd trudge about at 4 knots, listening on the passive sonar for the 'enemy' submarine. God help anyone who decided to smash around or bang anything aboard while this was going on. Or we'd stamp around with the active sonar pinging, searching for this elusive black pig. Active sonar is like you hear on the telly, except that when you are encased in a metal-hulled ship the transmitted pulse reverberates through the entire hull, and you also hear the returning pulse as it bounces off the contact.

When weighing anchor we sailors would muster on the sharp end, complete with stiff brooms and hoses coupled up and ready. In Portland, the harbour bottom was thick gooey mud, and as the cable was worked, more mud and filth would be raised, which we would energetically hose and scrub as the cable came through the hawse pipes on its way to the cable locker, round the capstans, with the occasional link being painted in transit, so everyone would know how much was left out. Occasionally, sea creatures would survive the ascent, and we'd be hosing off not only prehistoric mud, but also crabs and starfishes. The anchor would soon clear the water, and we'd slowly move ahead with the hook dragging through the sea. We had to bear in mind though, that as we revved up, the hook could start to wobble about in the increasing flow, so the trick was to get it out of the water half way between being 'automatically' cleaned, and having it smashing embarrassingly through the ship's side. We often heard almighty bangs as it hit us, but suffered no holes. Eventually, we'd raise it out of the water to the 'home' position, at which point we'd blast the remaining mud off it by leaving it hanging over the side, and increasing the hydrant/hose pressure to full pelt. Once we were satisfied it was clean (and remember those FOST goonies were always out to criticize something, even if it was only mud on the anchor), we'd haul it home, fasten on all the shackles, including the bottle-screw slip to drag it that last few inches, before hosing down the whole fo'c's'le while still getting under way a bit faster. Anyone who has never done this at 0500, in full foul weather gear, in the teeth of a gale, complete with driving, persistent rain has never lived. We'd then wait some hours till breakfast, or close up in the Ops Room for the first exercise. Still, we always had that day's exercises to look forward to . . . or the tourists' daughters that night, if we were allowed alongside.

There was something else we would always have to do before the anchor was picked up. There was an exhaust from one of our generators (known as 'donks' or donkeys) half way down the ship's side just beneath the bridge wings (i.e. the highest point on the ship's deck), and every time we flashed that up to give us totally shore-free power, it would churn out filthy black and blue smoke, leaving a huge black trail around and downwind from it. And every time we stopped, out would go the bosun's chair with the Duty hands, with his Duty ship's side grey in a pot, covering up the marks. Again. You would think that was all sailors were there for, painting the side, cleaning everywhere for everyone else to live, polishing everything not already covered in paint.

Gunnery exercises were always much more fun. One such exercise would involve shore bombardment. We'd steam up and down the coast off Lulworth (I think), ensuring stray targets such as grockle boats, fishing boats etc. didn't get between us and our target. Once we were absolutely sure, we'd open fire. It never sounds much – a 4.5 in gun throwing a 50-something pound projectile up to 10 miles, but the racket as it fired was enough to wake up long dead people. Every molecule on, in and round the ship would immediately be thrown ten left (off track) in reaction to the shell being hurled through and out the muzzle. Dust would fall from undusted places, unsecured glasses would jump from tables, and unwary people who hadn't heard the warnings that '"A" turret is about to open fiBBBBAAANNNGGG' would literally shit themselves. The first time I heard it, I jumped out of my new steaming boots – and I was ready for it!

On occasions, we'd fire just a few rounds, but on the shore support exercise, we'd fire, and fire, and fire shell after shell after shell. We would fire as many as ten rounds per minute – which is an awful lot of hard work – until you heard above the din, 'Guns' screaming . . . 'STOPLOADINGSTOPLOADINGSTOPLOADING–CHECKCHECKCHECK' and when the cry came back 'ALL GUNS EMPTY', you'd close your open mouth (previously opened to reduce the effect of the cordite blast), shake your head and get on with what you were doing.

The exploded cordite created an unforgettable and unmistakable stench as it forced the projjy out of the barrel. If the air-conditioning was still switched on, within seconds the whole of the interior of the ship would be filled with that stink, comparable to rotten eggs but worse. It was choking and acrid, and once in your lungs it took hours to get back out. Eventually, you'd hear the broadcast 'SPONGE OUT', at which time you'd know the racket was really over. The gun captain would then make his crew clean up the gun, put the tampon back in the end of the barrel (to prevent seawater invading the inside of the gun), put all the covers back on it, and there it would stand, deserted but menacing. Until the next time. Our favourite exercise, was actually the Z-Ex, which was always the last one, and entailed legging it back to your pit, laying on it fully dressed, shutting your eyes, and snoring, loudly. 'ZZZZZZZZzzzzzzz zzzzzzzzzzzzzzz . . . Ex'.

Of course, it was easy to whack the shells out, but we'd suffer later – 'ammunition ship' was the most loathed task in the RN. No smoking, anywhere, until it was over, no fags on you, no matches on you, no nylon on you. Then you'd sit in the 'mags' unloading shells (and the cordite) from the lifts, swinging them nonchalantly around and into the racks, trying to forget that one dropped could ruin your (and everyone else's within a several mile radius) marriage and career prospects! They were heavy too – a normal projectile would weigh 50 to 60 lbs, and the casing could be about 20 lb, both of which we'd throw at each other to stow, quite happily.

One of my Action Stations was the radar office, where initially I got a surprise I wasn't prepared for. This office was deep in the bowels of the ship, through and down several hatches and ladders. And it was incredibly hot as a result of all the valves in the radar gear. However, the first time down there, on the headset to the Ops Room, I was told to start the 965 air radar. I pretended I hadn't heard. When they finally sent someone down to show me – what took my breath away (in the new technological RN) was that I had to turn a wheel, which cranked the aerial. When it got fast enough, I could push a switch to engage the motor drive. Then I had to press a button to switch it on, to make it transmit. There was a similar set-up for the 293 surface radar, only not quite so clumsy, and I think a further one in the Ops Room to start the old navigation radar.

We would also close up 'Specials', Special Sea Dutymen – experts who would navigate us in and out of harbour, and be ready to react to any potential emergency. It was important to be selected to do Specials, as it meant you wouldn't have to get into blues and stand out in the cold and rain to enter/leave harbour. Instead you'd be in the warm and dry, and in Eights. Specials closed up for a variety of reasons: RASing, entering harbour and anchoring, to name a few, and would close up all over the ship, including the wheelhouse, DCHQ, gloom room, switchboards and tiller flat. That was not a favourite place – hot, right aft, below the quarterdeck, above the extremely noisy steering gear, with the knowledge that if we suffered a failure on that gear, you'd then be working your knackers off, aligning the rudders by hand pump. A terrifying prospect. Whatever, entrance to the tiller flat was by a small hatch, again secured by clips to correspond to the DC state. And frequently, when the tiller-flat pilot attempted to fall out, he'd find the door clips had been secured with enormous force by persons unknown, meaning he had to bang on the solid steel door until someone heard and released him. Not a job for the unwary!

It would be shortly before this Specials pipe that the Jimmy could make a broadcast, warning us of severe weather conditions and telling us to secure the ship for rough weather. This could be merely lashing down everything that might move – ironing boards, tea-boat, blocks – to rigging the upper deck lifelines and putting extra strops on everything else. We'd nevertheless rig the seaboat as a lifeboat, with the boatrope rigged and all the gripes hauled taut(er). Conditions like this were fairly normal for Portland, at any time of year.

My first run ashore in Portland was dressed in full Twos, with complimentary white gaiters and webbing belt, for I was Duty shore patrol. We had to sit in the dockyard Naafi all evening, watching everyone else steam into pint after pint. The next night we were alongside, I actually got ashore – remember this was my first proper 'run' outside Rosyth or Pompey or Guzz – and I can still remember the main drag leading from the dockyard gate in Portland as it was, with alternating pubs and food shops. I recall the atmosphere and smell too.

On another evening we went ashore quite early (as soon as 'secure' was piped) to try to empty the place of scrumpy and Merrydown. When we left the ship we were 'Channel Guard Ship', so there was only 'One Watch Leave' which meant that only half the crew were allowed ashore. We had done this before at Portland, often, as had all other ships doing their work-up. A different ship was 'guard ship' every night/day. Further to this, Tribal class frigates had two methods of propulsion – steam and gas turbine. The gas turbine (or G6 as it was called) could be flashed up within minutes, meaning we really could sail at the drop of a hat, in the time it took to fire up that turbine. That kind of information was nice to know, but meaningless to us. All we knew about G6 was the piped message before it was started 'Hands keep clear of the after funnel – G6 is about to be run up', followed by a muffled explosion, followed by an increasing roar as the turbine took effect. Then a large shower of soot emerged, covering anything down-wind of it. Not conducive to the health of the stoker(s), who wound it up just after we sailors had spent the last two hours scrubbing those wooden decks. G6 was usually kicked up before sailing so as to provide back-up power in case of a steam-plant breakdown.

As we stumbled back along the High Street, we heard the muffled explosion, saw the flames leaping out of our after funnel, thought 'Fuck – that's us' and improved our speed, but not necessarily our direction back through the yard towards the gangway. As we did so, we were met by the Duty PO, who told us to be quick (or words to that effect) as we were to sail. Yeah, Yeah, we thought, another FOST funny. Nevertheless, we hurriedly changed into Eights and foul-weather gear, ran back to our parts-of-ship, at which point, to our utter astonishment, we actually slipped and sailed. By now, we knew this was not a FOST funny. We were told by the Captain we were en route to just south of the Isle of Wight, where an oil tanker was stricken. We didn't get a lot of sleep that night, and as we had sailed without all the crew, we had to double up. The *Pacific Glory* was ablaze from its rear end, and we could see the glow even before we located it on radar. We weren't the first ship on the scene, but our engineers boarded it to assist bringing the blaze under control, and then assessed the considerable damage. Personally, I didn't see any of her dead Chinese crew, but we apparently picked a few up that night, as did others who participated in the rescue operation. Even so, there were twenty-seven very fortunate survivors from the tanker, and we Zulus were a lot less 'jolly' when we steamed back into Portland later that day for the rest of our crew. It is surprising how quickly a disaster like that sobered you up – in more than one sense. Mind you, it proved our training to be second to none – we showed we could respond instantly and professionally to any situation we were called upon. And that after only a few weeks of training.

At some point (lucky us), we had acquired our own helicopter – a 'Wasp' (so-called because of its noise and nuisance factor, buzzing round you all the time, I suppose), complete with pilot and aircrew. This necessitated a new set of instructions: 'No Smoking on the upper deck – helicopter ranged'; 'No smoking abaft the after funnel – helicopter being refuelled'; 'No personnel on the upper deck – helicopter at flying stations'. Even going into and out of harbour, the thing used to pose on the flight deck, surrounded by its workers smirking and smiling gormlessly. The only perk I used to get out of it was as helicopter lookout, when I would go to the gun radar platform to watch over the Wasp as it buzzed about. My job as lookout would be not only to track the thing with my Mark One eyeball, but to scream loudly if it fell into the sea, which it never did. However, I used to enjoy being up there in the fresh air, while we charged around the Portland practice areas at high speeds. On occasions, when we 'flew' at night, you were up there alone, in the pitch dark apart from the steaming lights, and while it wasn't noiseless, you'd really think you were the only person for miles. That far out at sea (the Atlantic, or wherever we were operating) you'd have a ceiling of stars and no cloud, but best of all, no artificial lighting to ruin your view of the skies. The bins then would be alternately trained on the Wasp then the skies. While it landed on to refuel or re-arm, you could lay back and stargaze. On that particular lookout post was a gadget designed to direct the guns. This had a powerful set of bins in it, but it was connected to the guns. We'd disengage the gun system (obviously we didn't want to give the game away), and peer through the gunsights at whatever there was to see. Being electrically operated, you'd gently twist the handle on one side to go left or right, then the other to swing up and down and be able to see much further, and this even enabled you to stargaze without twisting your head up.

We'd sometimes steam 'blacked out'. This meant covering all openings along the ship's side, and even turning off all navigation/mast/steaming lights. Normally we'd do this to 'hide' from the Wasp, to ensure he would be guided back under direct control, rather than see the light and fly towards it. Moonlit or starry nights were better, you could lay on the deck, gaze upwards and spot satellites and shooting stars easy as pie. You could even see the helicopter outside radar range if you stood up again. But put clouds up, and make it rain a bit and the whole scenario changed. We were only meant to spend thirty minutes as lookout – quite long enough in the rain, but we'd draw it out if the conditions were right, such as flying stations midday in the tropics. A favourite retort to anyone who'd say to us, 'You wouldn't do that at home, would you?', would be 'No, but there again, I don't get fuckin' helicopters landing on my fuckin' roof in the middle of the fuckin' night at home do I?'

Our shiny, navy blue helicopter lived in a little nest called a 'hangar' towards the blunt end of the ship. On the *Zulu*, and therefore all Type 81s, this hangar had a hole in the roof where the deck was on a lift. Once lowered, i.e. out of sight (and mind), the idle waffoos used to do their hardest work ever – putting the covers on the hole where the helo was now sitting. This only used to take a few minutes, but being waffoos they had to work out what to do afresh, every time they did it. So their evolution could take several hours, while we sandscratchers stood laughing. We did hear of a sister ship where an even more stupid waffoo than normal, engaged the lift in 'raise' while the covers were still on, destroying the helo as it went up. Again – hearsay!

At some point, we discovered why various items, mostly money, had been going missing from our lockers. Let me say that sailors trust other sailors implicitly, and rarely would anyone find it necessary to secure their kit locker. But we found stuff had gone missing. The mess we were in shared a ladder with the greenies, and our lockers were directly opposite it. Things went walkies. We found some of the money one day, tucked behind a trap (toilet) in the forward heads. We had our suspicions, and had words with the Leading Hand of the greenies mess, telling him who we thought it was, and why. The chap was charged, and immediately weighed off, curiously with bandaged hands, which occurred when a hatch cover accidentally fell on his fingers. That was a Navy tradition. It allegedly took several people to hold him there, and he apparently screamed very loudly while we were not present in the mess, having been earlier sent out.

CHAPTER 11

Our First 'Foreign' (Even if it was Only Hamburg)

Eventually the work-up climaxed in an orgy of exercises and thunderflashes and smoke and disasters, which we apparently passed with flying colours. At least, the 'staffies' could find no more to whinge and whine about, so we sailed for Portsmouth, and from there straight to Hamburg for our first run ashore.

We arrived at the top of the river, embarked the pilot up the jumping ladder, and closed up Specials, all the way down to Hamburg, where we finally moored. We were miles away from the main town, but right across the street from a cuckoo clock shop. I still have the clock and it keeps virtually perfect time, and cheerfully cuckoos, when allowed! As we went ashore for the first time, with our money conveniently changed into Marks, I forgot that while we drove on the left, in Germany they didn't – and marched out in front of a large tram. How I avoided it I know not.

The next few days was a blur of Hamburg, Lowenbrau beer, German fast food, more Lowenbrau and sightseeing, with just a bit more German beer for good measure. It was only when we sailed, got to the top of the river and turned into the North Sea that the snags developed. Too many sailors with a taste for English beer got a shock when, after drinking chemical beer for three days, we hit a force eight going back over to Rosyth. Me – I was sick as a dog for the first few hours of the voyage, but didn't know whether to put it down to my first real drop of 'roughers' (anything below a force eight was just windy, anything over was bumpy) or the beer. Whatever, I was not alone as we greenly pitched our way through high seas, with frequent trips to the aft heads (not so much motion as the for'ard ones), over to the peace of the Forth and back to the safe arms of the jetties of Rosyth. Subsequently, I have always claimed it was the beer, as I was never, ever sick at sea again whatever the sea state.

One of our perks as RPs was to stand on the bridge (in quiet watches), and gaze out over the sea, goofing at the ships we had just located. This was dependent on the sea-state – in bumpy weather, with the bridge windscreen wipers at full pelt, watching the green sea smashing over the bow, thundering down the fo'c's'le, hitting the 'screen', bouncing up that and then finally banging into those wipers was a truly amazing sight. We stood our steaming watch in the Ops Room, unlike the other seamen (Gunners, Sonars), who would stand 'watch on deck', providing bridge lookouts, stern lookouts (in case of man overboard), helmsmen and seaboat's crew. One night, a new young junior went on to the starboard bridge wing as lookout, and asked us how to report the light he had observed. Instead of telling him to say 'Bridge – Port lookout, Green three zero, white light – far', we told him the reporting routine was 'Bridge – Port lookout, Yo Ho Ho little white light, green three oh'. Then we legged it. He made the report, everyone on the bridge disintegrated into small giggling heaps – except the OOW who gave him a good bollocking, and taught him the correct procedure. The kiddy concerned gave us some stick afterwards, not that we cared – we laughed for days about that one.

When it came, we set off for our main leave from Rosyth with our duty free and rabbits from our Hamburg run – in my case my cuckoo clock, bottles of vino, ciggies and a large bottle of vodka. We freely imbibed from the carry out shops, and were three sheets to the wind before we boarded the train at Inverkeithing. When we changed trains at Waverley, we all opened our duty frees. This we mixed with the coke/lemonade from the buffet, and I can remember drinking the last of my vodka while going through Berwick-on-Tweed. The next thing I recall was waking up at Newcastle, absolutely sober, but thirsty. I drank lemonade all the way to Birmingham, changed for Northampton and arrived home quite safely.

CHAPTER 12

We're Going to the Fez

Going home for long leave, i.e. Christmas, was a strange experience, for although nothing had changed – except me, completely and forever – nothing was ever going to be the same again. And while I was ready for Mum and her question 'When do you have to go back', I found that I had nothing much in common with my mates John, Dave, Alan and Neil from Hardingstone, preferring to demonstrate my drinking prowess rather than go dancing around handbags.

Leave ended, I travelled to Rosyth and we began to make frantic last-minute preparations, before sailing amidst buckets of tears from RA wives. It was not in anyone's interest to do any winding up on that trip, so it passed uneventfully. We reached Portsmouth, re-stored, sailed right away into the Solent, and the Channel, and started on the several hundred anti-malaria pills, which, along with salt tablets, we ate every day until we got back to the UK eleven long months later.

We were to stop at Gibraltar first, and while in Pompey we had acquired 'crabfats' who were very mouthy about their self-assumed superiority, and who we were to deliver to Gib. They were going to join in WOD duties and upper deck pastimes, such as painting and cleaning, and were messed with us. As we turned left at the end of the Channel we drove straight in to a force eleven. We spent the next three days on the Bay of Biscay, tacking across seas, sitting with the sea ahead, astern, abeam, trying to find the most comfortable position. Obviously we all had our sea legs, but the crabs stayed in bed for three days, lifting their heads only to puke. Or to dash to the heads to puke and dump at the same time (called a 'grand slam', worsened by forgetting to remove your trolleys first). As I said, we were used to it, to the extent of deliberately and noisily sucking down and scoffing on greasy pork chops or bacon sarnies in front of them to provoke another attack of nausea. I can still see Jock Norrie, giggling, holding one side of his extremely large snout pretending to sneeze and letting go one end of a piece of bacon rind, so it looked like a large lump of snot had dropped. The target crabfat threw like a geyser, while we collapsed. All we had to do was mention 'bacon sarnies' or 'pork' after that for them to turn greener still! They never did do any duties, apart from clearing up their barfings. Well, we had no intention of clearing up – it was more fun to make them do it themselves.

We were all banned from the upper scupper, as it was considered too dangerous. There were provisions made – we had rigged up lifelines, to which you could secure yourself. And if you tied yourself to these, you had to tell someone you were going 'up' and for how long. So we stayed below, battened down, as much as possible – basically for the duration. We were allowed on to the bridge to watch the waves – one minute high above and all round us, the next below us – smashing and crashing not only over the fo'c's'le, spurnwater, 'A' gun and bridge, but in, round and down everything in between. While balanced on the top of the wave, we'd also hear the screw spinning crazily while out of water, before we assumed yet another astonishing angle, meanwhile dropping like a roller coaster back between more waves. This was one of the most impressive sights I ever saw, but it was only when we neared the shelter of Gib that we found we had not only lost several liferafts in the storm, but the decks and metalwork were bent. There was also damage to the spurnwater in front of 'A' gun which was bent over backwards, causing 'A' gun to be thrown off-line. Instead of pointing directly over the bow, the barrel now pointed some 10° to the right and several degrees up, while the aiming gear correctly pointed dead ahead. We lost the seaboat too – the one we had spent hours on, tuning the ancient engine, painting the old much-used planking a pretty, contrasting blue-and-white mix. It's probably floating around the Bay even now, I shouldn't wonder.

Because it was something else I never discussed with anyone else, it is difficult to describe the 'buzz' I got when entering any foreign harbour. Hamburg didn't count, as I was closed up and didn't see anything until alongside. Gib was the first time I had been on the upper scupper. What I got was an exhilarating mixture of anticipation and expectation and pure excitement. In the UK, after you had a few 'runs' behind you, you got to know what to expect, so runs in Pompey, say, adopted a standard format of drink, followed by food, followed by back onboard. Away from home the pattern was basically the same, but might be mixed in with a sightseeing trip, new faces, new cultures, new food, different modes of transport. So my feelings were more along the lines of what might happen, rather than what would happen. We knew we'd end up several sheets to the wind eventually, it was therefore exciting to anticipate what would take place before then. I never lost that buzz no matter where I went.

The most exciting part, really, was that of standing on the upper deck, at Procedure Alpha, or Bravo, watching everything that went on – the tugs, the manoeuvring, the expectant faces on the jetty watching your every move, the frenzied rush of work to get the wires and ropes across, to get the ship secured alongside, to get the gangway across and rigged. Then – as always – you went down below to change into working rig, to come back on deck to tidy up the wires, to lash ropes, to get awnings up, to repaint scars, to clean, skirmish the jetty, then, finally, to secure for lunch before scampering off for that all important first run.

In Gib we moored across the harbour from the massive old sheerlegs, long since demolished, and our first job was to paint the ship's side. This is a tradition – everywhere the RN goes in a warship, as soon as the ship is stationary, out comes the grey paint, the stages and the bosun's chair, and up and down go the rollers, brushes and elbows. This time, we had lost nearly all the paint from the stem and anchors, and strips down the side, all of which were quickly covered as the Jimmy prowled the jetty overseeing the repairs.

Ship's Side Party, as it was known, was instigated by the Jimmy at 'Both Watches' in the morning, whenever we were alongside. As soon as you got to BWH, and saw him leering over the side, you would know what was coming next, and immediately attempt to merge with the background. Fortunately, the way it worked was the better 'hand' you were at your normal daily work, the less likelihood there was of you being picked for SSP. So, SSP was generally staffed by the cabbages, who would have to go and find the stages and chairs, rig them, sort out their gear, don thick overalls (and in some cases life-jackets too) and descend over the side. The third-worst job was painting the stem, as this needed a bosun's chair, and delicate balance in order to keep in touch with the job. The second least favourite task was to have to do the side below the bridge wings – they were immensely high (or seemed it when viewed from the bottom). However, the worst was having to do round any of the sewage outlets, not knowing when someone would finish at their dumping stations, and flush their bowel contents out the side of the ship. You only did it once, after that you stayed above the drain and reached down.

By their nature, and due to gravity, the stages could only go one way – down. This meant that once you were near the waterline, you then had to climb the ropes back over the freshly scrubbed or painted bits. It was catch-22 – whatever you did, you got soaked or filthy. If anyone with a score to settle knew you were over on a stage, it was not surprising to find buckets of icy water being accidentally poured over the side, or even the ropes becoming suddenly unsecured, allowing one end of the two-man stage to tip its human cargo into the sea. It was usual to walk past the rope securing it and then kick it or shake it, just to watch the stage-monkeys jump and grab the rope – as if that would be of any help to them if it all collapsed.

Whatever SSP had to put up with while working, at the end of the day they had to restow the stages and ropes, return all their cleaning gear and paint, then go and get tidied up using copious amounts of white spirit to remove the 'ship's side grey' which now adorned their bodies and overalls, while we just washed our hands.

We had Rock-ape (Gibraltarian) dockyard mateys doing emergency repairs on the spurnwater, and I believe we flew out specialists to realign 'A' gun. We also obtained another seaboat, which was rapidly brought back into some kind of order. We were therefore forced to spend more days than we had planned. Gib is a wonderful place, and I will never forget my first proper run ashore there. The main drag, surprisingly called Main Street, is reached by climbing up out of the dockyard, which puts you immediately in touch with all the pubs. I mean pubs, not bars. Gib is British in every aspect except one – the inhabitants. There are Gibraltarians, and there are the Barbary Apes. The pubs at that time lined both sides of the drag, for as far as you could see. We went on that very first run with Jock Arthur, who steered us from bar to bar to bra t rba to b are . . . until we couldn't stand up any more. It was in the courtyard of one of these bars, surrounded by colonial tables and tropical palm trees that Jock first introduced us to JCs (John Collins) – gin, fruit juices and soda water, with a sugar rimmed glass. You could apparently drink these with no effect all day and night, which was most fortunate as that coincided with the opening hours – if you looked hard enough. We would start at the end of the drag with some Watney's Red Barrel, then as we moved further down the strip, we would slurp more JCs, ending up at a place called 'The Hole In The Wall'. We would then get a taxi back to the ship in time for 0100, which not only ensured 'big eats' but was an Ordinary Seaman's leave expiry time.

One day, just to be different, we boarded the cable car to the top of the rock. The view from there is unparalleled, from Spain to Africa, and a bit more besides. Unless it's raining. It was a scary ride on that cable car, it rises seemingly vertically for the first several hundred feet over nothing at all, then from the next pylon it is over rock to the next stations, where you can get out and walk further up or back down.

We also walked through the rock, along old passages said to have held munitions in the war, clear through to the other side of the island. We visited St Michael's Caves, full of brightly lit stalactites and stalagmites. We sampled the restaurants, of which there are many, catering for whatever type of food you want. We tried a steakhouse one night, and were served with litre glasses of Lowenbrau lager; we appropriated the glasses (I still have mine to this day). Jock also showed us something extremely odd – a Wimpy bar in the middle of Gib that sold alcohol. The shopping is great too – you can literally buy anything there if you look in the right shops. And it is a duty free place too!

So far I have not mentioned a thing called a 'grippo'. A grippo is someone who is so enthralled by the fact that they have met a real sailor, they willingly talk to you and buy you drinks and food all night. Obviously, the more they drink the drunker they get, but what they don't realize is that you are not, due to the fact that your 'alchofrolic' tolerance is far greater than theirs. Grippos can be met everywhere in the world, and it was in Gib we met our first. This man's family paid for our amusement all night until they had to get a taxi back to where they were staying, they were unable to walk!

Gib was also famous for being able to tell when the Spanish Navy was getting ready to go to sea. A huge pall of black smoke used to rise above La Linea on the other side of the bay as their warship (known as Smokey Joe) flashed up its ancient coal-powered engines, to finally sail creakily and slowly past our high-tech, gun-loaded, missile-bearing, gleamingly grey frigate *Zulu*.

CHAPTER 13

Africa!!!

It was with sadness that we sailed from Gib on a bright day, out into the calm Atlantic, turning left towards . . . and the smell of Africa, and regardless of what anyone tells you, you can smell it downwind. It is a smell like nothing else, of desert and animals and . . .

At some point we changed out of our Eights and into Tens or Ten A, which was shirts, shorts and sandals. How silly we looked, being made to wear shorts at our age, showing off repulsive white, hairy legs. We soon got used to things, spending every spare minute above decks, usually stripped to our nix, trying to get more than just our knees brown. We also gave our issue sandals the float test, preferring instead to wear the lighter, more comfortable versions sold by 'Snobs', the Chinese shoemaker on board. He lived in the bowels of the ship, handmaking shoes for us. He would have crates of sandals ready to flog to us, at a very reasonable price. Everyone turned a blind eye to our wearing of these – no one in his right mind wore the hard-issue version. I imagine that the floor of the Bay of Biscay, should anyone care to dive to see, is covered with rotting Pusser's issue sandals. Best place for them too.

Obviously, throughout our travels we changed time zones, and so we altered the onboard time as we traversed the zone. Now it became more important to observe good old Zulu time. Still, all meetings and exercises at sea between units were scheduled in Zulu, and we had to make sure we knew the right time to roll up for it. It also happened that if an hour was to be lost, i.e. put the clocks forward, we'd do it during the night watches, thereby doing a short First, and short Middle, whereas if we put them back, to gain an hour, this would be done during the Dogs, so we'd do an extra half hour in each. Clock changes clearly happened more quickly the further east or west you went.

Many exercises and drills later, we neared Freetown, Sierra Leone, and sailed up the brown, muddy river until we saw a ramshackle jetty in the middle of nowhere, to which we promptly tied starboard side to (the jetty). Virtually as soon as we secured the ship – two things happened. First, a fuel barge appeared alongside. Second, we heard a lot of shouting from our open port side. This emanated from dozens of hollowed-out logs, packed with brown bodies, fruit and 'souvenirs'. The shouting was to attract us to their wares, to which we feigned indifference. We casually pointed, asked 'how much?', laughed at their replies and walked further up the ship, followed by the canoes, and more shouting, 'How much you pay, how much you pay?'. Having settled on a price, you would then lower a heaving line with a bucket attached, into which your goods would be placed and you'd haul it up, put the money in, and lower it back down again. In principle this was a brilliant idea – no one got 'seen-off', we got our 'bargain' and the vendor got a few more days money to spend before the next cruise liner pulled in. The natives knew better than to come across the gangway, where several fierce-looking sailors would be gathered. All except one native. It transpired that a member of our crew got fed up with him and accidentally released a huge, very old shackle which he was coincidentally holding over the side. As gravity took charge, the shackle dropped into the canoe. It didn't stop, however, but continued through the canoe, out the bottom, and the canoe did its final 'float test', along with all the goodies it carried. The owner was incensed, and our man had to give him something in the order of £20 to shut him up. Well, the seller was brandishing a machete. He seemed to be remarkably richer on his money, so we must have got near the price. The shackle dropper then got immediate stoppage of leave, sad, really, as we were headed back to sea for the next several weeks.

We were allowed one watch leave there, into Freetown for several hours. That came as a shock – it was the first time I had ever been to a third-world country and seen beggars, pickpockets and general assorted dwellers, all trying to make you part with what you had. So, we found a bar, drank minimally and legged it back to the ship. Two visits down. Once again, we sailed, turned left at the end of the river and were occupied with exercises and drills for several more days.

It was one sunset that I heard the sun hiss as it set. I'd been told about this, but this particular evening, as we sailed south and the sun set off our starboard side, we leaned over the guard-rails, goofing at nothing in particular (a favourite pastime), the sun sinking lower and lower, becoming redder and redder as it went. There are not many sights more spectacular than watching the sun set over the ocean, but as it touches the water for the first time, it hisses. Then sets further and further, until it finally disappears, leaving just a memory and a red glow.

On 5 February, at the point where the water stops going round a plughole in one direction and reverses, we 'crossed the line' at Longitude 08° and thirty minutes West, and I am now allowed to cross the line at any future date, unmolested by any creature of the deep. I have the certificate to prove it. 'Crossing the line' involves the entire crew – one member plays 'King Neptune', who oversees the affairs, along with the rest of his outlandishly attired 'court'. These ceremonies include being shaved with a giant razor, having first been foamed up with a deck mop, or being dunked in flour, or whatever, while the rest of the members of his court laugh hysterically. You are perched on a 'plank' above a water-filled 'pit' on the quarterdeck (to be featured heavily later), while you are dealt with. At some point, you are tipped into the pit, emerging wet, but happier. The whole procedure takes several hours, in baking afternoon sun. Rank or rate does not feature in these proceedings, and in my experience there were clearly revenge attacks on certain officers and senior ratings, who were treated by the court with the contempt they fully deserved.

Before we sailed, those indolent swines at the Post Office had gone on strike, so after being away for three weeks not one letter had reached us. We would curse them for depriving us personally of any contact with our families. Normally, we would have had 'mail drops' from the long-range patrol Shackletons, but all they would do was fly ponderously past us – eight propellers all told, four props spinning, four feathered, waving as they buzzed us. They were nice to see though. Or we would come across a fishing boat, literally thousands of miles offshore, and we would stop and check they were OK, frequently dispensing bottles of brown liquid in exchange for fresh fish or, if we came across a merchant ship, we'd attempt to swap movies. However, as we sailed off Cape Town, our Wasp finally did something useful. Our pilot's father, an ex-rear admiral, had retired to Cape Town, and while picking up his father, our pilot also collected our mail for the first time since we sailed from England. The RN had, in fact, set up its own mail system, gathering letters from recruiting offices and Navy bases all round the country, before bagging it and sending it commercially to the next port the ship was to visit.

Our ship was often pursued by porpoises, who would race alongside. It amazed us that they could swim from side to side, under our bow without colliding either with each other or, more importantly, with us. We took to laying on the deck, as far for'ard as we could, with our heads over the sides, gazing at them for ages. And the flying fish, shoals of them. We watched frequently to see if any would headbutt the ship, but they never did, although we found one on the fo'c's'le one morning.

The feeling I got being right in the middle of that particular ocean was one of our insignificance in our surroundings, as well as our remoteness from shore. You felt that if anything happened, it would be forever before anyone reached you. We were literally hundreds of miles from anywhere – we could see nothing on the radar, there were no lights at night. Nothing. Just blackness all round by night, and sea and sky all round by day. Little wonder people in shipwrecks go mad before they are rescued. Pending what was to happen to us on our way home, these feelings were probably justified.

After several weeks of drills, and the fact that on our approach we cancelled our Sunday to get the ship sparkling for our arrival, we finally sailed into Durban, South Africa. The ship actually surfed on the huge Atlantic rollers into the harbour. We refuelled, with a two-hour stop at one side of the harbour, filled with last-minute preparations, such as Father forcing us to do unnecessary polishing of all the brass plates on the decks, until finally we moved to the main quayside. We had been warned about Durban, but our reception was unlike any I have ever received anywhere else. It was such an openly friendly place, and one day I will go back there. To start with we were 'sung' in by 'the Lady in White' Perla Siedle-Gibson. She had 'sung' naval ships in and out of Durban since the Second World War, and, unfortunately, we were the last ship to hear her sing. It was a very sad occasion when, a week after we left Durban, she died.

The cutting from the Durban newspaper at the time read as follows:

When HMS *Zulu* arrived at Durban on February 13, the lack of mail through the postal strike meant that the ship's company were not at their happiest. Then they heard from the jetty the welcoming songs of the famous Lady in White, and the ship was hardly alongside before the hospitality began to pour in, providing the best week that most on board can ever remember.

Very regretfully, the ship moved on, the Lady in White being there again to sing the ship out of harbour. A week later she died. The *Zulu* had been the last of countless ships to hear her greeting and farewell, and the news was received on board with great sadness.

It was appropriate that the ship concerned should have borne such a local name, and the welfare committee paid for a huge wreath to be sent to the funeral. Their flowers were the centerpiece of the tributes, and could be regarded as the whole of the Navy's token of affection for this gallant woman.

The story of the Lady in White – Perla Siedle-Gibson – began in the First World War, when she sang at Durban City Hall to some passing troops. In the Second World War, she was helping to feed about 500 troops, dressed at the time in a white dress and white apron. When the ship was pulling out, the boys called out to her to sing something and she cupped her hands to her mouth and gave them a song.

Afterwards she used a small megaphone, and her soprano voice was heard by millions of service men, in songs like 'Land of Hope and Glory', 'Tipperary', and the like.

After the war the Lady in White continued her greetings, and thousands of men of the Royal Navy will remember and mourn her passing.

She was at the *Zulu*'s cocktail party, and then went on to the ships company's dance.

As the *Zulu* steamed out, the Lady in White sang one of her last numbers for the Navy – a request from the ship. 'Wish me luck as you wave me goodbye' is always deeply sentimental, but this time the words had a special poignancy of which none was aware. They gave her three cheers, as so many had done before, and thus ended an era founded on the personality of a remarkable woman.

The papers were right, we had been warned that this was serious grippo territory, but we were totally unprepared for what was to happen next. Apart from the 'Lady in White' on the quayside, there were dozens of sightseers, all come to welcome us. We were dressed in our (now) brilliant whites, having entered harbour at Procedure Alpha. We also had a Zulu warrior (bearing in mind South Africa is Zulu country, and we were the *Zulu*), war-dancing on the bridge roof. Even as we put the gangway across, locals began to approach us asking if we could go with them for drinks, meals or tours. We just could not believe this was happening, but it was only the start. We had to wait until 'secure', which, as we were working tropical routine, meant being able to go ashore at around 1300. We could hardly wait to get back into our suits, and get ashore. We were told to wear 'rig' here, and we did.

I went ashore with my 'oppo', 'Sugar' Kane, and we'd got perhaps 3 yds away from the gangway before a man with his wife asked if they could take us out for the afternoon. We graciously accepted, and were whisked to a large hotel on the seafront, where we were plied with drinks and 'sundowners'. We were then taken to dinner (at the Smugglers) and I ordered my first, and the largest T-bone steak I had ever seen, let alone eaten since, accompanied by fries, onion rings, salad and mushrooms, with the steak on its own wooden platter. I had never eaten so much.

We met the same people the next day. They were on holiday from Jo'burg, and had two daughters, who we never met, but the parents were adamant they'd like my mate and me to go back to Jo'burg with them, to marry their daughters, and that they would take care of work permits, jobs – everything. We thought about this offer long and hard but declined. Nevertheless, we had another brilliant day touring Durban – visiting the aquarium, full of ragged-tooth sharks, garoupas (large fish) and all kinds of other 'never-seen-before' sea creatures. We also went on the go-karts, rode a rickshaw along the seafront, pulled by 'a real Zulu', and went inland to a 'real' Zulu reservation, where we witnessed dancing and drank 'Zulu' beer from a goat skin. In all we had a wonderful time. As a result of all this hospitality, the following day we resorted to sneaking off the ship earlier than planned, only to be picked up by yet another family, who took us down the coast for the day.

The next day, sad as it seems, we were exhausted by the attention, so we donned 'civvies', ran across the gangway and vanished into Durban, where we walked unmolested, before finding a club where we drank Cape brandy all night. We don't remember much about that night, except that wherever Navy ships go, the ship's company, as if by magic will inevitably all appear at the same night spot. That night was no exception. We did get 'grippo-ed', all of us, by most of the crew of a passing cruise liner. We drank all night with that crew, and introduced them to the wonders of 'The Zulu Warrior'; we had the monopoly on it as we WERE *Zulu* warriors. After several lessons that night, the stewards from this liner tried it – to rapturous applause. Emboldened, one of the stewardesses thought she'd have a go. She started it off, not realizing it was what we'd been setting her up for all night. We had so far refrained from the endpiece of 'the warrior' – the beer throwing bit. We sang it, she stripped it, until one pillock in the bar made a grab at her and she panicked, which was the end of 'Warrior'. So we waited until the next person volunteered to do the dance, and made up for it with him – I have never seen so much beer thrown over one person.

On this night, we also demonstrated another traditional naval dance, 'The Dance of the Flaming Arseholes'. In this, immediately following a rendition of 'The Zulu Warrior', we would have to hand a roll of toilet paper, one end of which would be tucked between the cheeks of the naked warrior's bum. He would then stand on a table. The other end, several yards away now, would be set aflame. The 'dance' was the contortions generated by the warrior attempting to extinguish the burning paper before it reached his bum, without using his hands, nor anything else except gyrations of the lower parts. This dance is extremely comical to watch, and very safe to do (usually), as when the danger point is reached (some inches to go), beer is thrown over the dancer, the paper, his bum – everywhere – to extinguish the flame.

I must mention the naval tradition of 'cake and arse' parties, seen on Daily Orders as CTP, or 'cocktail parties'. I should also point out the affection and esteem we held for our officers, politely known as 'the wardroom' but more generally called 'pigs'. They had their own cabins, while we slummed it in with loads of others. They were waited on hand and foot by stewards – we had to do it ourselves. There always was, and always will be, a great divide between the lads and the officers. It used to really gall us that we would have to show our respect by saluting them. It was made no better to be told we were saluting the uniform, not the contents. But it was almost unbearable when you had some pompous little 'snotty' (midshitman) who couldn't even spell HMS, much less tell you about it, and then you might get him on the POS as, for example fo'c's'le officer, where he had as much experience as the newest stores rating or chef, but was still expecting us to do what (dangerous) things he told us. Not that even some of the experienced officers had a much better idea.

The 'cake and arse' parties would usually be held on the first night a ship arrived in port, and would be held by the Skipper and all his officers, who would actually host the affair, with volunteers to staff it. Once you had missed volunteering for one party, you ensured your name was always down for the next one. I'll explain. The parties would always be attended by the local naval officer in charge and some of his staff, as well as the town mayor or local governor, and several hundred local dignitaries, rich or 'hangers-on', who would be there like a shot. What I didn't realize (as I was more involved in getting ashore that first day) was that it was an ideal place to secure a first-class grippo, who would normally have been targeted by 'the wardroom'. You would target a group of partygoers, or perhaps one, appearing at their elbow after they'd taken a mouthful of either 'horse's neck' (brandy and ginger) or gin and tonic, ensuring both were light on the mixer. You would engage them in conversation about how nice it was here, wasn't it, do you live here? Aren't you lucky being able to . . . anything to get their attention. Eventually, the alcohol you stuffed them with would take its effect and you would be asked out on a grippo run. Job done, get pissed with the rest of them, scoff some of the canapés, get changed, get ashore. Easy life.

There was a further bonus – the 'hat check' person would sit with a bowl, with some large denomination notes and coins in it, so when the hat or coat owner returned, he would assume his fellow partiers had put it there, and add to it. As the party thinned out, so the guests would be easier to 'trap', but as they got really scarce, they would be bagged by 'the wardroom', and taken back in there for further drinks and food, before being taken ashore. Some goers knew this, the unwary didn't, as we could throw drinks around more than they could. One perk after this was that when you were on duty, and CTP waiter, and when the 'pigs' had taken their guests back to the wardroom, their own chefs and stewards would prepare, serve and feed them on a 'special meal'. When enough people had eaten enough of this special meal, the remains would be distributed among the lads, specifically whoever got there first, that is to say the Duty watch! Not only were you out of your tree, but you got a free takeaway too. And still without going ashore. On the *Zulu*, the wardroom chefs and stewards were Goanese, which meant they created absolutely gorgeous curries, especially when they were washed down with the horse's necks we secreted into the nearly empty bottles as they became available, then hid for later collection once the fuss had died down. If asked, we would swear we saw a party-goer hoofing it with a bottle, that was why the wardroom flunky couldn't tally the empties. Stewards were almost the lowest form of life on a ship, and we would scream at them to 'peel me another fuckin' grape, you', in order to rile them.

The down side of the CTP was having to rig the fo'c's'le with canvas awnings, sidescreens and bunting (flag material draped everywhere), which would generally take the best part of a morning, assuming every sailor on board was turned to. Before that could happen, though, the whole area had to be repainted, or scrubbed, or polished. Only after this had taken place could the CTP take place.

All too soon it was time to sail, accompanied for the last time by the singing of that lovely 'Lady in White', and we sailed into the Indian Ocean and turned left. Our next destination was off the coast of

Rhodesia, to take over as duty ship on Beira Patrol, off Lourenco Marques, to support the embargo, and to stop the Rhodesians from getting any oil or supplies. 'Beira' and its connotations for Navy people can be summed up in few words: 'misery' and 'boredom'. We did four weeks, as well as passage there, doing nothing but sailing up and down and up and down and up. We were in sea watches, one in four, but after a week or so, you became desensitized to anything but waking up, looking at your watch, determining if you had just been shaken for your watch or if you were dreaming, going on watch, coming off watch, eating, working, sunbathing, sleeping. For four weeks.

We sometimes crept off our patrol line, just to be different. I think we spotted less than a handful of ships in that four weeks, which we would make heave to, before boarding and searching. Usually, whoever was trying to creep in, would either become aware of or be made aware of our presence, about turn and scarper.

I distinctly remember being on watch in the gloom room one day, watching the radar and generally getting bored stupid, when we decided to draw a picture on the old surface picture table. This surface plot was an old fairly accurate representation of what the radar was seeing, and had a travelling light which moved true to your course and speed. This meant any radar contacts on it also tracked at their respective courses and speeds. Except that where we were drawing was where the light was tracking, and pretty soon it all disappeared under our picture. At about that time, the OOW just happened to scan the bridge radar monitor and demanded to know why we hadn't yet reported the contact, the one he could clearly see with his Mark I eyeball. We responded instantly that we had 'just picked up the microphone to report it, and its course was 'x', with a speed of 'y', and that we were re-appraising it at the moment'. This quietened the OOW momentarily, until he worked out its true movement, at which time we again lied that it must have altered course then, because we made it the same as him, now. That was truly the first surface contact we had seen for weeks, and thanks to our drawings it nearly sailed past us and got into Beira. Ooops.

We had visits from the omnipresent 'Shacklebombers', who would now occasionally do a mail drop on us. This entailed them flying near us, dropping bright-yellow waterproof canisters into the ocean, from quite low in the sky. These would bounce and settle, and we would either recover them with the seaboat or launch the paraffin parrot to go and get them for us. This was followed by the joy of finding you had mail, and reading it over and over. Or the deep, deep depression of still no mail.

We would RAS every couple of days, with an on-station RFA tanker, either alongside with fenders between us, at which point we would take on fuel the easy way, or we would meet with her, underway, and take fuel on that way. RASing used to be fun, if you got the right job. Working on the dump where all the stores landed was a plum job, as was unloading each pallet in record quick time before the next pallet arrived. Generally, you'd have up to sixty seconds to do this, regardless of the cargo swinging over. If the cargo was large, easy. If, however, the load was forty-eight crates of ale – you would need to work harder and faster. To get the stuff away, human chains would again be organized above and below decks, with every available off-watch sailor forming part of these chains.

Unfortunately, items would go astray, like the odd box of nutty, or case of food, or even crates of ale. We figured that at the speed we worked, there was no way that anyone was going to be stupid enough to count every one as it arrived. Especially as crates or boxes would often 'burst' on being often 'dropped', spilling the contents all over the deck beneath our feet, and creating a dangerous hazard. Of course, we'd be too busy catching the next armful to bother about picking up damaged goods, wouldn't we? And the breakages were all immediately kicked over the side, weren't they? But the extra crates and food came in handy, and we'd often finish the RAS stinking of beer or chocolate, with more stowed in the mess or in POS lockers to look forward to. Perks of the job, we called it. Everyone knew it happened, but no one did much about it.

We could normally carry out light jackstays with ten minutes' notice, to swap movies, personnel (like Daddy-D or admirals) or THELMA (The Leading Medical Attendant) or the surgeon. People were normally shit scared of having to go across it, especially if they were ever so slightly unpopular, as it was well within the capability of the jackstay party to be a bit late in responding to the command to 'haul taut', thus allowing the transferee to get a dunking. Not that I ever saw this happen. Actually, thinking about it, when we did a big RAS, I imagine that nearly everyone on board was used, storing, steering, driving, whatever – the only goofers were normally on the RFA. It didn't matter that it was your make-and-break, or that you had just come off-watch, you still had to turn to in order to do the RAS. When all was complete, we'd cast off, let everything go, wave cheerfully, strike our skull and crossbones or whatever our 'flag' was, and go on our happy little ways. Depending on whether we were 'dump', 'jackstay', 'line' or 'stores', we'd either be knackered, very knackered, extremely knackered, or just plain out of it.

On one occasion, while refuelling, we detected a ship on radar, and in order to intercept it we had to do an emergency breakaway, meaning we just smashed the retaining gear and slipped the hoses. It was a pity that the supplying ship couldn't stop pumping quite so quickly, and it happened that everyone in the dump party got a fuel washdown, as did the fo'c's'le, the bridge – everything. It was weeks before we finally got rid of all the sticky black fuel and months before the smell eventually went from 'A' Handling Room.

Movies were very important to us. Every night, except the nights when we would hold 'Tombollocks' (tombola with money for prizes), we would have a movie in the junior rates' dining room. We saw all kinds of movies, U, X – anything, providing it looked appealing. We would jeer and scream like three-year-olds, especially if we had seen it before and knew what was coming. Anyone who died would be jeered at. Rudely. The more bloodthirsty or action packed it was, the better we liked it, and if it showed bits of naked female we'd demand the projectionist showed that bit again, until, happy, we'd let him show the rest.

On reaching our assigned patrol station, we would rendezvous with the unit we were to relieve, with them sailing past us at high speed, throwing flour-bombs, vegetables, blowing smoke, hosing each other down, generally relieving their tension. We would also be flour-bombed and buzzed by their parrot. We would, of course, traditionally pipe each other first, and sometimes 'cheer ship', for fun, before carrying all this out. And we knew we'd pass the honour on to whoever then relieved us.

We'd then settle in, and would 'fight' either the ship we relieved or the on-station RFA for the honour of holding the Beira Bucket. This was the mankiest bucket, bashed, battered and holed (currently in the museum in Portsmouth dockyard, where I saw *Zulu*'s name on it many years later), for which we would compete in all manner of games and contests. We'd have a boat race, which involved teams of sailors in a line, each with a can of beer. On the 'go', each would down the beer, before the next in line could see his off, and so on down the line. Rescrubs (reruns) were popular on this game. Or the 'Duck-Run Derby', which involved wedging coins between ones 'cheeks', running (like a duck, hence the name) to a pre-arranged place and depositing the coin in a bucket, in order for the next to go. We did too, such as have 'sensible' contests too, such as tug-of-war, with blocks rigged around the ship so you could pull parallel to the opposing team. You feared losing because your hands would be dangerously close to going through the block if you weren't careful. All these events would be held throughout an afternoon, finishing with a barbecue and ice-cold beer. We always had a large supply of steaks and sausages for the barbie, and had more beer than we needed. It was actually hot enough to cook eggs on the bare decks. We would also be dressed in just shorts, and sandals, and would never wear anything else until evening, when we might decide to wear a T-shirt over our shorts. We quickly turned shades darker with all this 'bronzy-ing'. The winning ship assumed ownership of the 'bucket', jealously guarding it until challenged, or until it had to be passed on.

We held 'set' (beard) growing contests. From the time we left Durban to just before we reached our next stop, we were allowed to 'grow', having asked permission first. The winner was judged on the fullest set, also the longest, also the absolutely worst beard anyone had ever seen! Another tradition at sea is 'quiz night', messdeck competing against messdeck, including senior rates and wardroom. The quiz was always extremely well contested, with surprisingly high scoring. Trivial Pursuit had not been invented then, but it could have been based on the devious questions we set. And here, for all you aficionados of naval history, is one of those questions. Name two things that run from aft to for'ard on the starboard side, and from for'ard to aft on the port side, of every Pussers' ship?

We held kite-making and flying contests, streaming miles of string astern as we chugged along at 10 knots or so, with un-aerodynamic contraptions held up in the far sky by sheer willpower. We also ran knockout tournaments, leagues and inter-mess contests based on card or board games, notably 'crib', at which I was particularly good, or uckers at which I developed an unerring skill. Uckers is derived from ludo, but has none of the associated genteelness. It is played on a square table, painted in the form of a ludo board, then covered in clear plastic. Uckers is played either in fours (in which case you help your partner), or head to head, in which case you go all out to win. It is an extremely tactical and psychological game. With us, before you agreed to play, you went through the 'You are not good enough to play me' scenes and 'By the time you are good enough, you'll be too fuckin' old' or, the worst, on getting challenged to play, you would reply, 'I won't actually play seriously, but I will give you lessons'. This would pre-empt the ignominious loss, whereby you would announce 'It *was* a lesson, not a proper game – just letting him see what winning is like. Anyway, I have "winning fatigue"'), which must be thought out many moves ahead, or you would lose. Before playing, you would decide on the appropriate rules, either 'far east', or another set. You also agreed the battle cry, generally 'uckers yer fuckers'. Having decided the rules, you played to the death. I have seen fights break out following defeats and participants thrown across messdecks for alleged cheating. I have also often seen the uckers table smashed up and all the bits getting thrown over the side.

One evening, we detected a cruise liner going about its business. We hailed it by radio and asked if they could drop mail off for us at their next port of call. Obviously it is not easy for a Shackleton cruising at over a hundred miles per hour to stop and pick mail up for us. The liner agreed, and 'Mail will close in thirty minutes', piped; we all excitedly dashed off or posted our mail as we stomped off after the liner. The Skipper hauled us in at speed from astern of the liner, and we passed a line across with our adapted rifle as we dropped the revs right off, bringing us to match the liner's speed exactly. By this time the deck of the liner was awash with goofers, all watching us. We passed the mail and the obligatory whisky, exchanged movies, then went up to full power, did a 'hard-a-port', tilted alarmingly, but most impressively, and sped off into the deep-red sunset, soon leaving the liner and its passengers far astern. Judging by the flashes, we were photographed countless times on that little jolly.

On one occasion a whale surfaced close by, and that certainly passed several minutes. We also had the biggest laugh I ever had, before or since. I have mentioned the pit on the rear of the ship, which is where we stowed all ropes, wires, fenders and other junk while we steamed about. This would be covered with boards and tarpaulin for protection. But when we were off Beira, we emptied it of this junk and filled it with sea water from the fire-main. We were then able to step in and out of it between browning sessions to cool off.

One afternoon when we were stationary, we nicked a joint of beef from the galley, a large hook, and several fathoms of strong string. We also acquired a barrel of fire-fighting foam, used to extinguish oil fires. This foam, allegedly derived from ox blood, was reputed to be a brilliant shark attractor, not that they needed that – we usually steamed with a 'gash-chute' rigged over the stern, down which went anything deemed to be gash. We opened and poured out the contents of the foam, holed it, and threw it over, for the traditional 'float test'. Unsurprisingly, it failed. But the foam was now in the water. We baited the hook, threw it in and waited, but not for long – we soon had a take. The shark we recovered was extremely surprised, exceedingly violent, and took a lot of smacking around the head before it was pronounced dead. Even at his size, nearly 2 m, he looked awesome. We stroked the skin, marvelling how it was smooth one way and like sandpaper the other. We argued over who was to have the teeth and or the fin. We decided we would give the fin to 'Snobs'. 'Snobs' was wary of us sailors after someone had ordered a pair of shoes, collected them, promised to pay on payday and left his name as M. Mouse. We never did find out who, but we had a good idea. 'Snobs', his tailor mate who made suits, shirts and trousers by hand, and the Chokey laundry crew were all to have their share of the shark too. The laundry crew were referred to as 'Number One', and 'Number Two', unless you weren't feeling too friendly, then you referred to them as 'Number Six' (after the very popular cigarette of the age). It was then that we noticed the baby clanks lounging in the pit, and before we could stop ourselves, we threw the dead shark into the pit along with the stokers. Except that the shark had been playing possum, and as soon as his head went underwater his tail wagged and he started to cruise, with apparently the mother of all headaches and a severe dose of arseache. The stokers came out of the pit vertically, screaming and disappeared below decks. We wet ourselves laughing. When we calmed down enough to be able to stand without any pain, we sorted out who should go to get sharky out again, and a rather large gunner went in, grabbed it and emerged holding it by the tail end. He then proceeded to smash the eating and biting end against the after gun turret until this time we knew it was dead. We processed it in the galley and ate shark steaks for supper. You needed to be there to believe it, but it happened. I have genuinely never laughed so much in my life.

We were eventually relieved, and zapped up the coast to Mombasa for some recreational leave, by watch, for several days each, and were allowed to go to a Service R&R place called Silversands. We moored in the middle of the river in Mombasa, amid much ceremony and manoeuvring. We completed our 1 in 4 duty, and boarded a coach for the ride up country. The journey took the best part of an hour, through the dense, green undergrowth, along dusty 'roads' and over a marvel of engineering – a bridge built by British squaddies after the Second World War. It was only when I got back to the UK and described Mombasa and this bridge, that my Dad told me he'd been one of the people who had built it. That was an astonishing coincidence, and he'd even been to Silversands. We reached the compound wondering what we'd let ourselves in for. We soon found out. We were 'barracked' into huts, situated among coconut trees, but more importantly directly on the starkest, whitest, softest beach I have ever been on in my life. The beach bordered the bluest sea I had ever seen too. To say it was idyllic would be an understatement. We quickly threw our gear out, and went exploring, only to find the Naafi open. This was a bar (called the Casuarina), and it was open. Before we could stop ourselves, we found ourselves rapidly downing large quantities of JCs and then going off to explore. We found the Naafi shop (most odd, to find a Naafi in the middle of such a remote place in Kenya), and lo and behold on the beach was the 'beach bar', where we drank some more as we strutted round in our new swimming costumes and shirts. We had bought these local highly patterned shirts during our one night ashore, and then wore them on every subsequent occasion. We discovered the beach bar closed late afternoon, but that a third bar then opened. We thought we were in heaven! When that one shut, the Casuarina re-opened, and we sat there all night getting more and more inebriated.

When we retired early the next morning, we apparently took the remnants of last night's drinking with us, for we woke up to warm and flat, but still palatable JCs for breakfast. That was after we had negotiated our way out of the voluminous mosquito nets around our beds. This was followed by the short walk to the dining room overlooking the beach. The waiter only spoke two words of English, although he understood everything you said. He was the tallest person for miles around, with more white teeth than I would know what to do with. You would ask for toast, he would grin, lazily and drawl 'Yiz Barsss', and trot away. He would return, you would eat the toast. That was if you weren't persuaded to give it away to the masses of longing brown eyes making you feel guilty at every mouthful. These eyes belonged to the resident troupe of monkeys, all of whom had a bright green-to-blue bum. They were very distracting, however we would feed them toast and they would scamper off to the nearest vantage point, eat and return to start over. It was the most entertaining breakfast I ever had. Asking for more tea, more bacon, more anything was also met with 'Yiz Barsss'.

We then started the rounds of the bars again, interspersed with lying on the beach. By the time we had left Beira, we looked like natives anyway – this was merely topping up and making the most of our rest and recreation. But soon it was over, we returned to the ship for our next duty, while the opposite watch took their leave at that wonderful place.

We got a couple of runs ashore in the main town of Mombasa, chiefly remembered for the huge iron elephant tusks that staddled the main road. And the Sunshine Bar, which coincidentally sold a local beer called Tusker. The market in the centre of the town, where you could buy anything you wanted, was also memorable. As long as you wanted something made of carved wood. Gaudy shirts were worn by everyone. Mine was bright green with migraine-inducing orange and yellow jazzy stripes, and I wore it to death. I got chased out of this market for offering too little money for what I wanted – just table rings carved into animal shapes, but I overdid the bartering and obviously insulted the stallholder badly with the price I offered. I got them in the end by sending a mate back to buy them at the asking price. I had no intention of facing the vendor again!

We had moored properly in Mombasa, meaning we secured fore and aft between two large buoys. This took the best part of a morning, and was probably the most technical seamanship evolution ever carried out by any ship, though we had practised previously. With the sailors working hard at this, the rest of the ship's company would be at Procedure Alpha, except for the waffoos. They would have previously launched the Budgie (helicopter), which would then fly round the ship and harbour with the lights on, trailing about a large ensign on a wire with a heavy weight attached to stop it getting embarrassingly entangled in the rotors, which would have caused a sudden end to the display. Things like this always impressed everyone watching – lots of noise, lots of visuals. Mooring involved us lowering the boats, then sending buoy-jumpers to secure the anchor cable to the buoy. The cutter crew then went to the stern, and secured to the aft buoy. We would finally use the capstans to winch ourselves in between the buoys. Once we were secured, and on hearing the 'still' piped, both accommodation ladders (laboriously made up over several hours previously) would be carefully lowered, both booms swung out, the jack, and ensign would be run up, and the ship would normally be 'dressed overall'. All this swinging out, lowering, and hauling would happen in perfect unison, and was, I have to admit, impressive to watch. Except the day we failed to secure the accommodation ladder, which slipped gracefully beneath the waves, making it necessary for our divers to go and retrieve it.

Once the sailors secured, the members of the greeny department would then all be kicked out of their beds, and they would have to rig floodlighting along either or sometimes both sides of the ship. They used to hate that, as it meant not only having to work for a living, but that one of them would have to remain on duty all day and all night just in case someone called them out to replace a dead bulb. Not that we'd ever get them out of bed to show them a bulb which was, by the time they arrived, working again.

Sometimes at Alpha, we'd have to do a gun salute for the local dignitaries, which meant (only the correctly trained) gunners would haul up the saluting cannons and secure them to the quarterdeck. They'd then assume their stern and serious faces, and with perfect timing (chanting BANG 'If I wasn't a gunner, I wouldn't be here' BANG 'If I wasn't a gunner, I wouldn't be here' BANG – five seconds exactly – try it yourself!) between salvoes, would fire the designated number of rounds, be covered in thick smoke, then have to put it all away again, which necessitated lots of noise and lots of attention.

Being moored in the middle of Mombasa harbour meant it was impossible to walk ashore, so we had to get liberty boats from ship to shore and back. However, we weren't too concerned if we missed our own seaboat, as Mombasa harbour used to crawl with small, brightly coloured 'K-Boats', water taxis for hire, very cheaply. It became a point of honour to get as drunk as possible, hail a K-Boat and demand to be allowed to drive it back to the ship. Or in my case, directly at the ship, ignoring the owner, who had to forcibly remove me just before I made the sudden, final, violent contact against 3,000 tonnes of grey steel. I was fortunate to get that far, that night. Having had far too much to drink, I'd fallen asleep in the toilet of the local château and my mates had all gone back on board without me. I woke up sometime during the early hours – I'll rephrase that, I was woken up by chattering, and on opening my eyes discovered many small brown faces looking over the top of the 'trap' at me. I ran out of there at a great rate, and hightailed it down the main drag, under the famous elephant tusks, back to the quayside. During our stay here we 'imprinted' – everywhere we went, we would add our names to our illustrious predecessors signatures, in pubs, on jetties, on dock walls, in fact, everywhere we could. I'll bet if you got to Mombasa today, you'll find 'HMS *ZULU*, 1971' painted in at least one place.

Once more we sailed, once more we turned left out into the blue, blue Indian Ocean, among the flying fish and porpoises, steaming, ever turning left, until we finally reached Bahrein in the Persian Gulf. On the way, we discovered more new terminology – 'sneezing', or 'caught a cold', or 'blobbing up', or 'catching the boat up', or 'squeezing up'. These were euphemisms for having ones leave stopped for several days, but only until the penicillin took effect, and cleared it up. This was in the days when the worst you got was Syphilis, not completely life threatening, if treated, or 'Gons', which went quickly with the injections. However, we were warned about 'Tokyo Rose', which is tame by today's standards. The painful part though, was having leave stopped until THELMA considered the patient fit to go ashore again. Having never been affected, I never found out – although I knew plenty that did. They should have taken the free noddy hats (condoms) from the gangway.

Another unpleasant side effect of living in close proximity to other people, was that if one person caught crabs we would all, eventually, succumb to them. This was partly because our towels and washgear used to be in close proximity, but mainly because the bastards would put a couple in your pit while you weren't around. So, if you discovered one of your so-called messmates could walk unaided, you'd steer clear, and inspect your pit closely before climbing into it. It is paradoxical that we should get crabs anyway – we must have been the cleanest people in the world, what with our daily shower and all. We discovered three cures. One was to go to the sick bay, talk to THELMA and ask him for some crab powder. Both the illness and the cure used to itch, so if you saw anyone with his mitts on his bits, you should guess he was attempting to dislodge his pets. Second, was to sit in a swimming pool or water for several hours until they drowned. But by far the most effective was to invest in a small bottle of scotch, and some sand. First you'd rub the scotch into the affected area and the crabs would all drink it, getting pissed in the process. Then you'd rub the sand in, the crabs would think it was rocks and throw them at each other in their drunkenness until they were all dead. Crabs and doses were actually the only reason anyone would normally report sick, stand fast accidents. It was so extremely rare we got colds, 'flu, measles or anything.

CHAPTER 14

Bahrein, Sand and Desert Wellies

As we neared Bahrein for a mini refit, we RASed with a Gulf State warship, who promptly got too close and created a large tearing hole in our ship's side. This was repaired with a large plate as soon as we got alongside.

The jetty we secured alongside was probably half a mile long, with us at the very end of it. The other side was where civilian ships would go. On the middle of the jetty was a small shop, selling fresh milk, some food, and extra-long, king-size cigarettes, which we would smoke to make our monthly allotment of 600 'duty frees' last longer, as these shoreside packs were cheaper than the ones we were able to purchase. When you consider that we were then paying something like 10p for a pack of twenty, these extra-length ones were good value.

One job I always volunteered for, was 'mast painting'. This entailed drawing all the 'safe to transmit/safe to rotate' keys for all the radio and radar aerials for the ship (just in case an overzealous but stupid flagwagger or greeny decided to transmit megawatts of power from an aerial near you, or decided to rotate the radar with you standing on it), getting several pots of paint and brushes, drawing safety harnesses (which were as useful as chocolate teapots, given that you tied them below you as they got in the way otherwise), then climbing the main mast complete with heaving lines (to haul up paint and brushes) ready for a several-day skive. Once up there (where no one else could come and check on you without being spotted fairly quickly), we'd do a spot of painting out on the yardarms – hence the harnesses, standing or swinging to get to the awkward bits. Luckily, the yards were over the ship, otherwise we'd have got wet if we fell off them. From the top of the mast to deck level was about a 50-ft drop, but it was 80 ft from top to waterline. We'd get odd looks when we descended – we'd be covered in paint, but brown too! The view, though, was worth the effort.

We also 'volunteered' to wash and repaint the funnels. This was a filthy job, but worth doing. We would climb inside the funnel and come out of a very small hatch on the top. Then we'd carefully creep to the edge, drop the heaving lines, and haul up the paint stages. Having ensured they were totally secure to our satisfaction, we'd gingerly edge off the funnel and on to a stage. Having got there, we'd have a fag in the knowledge that anyone who wanted to bollock us for doing so could have a bucket of stinking, sooty water upended on them, completely accidentally of course, before we got on with the job to hand. We'd take days and days doing the funnels properly.

The first night ashore, we went to the Naafi at HMS *Jufair*, at the end of the jetty. It was probably a mile walk, but all the booze was DF. Which meant a Bacardi (a double, obviously) would be less expensive than the coke to throw in it. Actually, you could buy a bottle of spirits for less than a couple of mixers. We would sit and drink all night, up to the point where we would cheerfully drink in excess of a 40-oz bottle of Bacardi and walk back to the ship quite steadily. There was not much else to do at *Jufair*. One night of the week, we would be permitted to use their chip shop. It only actually opened one night of the week. We were not allowed to use one of their swimming pools, but would sneak in anyway late at night for a dip on the way back from the town. That is until the night I nearly drowned in there, at which point we didn't use it any more. The only reason I got out was because even through my Bacardi-sodden drunken haze it occurred to me that if I sank to the bottom, I could kick, hard, and get back to the surface and shout for help. Which I did, and my mates got me out.

The night we first met the USN crews (Elmers as they are scornfully named) they moored where they belonged – astern of us with further to walk. The rumour says that when the yanks meet 'jack', they (the USN) are riot-act-ed – told not to try to outdrink, outsmart, outfight or outanything us under any provocation, as they would fail on all counts singly or collectively. Except some wouldn't listen, and as they came into the DF bar at *Jufair* – we saw it as our birthday and Christmas rolled into one. The USN run 'dry', whereas the RN don't. We had been used, by then, to heavy, prolonged drinking bouts. They had been used to their onboard luxury of Coke and ice cream. They would start to drink with us and lose track half way through our normal session, at which time we would leave them to sleep until we wanted to go elsewhere. We would carry them back, relieve them of their 'Popeye' hats, dump them at the bottom of their gangway and go back ashore, into the town in a taxi to continue our sessions. I still have a 'Popeye' hat, somewhere. We were also forearmed with 'the ready answer'. It was a foregone conclusion, that while in his cups, a yank would feel the need to ask us, 'How does it feel to be in the second largest navy?', to which we'd reply, 'Great, how does it feel to be in the second best?' That would always piss them off.

The *de rigueur* dress code then was Levis, well-worn and faded shirts (button-down collar, short sleeve, any startling colour, handmade by the Chinese tailor), and desert wellies. It was the desert after all and we felt entitled. Oh, and socks. We still only wore Pusser's issue socks. We would wear this outfit constantly, returning to the ship, throwing it all in to the laundry every fourth day (when on duty) for refurbishment, or repairs if necessary.

We would 'secure' at 1300, have lunch, then go ashore either to laze around the other pool at *Jufair*, or go into town to the markets to pick up some absolutely wonderful 'rabbits', ranging from gold to linen to real Persian carpets. The smell and the atmosphere in those markets was never to be forgotten. We would never drink in the town, we were too wised up for that, but would venture into the Gulf or the Moon Plaza Hotel, both of which had a night club. Full of sailors. From the *Zulu*. As I said – you couldn't get away from them. We found a back-street café that served superb food, and we would always make it a stop-off point between the hotels and the ship to eat the local food. I can still taste their gorgeous prawn masala with chapattis freshly cooked in front of you in the stone oven.

Sometimes we held 'banyans' (beach barbecues) and we would pile into the whaler or cutter, and drive to a lump of sand which became exposed for some hours each day. We piled the boats with beer, the barbie and food, and cleared off until we got bored, or it got dark, or the sand started to get seriously underwater, or until we ran out of beer. Guess which one usually drove us back. We would play cricket, bronzie, or snorkel around the crystal clear water, marvelling at the sealife, which was plentiful.

We didn't just sit alongside making the *Zulu* look pretty, we toured the Gulf from one end to the other, looking for smugglers carting diamonds or drugs or currency, and when we spotted them on radar, we heaved them to for a search. However, while on patrol, we stopped at remote islands to banyan. It became a standing joke that wherever we stopped, you could guarantee that within hours, a dhow (an Arabian sailing vessel) would stop, and the inhabitants would decamp to 'our' party to beg for food, which we would normally give them. At one of these stop-overs, the dhow stopped, off came the gopher and we gave him the bread. He reboarded the dhow and sailed off into the sea. We cracked laughing at what would happen to him – we used to carry a chemical with us to check our fuel for water contamination (or was it to check the water for fuel contamination), which was harmless, but if ingested would cause severe gastric disorder for some time. It may or may not have been laced into the loaf of bread donated to the crew of that dhow. I wonder if he ever scrounged off another warship?

We frequently took 'hands to bathe' which, as the temperature was usually about 110°F, would be very welcome. We would stop the ship, lower the whaler with armed sentry, put further armed sentries at strategic points on the ship's superstructure (in case of a shark appearing), lower the scrambling nets and dive off the highpoints of the ship into fathomless water. Then we'd climb the nets, climb the superstructure and dive off again. The 'midships' decks would be 10 to 12 ft above water, the Seacat launcher decks 20 ft, the bridge wings nearer 30 ft up. We would happily dive off all of them. The wimps would jump, the total wimps (i.e., the greenies and stewards) would climb down the scrambling nets. Whatever, we would enjoy ourselves thoroughly.

We did 'sea days', where we would take local dignitaries, Commander Naval Forces Gulf and Commander British Forces Gulf to sea for the day. We would be 'attacked' by aircraft, play with the minesweepers, fire the 4.5s, disturb the fish by dropping mortars, maybe loose off a Seacat, do a RAS, tank along at high speed, then return to base, hopefully having made a sale.

There was a permanently deployed fleet of minesweepers at the landward end of the jetty – it was a point of honour to be 'called round' there, which one day I was. I don't remember getting back on board that night, but I'm assured I did. Minesweepers, unsurprisingly, sweep up mines laid by other people. To do this, they stream large paravanes off the blunt end, which are connected by long lengths of wire. It's the wire that sweeps or catches the mine. Minesweepers (and other ships) carry 'dancans' (dan-buoys), which are carried rigged, ready to throw over the side to 'mark' items on the seabed, or for another excuse, as required for seamanship evolutions. In order to drop the dancan, you had to chuck a large weight over the side, which was attached to the can by wire. It follows, then, that the weight could be dropped long before the can was slipped, and thus needed a lot of wire, especially if the water was deep. Normally, wire on ships ready to work was laid down on the deck in correctly overlapping lengths, called 'bights', so when the weight (or whatever) was on the end, you kept well out of the way in case you got caught in it, and watched guardedly as the wire unravelled itself, and disappeared through special fairleads on the deck, right on the edge of the ship. Just to make that clear, the weight is chucked over, the wire then pays out by itself until it's all gone, at which point the dancan is slipped.

It was related to us that one of the sweepers had to rig a paravane for a sweeping exercise, and did so, readying it until all they had to do was drop the weight. Coincidentally, it seems, they had on board an illegal monkey, which they had been told to get rid of. Allegedly, they tied the monkey halfway along the wire, threw the paravane over the side, and the monkey apparently sat watching, interestedly, as the wire vanished before his very eyes, until with a rush, the monkey was taken through the fairleads, into the sea, never to be seen again. We had wet trousers when we heard that one.

We visited other ports on that tour. We went to Bandar Shapur and took some station leave to Isfahan, a place I remember for several reasons. The first, and most memorable, was stopping the coach halfway there (in a village where Moscow was signposted), and buying Fanta Orange from a tub of iced water. Second, the hotel we stayed at fed us soft-boiled eggs for breakfast. After months of either fried or fried, you would never believe the luxury of soft-boiled eggs. Third, the beauty of Isfahan – old buildings and bridges, and the most eyecatching mosque ever, exactly what you would expect to see in Persia. On the way to Isfahan, we crossed miles of desert, but snow was visible on top of the surrounding mountains. There we were in heat of more than 120°F, yet we could see snow.

We also visited Dubai and played volleyball against the sons of Sheikh Rashid Bin Said Al Maktum (the Ruler of Dubai). We made trips to Bandar Abbas, Qatar, Abu Dhabi, Muscat, Damman – and nearly every island in the Gulf. And all the time we wore our desert wellies.

One sunny day, my mate Arthur had a berserker, refusing to obey orders. This started when he was offered a 'blue card' job (a job with no duties), later rescinded. He took exception. He was quarantined in the diving store, and the story we heard after he was carted off to DQs was that when he was ordered off the bridge wings where he was waiting for 'Captain's Table', his response was 'make the bastard come out here to me – I'm not playing anymore'. Unsurprisingly, he came out of DQs some months later, and was subsequently discharged – SNLR. It was a great shame. He was a nice bloke who I missed, and, after all, we had been together since that first train journey to Plymouth.

Captain's Table is held weekly, normally, at sea or in harbour, but can be held for sudden serious 'crimes', such as Arthur's case. It is held to answer request forms or to punish defaulters. Everyone wears 'blue suits'. Requestmen are marched on, have to salute, and have their request read out by the 'Jossman' (Master at Arms), have a few kind words read out by their Divisional Officer, have a few more patronizing words spouted by the Captain, then (generally) have their request granted. You 'request' to be promoted, to have a long service/good conduct badge, to get married, anything 'pleasant'. Defaulters, however are marched on after all the good boys, given 'off caps' (hence the expression 'get your cap' when you need to 'troop' someone, or 'get two hats, an' take a lifejacket 'cos you're in DEEP') then stand before the Captain. Normally, if they've got this far, it's because their 'offence' warrants Captain's punishment, or worse (i.e., court martial). It also means you've been through Officer-of-the-Day's Table, and been passed on, and possibly through Jimmy's Table too. The defaulter's charge is read out by the Joss, his DO says some mitigating things, then the Captain awards his punishment. If you are in front of him, you are guilty, no two ways about it, unless you can spin the shit to such an extent that he believes you. At OOD or Jimmy's, you are given the opportunity to plead guilty, not guilty, or no plea. The latter means it wasn't your fault, and that you intend to blame someone or something else in the hope that you won't be so severely punished. If the Captain finds you guilty, you get stoppage of leave, or reduction in rate, or stoppage of pay, or a fine, or any combination of the above. He can also send you for a 90 day 'holiday' (in DQs). Anything more than that, he'll offer you a court martial. That means going ashore and being 'weighed off' by total strangers. You then stand a fifty-fifty chance of having your 'pun' increased, drastically, or of getting off altogether. This second option is most, most unlikely. You really have to come up with something good at this stage!

Perversely, a favourite pastime is trying to second-guess the punishment, with an appropriate sweepstake on the outcome. We would take great pleasure in winding up 'the accused', telling him sea stories – '. . . when I was on the XYZ, we had a bloke did that – he got ninety days'. We would normally be fairly accurate, with practice, although various other factors would need to be taken into consideration

It helped if your recent appraisals were good, too. Periodically, you were lined up in front of your DO, where he would read your report on what a good boy you'd been or how you'd performed in your work and

Telephone No.: **37518**

Careers Office,
Royal Navy and Royal Marines,
Newilton House, Derngate, Northamtpon

Date 24th March 1969

Dear **Michael,**

With reference to your application to join the Royal
Navy/R~~oyal Marines~~, I am pleased to inform you that, provided
you are in all respects still fit, you will be offered a
vacancy for entry to:-

H.M.S. Raleigh at Torpoint near Plymouth on

~~xx~~ Monday 8th September 1969

Further details will be sent to you nearer the date
of entry.   In the meantime, if you get a job or change your
employment, please forward the name and address of your
employer, the date you started and the nature of your
employment.

Yours sincerely,

for   Lieutenant (Careers Service),
RN/RM.

ow it all began – March 1969. My letter of acceptance into the Royal Navy.

Bear witness thatone. M. Payne
of Her Majesty's Ship Zulu
did on this 5th day of February 1971
cross the Cine at Cong. 30 West and
that the aforesaid having observed
the proper rites of ceremony, was
baptised at the hand of His Most
Gracious Majesty King Neptune, who
according to the Caw of the High
Seas, pronounced him a Son of Neptune
thereby permitting him to cross the
Cine at any future date unmolested
by any creature of the Deep.
Certified this day above written and
given under our hands and seal.

*Been there, done that – February 1971. The
certificate I received when I crossed the equator for
the first time.*

Your friendly BP station. Zulu *fuelling abeam from a Royal Fleet Auxiliary tanker, November 1971.*

This was what Beira patrol was all about – intercepting one of the sanction-busting tankers that refused to stop, November 1971.

You don't get this many spectators if you catch a fish on the canal bank at home. This was the shark we captured in November 1971.

Away seaboat's crew, November 1971.

Prepare to tow for'ard. This was not just a drill, but for real, when Zulu's main gearbox seized in the middle the Atlantic, and not an AA man in sight, December 1971.

HMS Zulu *in Grand Harbour, Malta, spring 1972.*

'lag K at the dip – HMS Tartar *preparing to take her helicopter on board.*

The author – 'every hair a rope yarn, every finger a marling-spike'. This was the photograph that caught my future wife's eye.

Ceremonial divisions, Tartar's *ship's company parades on the jetty, alongside the ship in Vera Cruz.*

Steam past for the Queen, Tartar's *ship's company cheering ship for Her Majesty and Prince Philip, off Vera Cruz, 1975.*

A real bringer of tears to the eyes of old matelots - the 'Gully Gully' man, Port Said, December 197

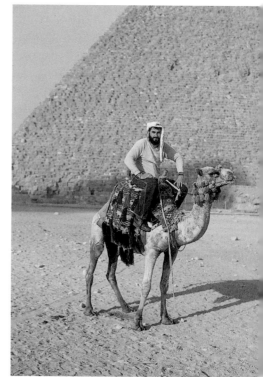

Between the wars there was a famous recruiting poster for the Navy which featured two jolly jacks in uniform, riding camels, over the slogan 'Join the Navy and See the World'. I did and I have, AND ridden a camel as well.

attitude, and also your behaviour. If, therefore, you were a snivelling arse-licker who had never been trooped, and never got into any trouble ashore or aboard, your summary would be V.G./Sup.(erior). For the rest of us, we'd get V.G./Sat. or G./Sat. or a mixture of them. You always knew what would be said about you before you got there, but it was, nevertheless, a great help if you stood in front of Skipper to hear your DO plead your exemplary record and your V.G./Sup. record. So a good appraisal always reduced your sentence. Slightly.

Sadly, we also lost a crew member, who died in a freak accident involving a lorry. This was a terrible shock to us, and something we never expected would happen to a mate. Navy tradition after a death requires an auction, where everyone bids for various items of the dead man's kit. Even if you don't want it. Once purchased, you then return it to the auction, where it is bid for again and again. The money raised, along with his kit and possessions, is then sent on to the family. His death frightened us and shook us badly, making us realize how easy it was to become the victim of an accident, and that we weren't as tough as we thought.

We came back one night, and, as usual, the hurricane fan at the top of the mess was whirring away, turning slowly from side to side. This was our only form of air-conditioning, so we would run it continuously. Jock Arthur, who slept closest to the fan, threw himself out of bed one night, drunkenly, screaming about the rats in his pit with him. We all turned out, put all the lights on, and nervously scoured every nook and cranny in the mess searching for our new pets. After some time, someone noticed that Jocks' sheet was flapping every time the fan pointed at it. 'There's your rat, you prat'. And we all returned to our beds.

Peculiarly, every week, an old battered freighter/steamer would stagger towards the jetty, tilted drunkenly. Eventually it would grind to a halt, generally by hitting the jetty, then disgorge hundreds of sheep and people. After a few hours, it would stagger back to sea, and disappear for a further week. God alone knows where it used to go when it left Bahrein.

Occasionally British freighters would tie up, and we would make our acquaintance with them. They, you see, could have as much booze as they wanted on board, which was very handy after closing time.

We finally sailed from Bahrein in late summer, and headed for Singapore. We stopped at Cochin in India, which put me off going to India ever again. We tied up as usual, but were besieged by onlookers, raggedly dressed women, men and kids, all holding their arms outstretched begging. Many of the beggars had missing or deformed limbs – it was a pitiful sight and one I will never forget. Apparently the women were offering themselves in exchange for a bar of soap. We threw them the soap anyway. We went ashore in the afternoon to one hotel, near a market. We spent all our allocated money on some terrific rabbits, got back in the rickshaw, and went back onboard in time for supper. We were only allowed to 'change back from rupees' what we had 'changed into rupees', so we didn't spend a great deal of it. We were offered many times the going rate by the taxi driver for our sterling though. When we got back, there was a man on the jetty with a mongoose and several snakes, one of which was a cobra, which he thought we ought to watch fight. For a sum. A very large sum, in fact, we thought. We watched the mongoose 'fight' another snake. The mongoose was winning when the man hauled it off. We never did see the cobra – we refused to pay him his fee, got bored and wandered off. The smell from Cochin was appalling, and it took a long time before it cleared from our nostrils. A very sad visit to a very sad port.

CHAPTER 15

The FES, at Long Last

We reached Singapore, and eventually moored at Sembewang dockyard. I was 'specials' that day, so I missed all the sights, except that I saw them all on radar. We were still working 'tropical' routine, fortunately, as every day, without fail really, it hissed down with torrential rain, then cleared, and was nice for the remainder of the day. We secured alongside HMS *Triumph* – an old carrier converted into a factory ship, and commenced a month-long mini-refit. The whole ship's company therefore moved into HMS *Terror* for some weeks. We were back into the routine of trekking down to the ship for 0700, turning to until 1245, securing, back to *Terror*, then see what developed. There was a terrific swimming pool at *Terror*, mostly for families, but we were allowed in if we promised to behave. Or we would go to one of *Terror*'s bars, drink pints of draught Tiger beer (only available otherwise in bottles), watch the 'chitchats' (small lizards) climbing walls, ceilings – everywhere, and generally laze around. Chitchats have an aversion to glasses being thrown at them, which is why you could never hit them. Or was it the fact that after several delicious glasses of ice-cold Tiger, your co-ordination went.

On the *Triumph* were several 'shops', whose owners, I remember, raided our messes as soon as we secured, looking for clothing to launder or repair. I don't remember the very large man's name, though he was a naval legend at that time, however. He would haul your gear out of the communal locker, throw it disdainfully on the floor, screaming 'Fuckin' do'yard job'. i.e., badly needs repairing or cleaning. You'd negotiate a price, he'd repair or clean it and return it to you in far, far better condition than when it left. Or there was the tailor, who would tout his wares and samples. You would order some shirts in a particular colour of a certain style for a fixed price. Without fail, he would return next day with the shirts, all exactly as you expected, all a perfect fit. Emboldened, we also purchased immaculately tailored trousers and suits. There were also snobs who sold many, many pairs of shoes. There was a 'drinks' man, who offered different flavoured milks. However, you ended up asking for 'cho'la miw', or 'green miw', or 'ping miw' which is what he called them. These were lifesavers for those trying to dispel the effects of the night before, having missed breakfast, but desperate to be rid of the remains of the 'Tiger'.

We had to spend duty watches on board, but in better conditions than Rosyth, however. The dockyard canteen was just across the jetty, and we would send the junior watch person with a 'fanny' to fill it with Tiger, which we would dispose of. We would mess from *Triumph*, queuing in batches to eat our evening meal on board. HMS *Intrepid* was there at the same time, and my mate Glen (from *Raleigh*) was aboard. We exchanged pleasantries, ale, stories and separated once again when she sailed.

There was a duty free shop on the base, which is where I bought my first sensible camera – a Pentax, with which I took thousands of photographs. I finally decoded the manual, learned how to use it properly, how to exchange speed for aperture, and it rarely left my side throughout the rest of my naval career. At that time the trend was for multi-stereo systems, portable ones that looked like briefcases, with cassette/radio/record player, detachable speakers, battery or mains: I think everyone bought one of these except me. And in the markets in Singapore you could select some records, return later and the stall owner would have recorded them on to cassette for you, in perfect stereo. We spent a fortune there too.

Sembewang village was just that, and comprised several bars (knocking shops), restaurants and assorted other stores. It looked like a cross between a wild-west town, and a suburban high street. However, the choice of entertainment was limited, though cheap. I should say Cheep, as the song blasting out of every bar was 'Chirpy Chirpy Cheep Cheep' (or 'Sembewang is cheap, cheap' as we paraphrased it). We would therefore fill up with Tiger in *Terror*, adjourn to Sembewang until closing time, then move on to the city for the nightlife. This would normally be a place called Bugis Street, which was the place to go. Populated by 'Kai Tais' (transvestites) who would parade up and down all night, trying to scrounge drinks. Off us? More chance of being hit by a meteorite. It was, however, one of the best black cats of all time, to be able to say you had started a session at lunchtime, played it out all afternoon, gone ashore that night, ended up in the city – seen the sunrise over Bugis Street with a bottle of Tiger, then gone back on board courtesy of a very fast black, and actually made it without being adrift.

There is a strange place called 'The Tiger Balm Gardens' in Singapore. Tiger Balm is an (apparently) illegal substance, something like Vick's mixed with heroin. Allegedly, it cures many ills, and was freely available in Singers. These gardens are full of contorted statues, montages of wild cruelty and hideous 'apparitions', all representing legends and folklore. The gardens were unlike anything else I had seen in the world and absolutely enthralling.

We would return from a run, via an open-air 'restaurant', where we would sit alongside an open sewer, watching the chef prepare what we wanted. Normally Heinz tomato soup with bread and butter, followed by the local dish – nasi goreng – and washed down with more Tiger. One night, one of our crew rolled off his chair into the sewer – and had to be rushed on board for emergency medical treatment (mostly injections!). Eventually, replete, we would go back to our rooms at *Terror*, and catch some sleep before starting again. The rooms in *Terror* were first class, and looked like the colonial apartments you would expect in such a place. We had an open balcony and slept just four to a room. We took to spending our off-duty aboard time dressed in multi-coloured bedsheets which you could wrap round your waist and which were considerably cooler than shorts. We wore these for months until it became too cold on the way home.

At some point, between the torrential rainy season daily downpour, and the Duty watches, and the runs ashore and the camera learning, I became an Able Seaman. I also upgraded from a basic RP to an RP3 (third class). Eventually we moved back on board *Zulu*, and sailed for Hong Kong – the highlight of our eleven-month tour, and something I particularly looked forward to. I had heard so much about the place – could it all be true?

Unfortunately, something had bitten me in Singers and I spent two weeks in sick-bay with severe pain in my extremely swollen knee, and frequently had to remove the pus that built up inside it. This was accompanied by large doses of antibiotics into my bum, several times daily. Admittedly, I got out of the exercises we took part in, but I was desperately disappointed to miss the first few days in Hong Kong.

When I finally surfaced, limping, we went to the Fleet Club, where we met the Yanks again. We took the ferry to Kowloon and played in the bars and clubs. We toured the shopping malls, and took a bus trip up country to the China border, where we had mud thrown at us (right through the bus window). Fortunately, the bus driver had the good sense to drive off, otherwise there is no telling what would have happened to the person who threw it, or what the repercussions would have been for us beating ten bells out of the locals.

We went up Victoria Peak in the tram railway. Almost vertically, but once above the skyscraperline, the view improved. By the time I got to the top, the view over the whole of the harbour was absolutely amazing. And you could see in all directions, for miles. One of the best views in the world.

One night, having saved up for this for months, we visited the Tai Pak floating restaurant, having previously made the reservations. We ate an eleven-course meal, comprising lobster salad, abalone with green kale, Fried stuffed crab claws, sweetcorn with crabmeat soup, steamed fresh prawns, deep-fried chicken, baked lobster with onion sauce, steamed garoupa with chicken fat, fried rice, wan ton soup, and fresh milk punch. We were in there for hours, and hours. I remember the menu exactly – I kept it!

In those days there was no tunnel across the bay, you either got the ferry, or got stuck when they stopped running. Alternatively, you could pay an exorbitant rate for a sampan and be rowed across. That was the usual choice, that or be adrift and fined more than the sampan price.

Attached to HMS *Tamar* (the base in Hong Kong) was the jetty where we moored, and no sooner had we tied up, apparently, than we had an offer to paint the ship's side. As I said earlier, doing the side was an absolute drag – you needed to be volunteered to do it; you avoided it at all costs. Jenny's Side Party happily turned to, primered, undercoated and repainted the whole lot while there – it looked magnificent when they had finished it.

At most places we visited there would be a market set up on the jetty alongside us, in order to induce us to part with our cash. Hong Kong was probably the only place where the markets were allowed on board, in both 'waists', spread around, much as car boot sales nowadays. We got some good last-minute rabbits from there.

CHAPTER 16

'Time to Go Home, Time to Go Home . . .'

We sadly left Hong Kong for the return trip, counting the days until we got back to Rosyth, and now we were 'Homeward Bounders'. We stopped at Gan, in the middle of the Indian Ocean, now known as the Maldives – an RAF base at that time, populated solely by RAF people. We had the inevitable banyan and game of football and then sailed, rapidly. I don't know if crabfats would volunteer for Gan, or whether they were volunteered, but there was nothing, and I do mean, nothing to do there.

We spent a week at Victoria, on the island of Mahe in the idyllic Seychelles, where we spent all our free time disappearing in taxis to the beaches on the far side of the island, where the sand was as fine as flour on the beaches, which were again unparalleled. We tried to locate the famous turtles, but never saw any.

While we were in Singers and HK we had started to lose our suntans, and were now glad of the opportunity to top them up. We left Mahe, and sailed back to Mombasa. This time, no station leave, but we did safari up country to Tsavo, with camera and several films, in a minibus, scouring the park for different animals. We saw, as I recall, elephants, lions, crocodiles, antelopes, zebra, cheetahs, giraffes, more elephants, monkeys, gazelles, hippos, hyena, impala, more giraffes, more antelopes – and ended up at Lugard Falls. We had tea at Voi Safari Lodge, then returned, exhausted (we got up at three in the morning to do this one), to the ship late in the evening. This was one of my most memorable days.

We sailed from Mombasa straight back to Beira – another month at sea, scanning the radar, topping up the tan, fighting once again for the 'bucket'. We returned back to Durban for another few days. We then sailed to Simonstown to refuel, then to Cape Town harbour, just to see Sugar Loaf. At last we set sail properly for home.

It is a fact that while you serve in any ship you become so used to the background rattles and noises that you actually become attuned to the ship, that you instinctively know when something amiss happens before you are told about it. Or even before something happens. One night, as we sailed northwards up the west coast of Africa, while passing the mouth of the River Gambia, we were in bed awaiting the 'shake' for the Middle. I think we all woke up without exception, and looked at each other in the lights from our bunks. Then came a loud bang. The *Zulu* shuddered, the propeller stopped turning and we cruised to a halt. Hundreds of miles from shore. We had had a major fire in the gearbox, which fortunately for us was quickly extinguished. Those practice drills, daily for eleven months, served their purpose that night – it was 'out' before it knew what had hit it. We sat there motionless for several days, while (luckily for us) the same sweepers that were in Bahrein with us caught up. They were returning from their deployment too; they arrived one morning, hitched up tow lines and dragged us to the nearest port, which was Dakar, in French west Africa. As soon as we arrived there, we were well entertained by the French Navy, who could not have been more helpful unless they had actually held the wine bottles to our mouths.

It was very close to Christmas by now, and we had specialists flown out from Rosyth to come and make good the gearbox. They couldn't immediately, and it became high priority to get several of our crew home to UK, as they had weddings arranged. They were flown back; we sweated over whether we'd make it. After several days (and several large hammers) the 'mateys' freed up the gearbox enough for us to connect G6, and we came home all the way on that. This was unfortunate – as G6 was a thirsty beast only used sparingly, so we had to RAS, it seemed hourly but was probably daily, all the way back to England. We were also curtailed to the maximum G6 speed, which was well below normal cruising speed. We arrived in Rosyth just days before Christmas, actually only slightly later than expected, and headed for home for well-earned leave.

We were all loaded with rabbits, all looked deeply suntanned, all had new suits from the tailors (mine had a rich red lining), and all ran like hell to get the taxis to Inverkeithing for the train to Edinburgh, for the fast trains south and home.

CHAPTER 17

After the Lord Mayor's Show
. . . Comes the Med

Christmas 1972 was over far too quickly, and back I went to Rosyth. The clanks, along with the dockies, finally separated the gearbox bits from the engine through a large hole specially created in the ship's side, rebuilt the lot and then patched it all up. We were away again after the inevitable 'basin trials' and power trials. We refuelled and once more headed for Gib, and the prospect of three months in the Med.

We were designated Gib Guard Ship for a month, and in that time were twice called out to 'escort' Russian warships. On one of the 'escort' duties, as apparently the two fleets were changing over, hence our escort, we saw a brand-new Russian aircraft carrier, the *Moskva*. However, when we next saw it it seemed to be the *Kiev*. Or was it really two ships? Whatever, they were operating helicopters that flew close to us for a gander, while their version of our Harrier jump-jet took off and landed behind them, as, for once, we were the observers.

One day, while at sea, I was 'piped' to the Air EMR, and informed it was my turn today to be a passenger in the parrot while it did a one-hour sortie looking for surface contacts. I was briefed (do NOT jump out), strapped in (the rear seats were removed and we sat on the floor with lap belts), and we launched with a jerk. For 'flying stations' the ship hurtles into the wind at high speed, to get extra lift for the parrot. As you lift, therefore, so the ship clears from underneath, the parrot breaks to port and up you go. Like an express lift, your stomach is still on the flight deck. The pilot then demonstrated the art of high-speed manoeuvring, so if I looked to the right, I could see the sea. I thought I would have seen the horizon, really. They also removed the doors – there was nothing but a lap belt, then, between me and the sea. It was totally exhilarating. To land, the parrot would slowly catch up with the ship, hang over the port quarter, wait until signalled, then scat across and down. With one hell of a bump. I volunteered to go again, but never did.

During one exercise, we were in contact with an American Orion, which was flying and flitting about reporting surface ships back to us. Later in the afternoon, we were called by another warship, also American, the Orion asking if we had heard from him recently. We had to confess we hadn't, not for several hours, but said that as we weren't controlling him, and as he had only spoken to us sporadically, we weren't surprised that he might have gone 'off task' without telling us. It was then, with great shock, that we heard later of reports that an aircraft had been seen to fly into a hill. We legged it there, but too late obviously. The Orion had for some inexplicable reason, flown straight into a mountain, killing everyone onboard. We never did find out how they'd managed that, all we saw was the smoke from a distance.

We also engaged the local MFV to take a large party of us across to Tangier for the day, another unmissable experience wandering round the souks, looking at the sights, buying souvenirs, smelling the spices and tasting the food. A terrific day, especially the camel rides!

We also visited Naples, where the local kids, all expert pickpockets, would tap your pockets as they walked alongside you. We then took a ferry across to Capri, to see Gracie Fields. In 'rig' of course. We hadn't planned this, although we were aware she lived there somewhere. We went to the front gate of her villa, knocked, explained who we were and why we had come there, and were let in to her home without hesitation, spending a wonderful afternoon talking to a lovely lady. We had tea there, and returned to the ship. We spent a weekend in Rome, driving up in a coach to a hotel on the outskirts. We ate all the native, real, proper, genuine Italian food, we toured the city in the coach and saw every tourist trap going. We walked and admired the Colosseum, the Trevi Fountain, and took the photographs to prove it. We visited a cameo factory, where a man was making jewellery out of silver with cameo settings. I bought a ring, with the head of a centurion in it, but it broke one day and I could never find anyone who was willing to repair it for me.

The night we were in Rome, we had the obligatory party in our hotel room (I can't for the life of me remember how many people shared the room), but we found a bar nearby, after we'd got back from a short 'run', and purchased several bottles of the local devil's brew. It was warm, so we put it in the wine cooler in the bathroom ready for the proposed evening party. The first person who saw our Roman wine cooler collapsed laughing – we had used the bidet.

We toured Pompeii, and saw all the sights including the man apparently zapped by the lava. He was displayed for all time in the museum, actually as he was when the lava hit him. We spent hours there, and it was amazing to remember that people actually existed there – the graffiti, the wheel ruts in the road and the mosaic saying (in Latin) 'Beware of the dog' were particularly memorable. Another grand run.

We 'stern-moored' in Naples, meaning we approached a very narrow jetty backwards. When we got close, we dropped one anchor, veered to one side and planted the other one, then reversed so that only the stern was on the jetty. We'd then secure the stern, set the tension on the anchor cables and stay there. Leaving was just as hairy – let go aft, winch in on one anchor while releasing the other, raise the first one, winch over to the other, raise that, Simple, but time consuming. At least the mud was warmer here.

We finally left Naples and resumed exercises. We had by that time teamed up with a Mediterranean fleet of warships from Med nations. The idea was that we exercised constantly with them, but weekly we would sail into a host port for some leave. Hence the start in Italy. We then visited Patras, Thessalonika, Messina, Taormina, Valletta, Izmir and a small bay on Cyprus. Here, unfortunately, I fell over a cliff while returning from a banyan. Luckily, I was drunk enough to bounce, but it scared my oppos! In Izmir, I was the Duty boat driver – we had moored some miles out of port along with the other ships. I drove the boat ashore one night to pick up liberty men and wondered why the rest of the fleet boats were all alongside even though they were full of respective 'tars'. I put the boat out – and sailed slap bang into a typhoon – well, it felt like it. It was a severe squall, and by the time I had got the whaler back to the *Zulu*, it was slightly full of water and the liberty men were all drenched (including the officers, who sat at the front where waves break over) and exhausted from baling the whaler as I bravely steered through the driving rain back to the ship. We emptied the boat of men (up the accommodation ladder), hoisted the boat a little way on the falls, took the bung out, then sat back and watched the water drain out. And by the time we had it fully hoisted, the squall disappeared as quickly as it had come. So we put the bung back in, lowered it and returned for all the crew who were by that time waiting on the jetty and wondering how they would get back.

On board all Navy warships are 'booms', which can be swung out from the ship's side. At Procedure Alpha, or when anchoring, all the booms and ladders and boats would be swung or dropped at the same time. The ladders require very many sailors to position them, even after the many hours required to build them. However, the booms are lumps of wood, with ladders and ropes and wires everywhere. If the ladders are where sailors climb on and off the ship to the boat to/from ashore, the boom is where the boat is itself moored while doing nothing. So after dropping off the liberty men, the boat would approach the boom boatrope and secure to it. The crew would then disembark the boat via the ladder hanging from the boom, then get back inboard by traversing the boom. Piece of cake – usually. However, it was more common to have to do this in a swell, sometimes in a heavy swell. That would make mooring the boat difficult, as you would need to judge the approach to the boatrope exactly. Then hope that the bowman could actually grab the rope and secure it before the boat dropped away on the bottom of the wave, dragging him overboard if he wasn't careful. Once secured, it then became dangerous. You'd have to go to the pitching bows of the boat and pull the boat up on the boatrope until you could reach the ladder. You'd then ascend the ladder to the boom, except that the boat would want to drop back with the tide, which meant the ladder developed its own malevolent personality. Even dry those ladders were evil; wet, they were virtually impossible. We'd also be wearing plimsolls to attempt this. If you managed to leap at the right time, you'd be half way up the ladder, then have to get from beneath the boom on the hanging ladder to above the boom so you could seize the guy wire, and carefully walk sideways until you got back aboard the ship. By this point it would be time to take the boat back again for more liberty men.

Getting back to the boat was more dangerous – cross the boom, feel for the ladder, swing underneath to it, keep your weight on the ladder until the boat appeared beneath you and let go. All things being equal, you'd fall into the boat, start the engine, propel it forward, and let the rest of the crew in. As I said, couldn't be simpler. Now throw in driving rain, a heavy swell and do it again at 0200, in pitch dark, having been roused from sleep five minutes earlier. Soak your plimsolls in the oil and grease from the bottom of the seaboat and try it again.

It was also in Izmir that I ran out of money, but managed to swap an extremely cheap watch for a genuine Afghan coat. Unfortunately, on getting it back to the ship, it turned out to contain its own zoo and so was consigned to a carrier-bag full of 'crab' powder until we returned to the UK, where it was declared 'safe'.

We had a final few days in Gib to buy souvenirs, where I eventually cracked and bought a stereo, which I promptly blew up, having not read the voltage label. I returned it, swore blind it was duff when I got it, and had it replaced. I also purchased an Omega watch, the like of which I have never since seen, and which still keeps perfect time. That watch didn't leave my wrist or pocket for the next eight of my naval years, in case someone fancied it more than I did.

We then returned to Rosyth – some glad to be home, most sad to be at the end of the commission. We had enjoyed thirty months together, seen some wonderful sights, bought great rabbits, got older, and much, much wiser. I was sad to leave the *Zulu* – she held some good memories for me. I never saw her again. I wonder if anyone ever found out about the pumpkins and other odd fruit we used to ferment into wine? Or discovered any of the crates we stowed away during RASes, and forgot about? And whatever happened to her anyway? I spent two-and-a-half highly formative years on there, and enjoyed almost every minute of it.

CHAPTER 18

A Shore Draft

I left the *Zulu*, had several weeks decommissioning leave and rejoined HMS *Dryad* for a 'twos' course, intended to make me into a 'second class RP', instead of the 'third class' I was at that time. Before leaving after a tour, all crew would request a draft to a unit they fancied. I fancied (and was recommended for) the 'twos' course, but was nevertheless surprised when I got it.

I must first say, that after two-and-a-half years of not being able to look out of a window and see daylight, it made a very pleasant change to draw curtains and see fields. The mess at *Dryad* was at the edge of the base and overlooked pastures, and it was cows that now kept me awake rather than stabilizers and steering gear. Looking back, being in a steel box was like sensory deprivation.

The life at *Dryad* was now at my fingertips – I was nineteen, had seen the world, got the T-shirt (worn frequently) and read the book. Surprisingly, my fellow course-goers between them had not been to as many places as I had. I counted myself as fortunate to have been on the *Zulu* for that commission. They had, though, their own wealth of experience to recount, and we learned an awful lot from each other.

We would frequent 'The Beast' in Southwick, which was a five-minute walk there, but took anything up to an hour back. The Beast didn't sell shorts, only Gales Ales and, a variety of wines of different flavours. A different one for every day of the year, I think. We would either buy by the glass, or by the bottle, or we would hold a bash and get Sid's missus to fill a large bucket with assorted bottles, lemonade, beer and fruit slices. As the level sank, we would augment the contents, with wine, crisps, nuts, scratchings and more wine. As the night wore on, the tastier the contents of the bucket became, conversely the weaker it appeared to be, until the mixtures of lemonade were omitted, meaning what was left was pure wine. We had some great nights in there, as there was no defined bar, just a couple of rooms, one of which had comfortable armchairs and an open fire. We would sit there for hours, then crawl up the back road to *Dryad*, followed by 'Dot's' for the inevitable SRE. Occasionally, we would race back to the Naafi ready for last orders, or send an advance party there to get them in, prior to our arrival, so we could sit there until the 2300 Naafi closing time.

Just for a change, we would go to the other pub in the village, which was a 'normal' pub. Very infrequently we would go into Pompey for the night, but there had to be a good reason for that, such as going to see live bands at the Guildhall.

The weeks there passed in a blur, punctuated by weekends at home or in Pompey if there was something to entice us there. We were fiercely team spirited, and we would rarely go round with other 'courses'. We would, however, team up with Wrens, and it seemed an unofficial contest to get the largest bunch of tables together in the Naafi in the evenings, in order to create the biggest 'gang'. My course would normally win that, with all our tables haphazardly arranged, but deliberately right up the middle of the club. The war cry in those days was 'Cheese Toastie'. All through the evening, the Naafi served sarnies and would put them in the toaster, hence that cry, which used to really get on our nerves. We would drink in rounds, with everyone getting theirs in. Sometimes, we would have 'club night', or 'folk night', which was merely an excuse to sing, volubly, along with the man holding the microphone.

'Zulu Warrior' was a favourite song, depending on who you could coerce into performing it. As was that (now hijacked) old faithful 'Swing Low, Sweet Chariot', which we knew all the words and all the verses to. We would, for variation, hum it, then mime it. If you have never seen anyone, let alone several dozen (or more) people in a line, miming silently but in perfect time to 'Swing Low . . .', then you are in for a surprise. It is very easy, and you can make anyone understand the chorus, amidst a great deal of laughter when the mimes become obvious.

Interspersed with the serious drinking songs would be gentle melodies about a crow in a tree (my favourite, and rarely did I ever find anyone else who knew the words to it), or about 'Chiefy put me dayman (you can have my tot)' or about a gentleman called Sambo and the bee. We even knew the 'Eton Boating Song', clearly with our own words, mainly involving hard boiled eggs, and several others about 'My Brother, Sylvest' and much more. It was clear that the more songs you had in your repertoire, the better it was for you. All were guaranteed to get a laugh, especially if performed in front of a previously untainted audience.

Eating at *Dryad* was fun. We would queue, starting an orderly rabble outside the dining hall well before the correct time, merely to allow ogling. This would take place between Wrens and sailors, and go on until the doors were opened. It was also traditional to get there even earlier on 'new intake day' as new Wrens arrived from their initial training at HMS *Dauntless*, to be the first to scan them for anything interesting. We, then, would normally be the first sailors they'd ever seen, live, and we would clearly often take advantage of that.

After many weeks, we took final exams, did our final 'models', received our next drafts, said goodbye to all the course mates and Wrens we had come to know over the preceding very enjoyable weeks, and disappeared into the railway stations.

CHAPTER 19

Another Shore Job

I was drafted to HMS *Victory*, and was put on a requested educational course to top up my GCEs. This meant being in class all day, cramming for English and geography. For this period, I had a blue card, which meant 'no duties'. Great, ashore every night, home every weekend I could afford it. Along with my friend Glen (who was coincidentally on the course), I sailed through all the exams.

My first day job after that was being attached to the registry, where I carried round all the internal mail throughout the base. That opened my eyes when I had to make the daily delivery to DQ's (Detention Quarters), which was reputed to be not too dissimilar to Butlins. It seemed a harsh regime there, not one I fancied, so I'd skid in, then out, quickly. The 'warders', all senior rates from the Navy and Marines, were seemingly hand picked as the most unpleasant shites the Navy paid. Even when I went in there to deliver their mail twice daily, you could not even start a conversation or get one to speak coherently or pleasantly to you.

I was detailed after that to another blue card job. I worked with one of the last Navy sailmakers in the sail loft, where we would repair marquees or sails from the RNSA boats, but not too hard or too fast. The reason it was a blue card job, was that we used to hire out marquees to local functions, at a cost, and not only had to deliver them, but also to erect them. The three of us, along with as many volunteers as the hirers could muster would take the best part of a day to do that, generally on a Friday. We would then go back either on the Sunday, or first thing Monday morning, to drop it and stow it. We would then have to air or dry it, before taking it out the next weekend. Not that it was all drawbacks, the hirers would normally 'treat' us, not only while in progress, but generally afterwards too. As 'the loft' was off the beaten track, we rarely received visitors. We were exempt from rounds because of the nature of the job, and exempt from duties, so life was pretty easy.

I was 'messed' right across the road from the Naafi dining hall – very central. As usual, a clique developed, with the whole gang trooping around together on jaunts here and there. One of them ended up in the

Fire Brigade, with John, a mate of mine from my home village – I don't know who was the most surprised of the two of them when they realized they both knew me.

It was an extreme shock when one day I discovered I had been volunteered to take part in an honour guard for the Prince of Wales. It was an even greater shock when I started to drop the SLR every other movement. I made a rapid visit to the sickbay, where my elbow was X-rayed; they decided to schedule me for an operation, and promptly excused me from the guard. That was close.

A couple of my 'run ashore oppos' were at that time guides on the wooden HMS *Victory*, in permanent dry dock in Portsmouth Dockyard. In those days, that was the only place civilians could go in the yard, and they would spend hours queuing to traipse around the *Victory*, peering at where Lord Nelson fell and where the crew lived. We would infiltrate these tourists at weekends, being attentive to everything our oppo would have to say, prompting questions here and there. We would then be first off the ship, but in full view of the assembled tourists, we would loudly announce our thank yous and give them some money (usually a fiver borrowed from them some hours earlier). That would normally precipitate a shower of further dosh from the grateful grockles, which we in turn would thankfully divvy up later, going ashore on the proceeds.

On a Sunday, we had major choices. We could either stay within the base, go to the Naafi, and watch the (ostensibly) live folk singer, which was guaranteed to get a laugh, especially the day one announced he was going to sing a song by Tam Pax, sorry Tom Paxton. The 'splits' didn't find that at all amusing. Or we could go ashore, and after the pubs shut at lunchtime, we would catch the Isle of Wight ferry, and make one or two crossings until the pubs opened again. The fact that the IOW ferry bar opened as soon as they left the jetty was neither here nor there – we just used to go for the sightseeing.

For two weeks in mid-summer, I was drafted to HMS *Bacchante* (known as the Bagshanty) which was Guard Ship for Cowes Week that year. I was boat's crew, meaning we ran between Portsmouth and Cowes over the sandbanks to fetch/return crew/stores. At night we ferried yacht crews from wardroom – sorry – ship to yacht, or back, taking great care to avoid causing a wake enough to rock the sleeping yachts and their crews. Not that we'd do that of course, unless provoked by, lets say, not getting a tip. Those weeks passed quickly, and it was soon back to barracks. Many years later, while touring HMS *Victory* (the real one) with my wife and some friends, I met the man I crewed with – we recognized each other immediately, and dredged up all kinds of memories.

Ships refitting in Pompey did what we used to do on the *Zulu* in Rosyth – live ashore and march to the ship. It came to our notice that the officers of the ships would traverse *Victory*, short cutting to their ships. We especially came to like one officer, a very green, obviously straight-from-university lieutenant, small and inoffensive, with an oversized cap, held up only by his protruding ears, it seemed. We noted how he would blush when saluted, so we took it upon ourselves to line up one behind the other to get the blush. We would also hammer round the blocks to do it again. I don't know if he ever caught on, but he must have generated plenty of heat and then arrived with a tired right arm! The blush, incidentally would be followed by a very sheepish grin. He was lucky – for a start, we'd normally go miles out of our way to avoid saluting 'pigs', but fortunately the 'rule' was only to salute the same officer once per day. And if they carried their cap under their arm, we could totally ignore them.

Towards the end of the summer, in among more concerts, weekends, and other mixed fortunes, I received another draft. Bearing in mind that the 'scare' ships this time were the *Blake* and the *Tiger* (not popular), I was extremely pleased when I was told that mine was to be HMS *Tartar*, another Tribal class frigate, based in Pompey, but more importantly, it was going on a tour of the Windies.

I then served out the rest of my time at *Victory* in the loft, with weekends mostly at home, but with several others tear-arsing around in Vic Jelley's old MG, visiting the motor museum near Southampton, the New Forest, or wherever else we could scrape up enough petrol to go.

CHAPTER 20

The Tartar *(of the Title –*
See, I wasn't Lying) in Pompey

I was extremely pleased to join the RatRat – I was welcomed on board by my peers, as, as an RP2, it meant I was in charge of the Ops room watch, along with the other seven RP2s, meaning that when we sailed, we were actually one-in-eight (watches) instead of the one-in-four the rest of the crew were on. Also, as a '2', I had credibility, could play uckers, talk sensibly about a wide range of naval topics and spin the shit when I had to.

Unfortunately, within weeks of joining her, I was taken off to have my elbow sorted, and went P7R for six weeks. More unfortunately, I had to go back to *Dryad* to recuperate. More 'Beast', more 'toasties'. While I was up there, the *Tartar* did basin trials, and in doing so, the hawsers holding her parted and she took off towards the caisson separating the ocean from a dry dock, which contained a submarine. She was stopped following some extremely quick thinking by the OOW, who had the engines reversed in record time, so no serious damage was done. *Tartar* had just completed a long refit, and my first shock was to see the officer we had tormented was the electrical engineer, and, although he didn't recognize me – he still blushed and grinned.

Portsmouth was at that time divided into two drinking areas. 'The Strip' was where I had previously been, with the pubs full of students and sailors and the floors with sawdust (to save putting it down after the event). Then there was the main drag, where I had visited during my *Victory* days. Even I was amazed when my mates on the *Tartar* introduced me to pubs I wasn't aware of. We quickly made friends, George (later to become my best man) and me were virtually inseparable for nearly three years. Being a '2' made it easier to be accepted, that and the fact there was a juniors' mess on board, which kept them out of the way. Attitudes changed quickly as you ascended the ranks. It meant I could now pass on my knowledge and experiences to these juniors. It was strange to think that just two years previously, I had been on the receiving end.

Comradeship was very strong on the *Tartar*, and gangs of us would go ashore. If one person was broke, he would have a 'free' night and we would buy his ale. The next night, you might be skint so you'd have your ale bought – bearing in mind that even then you could still go ashore and get smashed on a couple of quid, including the snack on the walk back to the dockyard. We had our favourite pubs, and queued outside the preferred ones at 1755, waiting for opening time. My favourite was the Borough Arms, full of students from the local poly. That particular pub had three things going for it. First, the best jukebox I have ever seen. Second, most matelots kept away from it, as it had a dubious reputation even for Portsmouth. Third, they still sold scrumpy from the wood, and if you were fortunate enough to get the last pint, you'd find you got a free meal from all the bits of apple at the bottom of the barrel.

We used to occasionally 'smooth it', either by going to grab-a-granny night at the weekly disco at the dance hall in Pompey, where we'd wear a tie with our short-sleeved shirts, jeans, and jackets. That place would keep a stock of ties on the door, just for passing trade. Or we'd go to the 'Still And West' in Old Portsmouth, where we'd drink outside overlooking the harbour entrance, shouting encouragement at passing warships or ferries. They sold wine (like at Sid's) there, and scrumpy, beer and Guinness. I had never drunk that before, but quickly appreciated it. The first night me and George had leg failures on Guinness, we woke up to find we had acquired a whole length of flashing lights, which used to guard a hole in the road in Old Portsmouth. I have absolutely no idea how they got there, how they (or we) got past the Mod Plod guarding the dockyard gate, or up the gangway, but they made a terrific splash as we gave them a float test only moments before Colours the following morning.

We also got into the bad habit, but naval tradition, of stopping for 'big eats' in the form of a Chinese. Our favourite one was close to the station and run by one 'Charlie Chop Suey', who would see us walk in and get the kitchen staff cooking it before we'd even ordered. Charlie was terrific, nothing was too much trouble for him – he would even let us put our meal on the slate if it was near payday because he knew that we'd be back and pay for it with our next meal.

If we felt really flush, we'd go down to Southsea, spend the evening in the bars and discos, then stagger round looking for a taxi back. We'd stop at the snack bar to ensure a supply of milk for the following morning, although if you spoke nicely to the QM, he'd ensure he skimmed some off the top of the milk churn delivered daily (so we sailors could have fresh milk with our cornflakes and in our tea). Fresh milk was obviously unobtainable at sea, but we ensured supplies by freezing vast quantities and thawing it out periodically. Apart from that, we'd have 'metal cow' (powdered milk), or the least favourite – tinned milk, something I still avoid.

Scarcely a weekend passed without being called 'up-homers' by one of the locals, where he and his wife would give a good Sunday dinner. Our special favourite was to go to Blackie's house. He was a gunner, with an alarming ability to dispose of Bacardi. His wife, Barbara, made a splendid Sunday lunch, uncomplainingly, when we got back from the pub late. We'd sit around in armchairs at Blackie's, eating his food and all of us chatting away. Blackie left the ship sometime while we were in the Windies, never to be seen again. I heard subsequently that he had accidentally had his back broken. I really hope not, or if he did that he recovered sufficiently. Budgie was another favourite – we lost count of the times we went to his single-room flat for meals with him and his wife.

Not that we needed an excuse to get away from the food on the *Tartar* – it was simply the best food I ever had in the RN. We had a choice of at least two joints for lunch, with amazing suppers. You could normally tell what was being served – the length of the queue back up the Burma Road would be in direct proportion to the 'goody rating' of what was on the menu. Mixed grill was favourite (especially if this was served with mushrooms), but strangely this were only ever dished up on a Saturday. Second in the running was Chicken Supreme, something the Chinese wardroom crew would knock up easily, but which I have never managed to recreate, try as I might. Breakfast was always good – we were allowed to fry our own eggs rather than carve a lump from the scrambled tray. Actually, my taste in food was (and still is) wide ranging and varied, but I could never hack Spanish omelettes, which went on the menu when the caterer ran out of ideas. Disgusting looking things.

As a sideline, when we did the Morning, one of the chefs used to be treated to a cup of tea when we woke him at 0430 (ish) to start cooking – he would then bring us fresh bacon sarnies later, right before we slid off for the first of two breakfasts. The chef we used to do this trade with was a bit of a wag (for a chef), and if he was Duty chef for '9-o'clockers' (supper every evening), you had to be a bit cagey what you ate. For example, if it was 'cackleberries' (hard-boiled eggs), you had to make sure you cracked the eggs somewhere safe, or you might just get one of the several uncooked eggs thrown in for fun. We got wise to that after a while, and would either threaten him, in which case he'd keep yours apart, or you'd use the old trick of spinning the egg quickly on its base. If it fell over – uncooked, if it continued – cooked perfectly. Nine o'clockers (actually served at 2000) is a Navy tradition, like rum was, and it could be anything – cake, sandwiches, crackers (at which point you would have a side bet as to who could actually empty their mouth of three cream crackers inside one minute. impossible to do), with cheese, ham, eggs, corned dog, 'herrings-in', meat paste, whatever lay at hand when the Duty chef decided to get it ready. We would, generally, toast the bread first and lash it with plenty of butter, or we'd nick as much as we could of whatever there was available to take back to the mess if it was our 'turn'. If you were tardy getting there, bad luck – it would all be gone in moments. It was like a flock of vultures descending. If you were lucky, the Duty chef would still be about, and you might be able to con something out of him. More often than not, they'd put it all out, and that was it. During the in-sail movie, we'd shut down the projector to allow hungry sailors to feed, even though they'd been troughing nutty since suppertime anyway. Once the last hand had sat down again, we'd recommence the movie.

Again, we had a central dining room on the *Tartar*, four rows of tables, with benches either side. We would then eat as quickly as possible, for two reasons – first, to let someone else sit and eat; second, to get back to the messdeck for a rest/clean up for rounds/continue the card school/have a fag or anything else not listed.

In the dining room was a speaker for the SRE – Ship's Radio Equipment. The SRE usually played World Service, local radio, tapes from home radio or records (*The Navy Lark* was always a good bet) on the ancient 'deck' in the SRE office. We used to be able to take our own LPs in there and knock out a show for a couple of hours. The dining room SRE, however, could be a bone of contention, especially for George. If there was something playing which he took exception to, or if he judged it to be playing too loudly, he would go to the SRE and turn it off, saying 'This is a dining hall, not a fucking disco. If you want to dance fuck off to your mess and do it there – I want to eat', and go back to his meal, defying anyone to turn it back on again. And woe betide anyone who did! Of course, we (George and me) knew he was only winding everyone up, but no one had the nerve to turn it back on until he left the area!

All our meals were planned in advance, and promulgated outside the galley. We always knew when the best food was going to be there and got in the queue. Navy shorthand decreed that RB+Y/P was roast beef with Yorkshire pudding – you get the idea, so we would know whether to eat on board or get ashore early for a pork pie, with a chinky later.

The meals were organized by the ship's caterer, normally an overweight Chief PO, never anything less than a PO. He would sit in his office discussing the menu with the CPO or PO Chef, and would then have to ensure the food was fresh and available for us to scoff at scran time. One of the 'high points' of eating Navy food at sea, after several weeks without fresh supplies, was that we would fall back on tinned junk, such as powdered potatoes known as 'pom' – disgusting. Warned with that, you'd know the next few meals could be tinned veg, tinned meat, powdered egg, everything 'out of a tin'. Bread would be non-existent, so a chef would have to be on duty all night baking fresh for us. The tantalizing smell would permeate the whole ship, especially the gloom room, where we would be the first ones there to congratulate him, 'brilliant bread chef – any chance of a couple of rolls with a bit of bacon in. We'll wet the coffee, see you in the Ops Room in, wot, ten minutes?' We'd also by then have run out of fresh milk (unless someone was careful enough to freeze some), which meant we had to make do with 'metal cow'.

We'd get stews (potmesses) and unidentifiable mismashes, just to ensure we used up the old food to save having to ditch it when we got back. Other delights created for supper, to clear the food supplies, were 'trainsmash' – a mixture of tinned tomatoes, cheese and eggs, 'babies' heads' – individual steak-and-kidney puddings out of a tin, 'cheesyhammyeggy' – egg on cheese on ham on toast (still something I'll eat at the drop of a hat) and 'shit on a raft' – kidneys on toast.

There are many offices aboard Navy ships, from where scribes sit (doing very little), to the regulating office (where the cementheads used to read QRs and AIs – Queen's Regulations and Admiralty Instructions – all day, contemplating who to pick on next), the radio office (where the flagwaggers sat playing with themselves) and other special offices for various heads of department. You could always get five or ten minutes in an 'office', apparently disappearing off the face of the earth. Eventually, you'd get 'piped' to wherever you were supposed to be, in which case you'd already have an excuse for your boss. Your excuse would be 'Well, I went down to stores, for a new pair of bats, but he wasn't there. I was just on my way back, when you piped me.' Another 'JUST' rating.

We spent weeks attached to Middle Slip Jetty in Portsmouth, and being summer, we would turn to on the upper deck, keeping a watchful eye out for the 'belles' sailing past, packed to the gunwales with grockles touring the dockyard. 'See the ships' the sign would proclaim, 'Sail on the Southsea Belle', and there they were. The game then was to jump up and down, waving frantically at the grockles, screaming 'If you got a bit last night – wave', knowing they couldn't hear you above the din of their engines and the constant cackling of their tour guide. They would inevitably wave back, at which point we'd wet ourselves with laughter – it had worked again! The grockles went away happy – if only they knew.

We used to enjoy ourselves though, apart from going ashore every available night. We had a mixed mess, with all ABs and LSs in. We got on well, we could predict who would say or do what next, and several of our games involved catching people off-guard. One way was to wet the tip of our forefinger, creep up behind someone not paying too much attention, then ram it into his earhole. This would crack everyone else up, except for the poor sod who now had an ear full of someone else's spit. The other was to wait until someone sat down, then drop on his lap and fart loudly. This also used to guarantee crack-up, unless you were the one being sat on. When we wore shorts, we'd sneak up behind someone, grab a handful of leg hairs, yank hard and run off with them. The pain from that is worth smacking somebody for.

I was drafted into the 'Tartar Rifles', otherwise known as the Internal Security (IS) platoon. This was to back up our detachment of booties. We went to Whale Island daily for a week, relearning how to strip, re-assemble and fire SLRs – and how to do this in the dark, by touch. We were also trained how to prevent natives from furthering their proposed riots. This was achieved by marching up and down Whale Island, waving rifles in a threatening manner. We fired on the ranges, 'shotgun style' (open sights) at night, then got acquainted with SMGs' bootie style (at anything, anywhere, as long as everyone else was behind you), then finished off firing GPMGs (General Purpose Machine Gun).

Following this we went to another base to practise riot control. This involved several dozen ratings from this trainee stokers' base pretending to be yobbos, with our IS platoon task being to control them. We did, but not before it got out of hand and our baby gunner (deputy gunnery officer) tried to stop a house brick with his chin. The brick was deliberately thrown at him, we knew that, as all the other bricks thrown were made from heavy sponge. Obviously Guns came off second best, bringing the proceedings to an abrupt pause. We did get our own back on the little moron who threw it. We were taught total self-control, even though we would potentially be surrounded by hundreds, possibly thousands, of irate rioters, and how to run snatch squads. We combined the two, waited for the rerun, bided our time until the right moment and grabbed the brick-chucker. We then gave him a thorough slapping while official eyes were averted. We were told to remember that we would be armed with weapons that would fire a round through a human body. We were shown films of the effect of a round fired from an SLR through a tub of soap (said to be fairly comparable to the human body), and told to remember that while we knew our weapons would be loaded, it would come as a surprise to any rioter when he felt a 'sharp stabbing pain in the right eye, followed instantly by a fucking big hole in the back of his head'. We were told not to aim for legs, that was only in the movies. If you fired, you fired to kill, not to injure – an injured person could still do damage, a dead one could do nothing but lie there. We were also told that by law we had to warn someone running three times to halt before being 'allowed' to open fire. Hence 'STOPSTOPSTOPBANG!!!'

Volunteers were called for to go to Loch Ewe, a remote loch in western Scotland, for a week with the booties. We volunteered. Before we had got out of Hampshire, one of the married men was at it in the train toilet with a lady he had just met. We drank all the way to Waterloo, went to King's Cross, got the overnight sleeper to Inverness, then caught a further train to Achnasheen. We detrained into a coach, which took us through Kinlochewe, up Loch Maree and Gairloch before heading up Loch Ewe through Aultbea and up the coast to where we were to reside for the week – in an old naval base, unused recently, but it had been an anti-submarine or torpedo something or other. To say this place was desolate was a severe understatement. Fortunately, we had taken some sensible precautions, such as bringing vast quantities of beer and whisky. This, however, was not really necessary as there were crates of the stuff already there for us to quench our thirst.

We also noticed that where we were staying was only a short bacteria flight away from Gruinard Island. Anthrax had been tried there many years before, rendering the entire sheep population dead, and preventing life of any sort on the island for many years afterwards. We sniffed the air very cautiously after we found out about that.

We soon found the short cut back to Aultbea – a 7-mile walk back down the road we'd just arrived on. We weren't prepared for the next morning – the booties dragged each of us out of our pits, throwing us into that nasty, cold loch. All this before breakfast. I should point out that if the marine was told to jump off the ship as it sailed, he would, such was his belief in 'The Corps'. It did though let them in for stick – we'd tease them with remarks like 'Royal Marines, running round the world – GO. What kept you laddie', or 'Royal Marines, jumping in the air GO. Who told you to come down'. It never failed to get a bite. Mind you, they got their own back with this throwing into the loch business.

We spent several relaxing(!) days there, swimming, crossing the loch to the island, exploring everywhere, walking steadily to Aultbea, and unsteadily back, after hunting for cockles on the beach while waiting for the pub to open. The booties then decided to go yomping up An Teallach – a 3,000 ft mountain – and what's more, they expected us to go with them. We got back into the coach, drove to the base of the mountain and camped out with the survival rations etc. Next morning we tried it, but with our sailor senses dulled by weeks of inactivity (and alcohol) we gave up and left it to the booties. We returned to the croft and tickled some trout instead.

We got back to the base, and found we were returning to Pompey next day, so we had one final hoolie there, where I remember Dago Robson clearly calling the wife of the ship's bootie officer a 'Dumb Cluck' because she couldn't understand what he was gibbering about. Luckily for him it came out as that instead of what he really meant to call her. She was actually quite fortunate – Dago normally could only manage a high-pitched whine rather than speech when pissed. We, though, could understand – it was either a waz, a drink or his pit. Dago persistently asked everyone 'How's yer neck, Rabbithead?'

The *Tartar* was recommissioned in January 1974, and was the tenth to bear the name – the first was launched in 1702, and lasted until 1755. The motto was 'Without Fear'. They got that right. We never ran away from anything! Further, the Tartars, led by Genghis Khan, were renowned for their ruthless ferocity and fighting expertise. That would certainly come into play during the commission ahead. We also had our ship's mascot – 'Dago', the three-badged AB, who would dress up as Genghis for each event, such as the CTP, open day or for sailing at Alpha, standing on the bridge roof brandishing sword and shield, and with straggly beard (his own actually).

CHAPTER 21

Another Crack at Portland

During the weeks leading up to Portland, we did the same things as I had done on the *Zulu* – basin trials, compass swing, hurtling up and down the Channel and Solent, staying out overnight, working up Ops Room crews, while the riffraff stayed below out of the way. One weekend, we were sent to live ashore at *Victory*, while the whole ship was defumigated and blitzed against the cockies. We'd see them scuttle away whenever you switched on the dining hall or galley lights, so we knew it was well overdue. Funny, I hadn't seen any on the *Zulu* – must have been that they couldn't survive up North.

We had newer radar than the *Zulu*. We had 993, which was a very uprated 293, and 1006, which was very much better than the 978. But it still didn't stop us reporting 'Nab Tower' in the middle of the Solent. It took us all a while to get used to that one. Any RP who has ever forgotten to take account of the tide will appreciate this gaffe, followed by the derisive laughter from the bridge, and severe tormenting from their colleagues when off-watch. Of course I never did it . . . We would also get the lighthouse off Portland travelling. Mind you, we never reported the Nab to the OOW deliberately to hear him say 'Roger – report'.

Being i/c of the radar watch at steaming stations was great. I learned how to tell the course and speed of a contact on radar by eye without having to work it out on the old mechanical plotting tables (this was a long time before computers assisted the operators), which made me favourite for any exercises we did with other ships, where we had to work out what they were doing and report to them, We would get points for 'near' and massive points for spot on, which I could do within moments of them changing course.

I also got good at playing with the air radar. The day we exercised with a shore base, reporting all air contacts within a 12,000-square-mile area, we did such a good job on the air side that the shore controllers were forced to admit they had never heard such accurate or good reporting. Our boss Lt Johnson was over the moon that day, as were we. I got him a beauty. I would do raid reporting over the radio, to other ships and units. I had to wear a headset to do this, which I would talk into, but as the transmitter switch was on the floor, I had to consciously press it with my foot, which meant leaning forward slightly. I would be talking over the radio pretty much incessantly, reporting the air contacts that we could see to other units without the benefit of 'air' radar, who could therefore not 'see' them. I had to break the 'chat' every few seconds to allow other units to butt in, if necessary. All the time, we would use callsigns to attract the attention of the other units. Occasionally, this 'butt-in' would be a deaf dimwit asking me to rereport something, which I would do. Once Johno was engrossed in my reporting, I 'broke', waited a few seconds, leaned forward as if to transmit, 'called' his callsign, and said 'Are you fucking deaf – I'll tell you this once more, then swim over and smack you one'. The rest of the team cracked up, Johno's headset flew off as he dashed over to me, screaming 'Did you really say that, did you? Did you?' I then confessed I hadn't actually transmitted, at which point he saw the funny side and laughed, with relief. His opposite number was known as 'Golden Bollocks' (Gordon-Lennox), who could also be relied upon to be on the receiving end, if he was in a good mood.

I have to say that while we were on watch, with anything between four and twenty plus people closed up in the plastic palace, we would all talk incessantly about anything or nothing. Most likely, the subject would be what we did on our last run, or how we'd spent the past few days winding someone up, or how we were going to 'fit' someone who was winding us up. The conversations would last for hours and cover all manner or topics, all running from one to another. The best topics were either 'when I get ashore in . . .', or 'my pasha back home . . .', or we would resort to the inevitable black catting. 'When I was on the. . .'.

When we met another Navy ship at sea especially one of our own (we'd normally do this at a prearranged rendezvous time), those in the Ops Room would normally have to hold an exercise of some description. Before closing with them we'd be talking on the VHF radio nets. But before we could do that, we'd have to prove to each other we were who we said we were. How we could possibly be anything else in that particular place, at that exact time I know not. Nevertheless, we'd have to exchange details. We'd normally use our unique international callsigns, but if we felt compromised, we'd use other previously published, coded callsigns. Whatever, when we finally got through, we'd 'authenticate' each other using a numerical code. This entailed asking the other unit(s) to 'authenticate' a two-number/letter code. If he responded with the correct answer, we'd know he was on the level, especially if we'd challenge with 'Authenticate Foxtrot Oscar' (foxtrot oscar being Navy shorthand for 'fuck off'). They'd have no alternative but to authenticate the answer and respond with it. They'd probably then ask us to 'Authenticate Oscar Delta' (oscar delta being the shorthand for OD, ordinary seaman, or just plain prat). It would degenerate from there, us feeding them a long string of code, which they would have no option but to decode into something very, very insulting. Sometimes, we'd then be 'called', demanding 'I to I' that is PRI (Pilot Radar Instructor, senior radar rating on board) to PRI. We'd then pretend to be him anyway and reel off further abuse. Not that we'd deliberately do that to antagonize anyone or to make the matter worse, but when everything finally settled down, we'd all chat like old mates, which we probably were anyway. Every ship's radar crew would know at least one person on another ship, and we'd break the ice and calm the situation down from there.

There were also Falcon Codes, which were used by the ship's warfare officers to exchange insults after particular cock-ups. For example passing 'Falcon Code 12' to the PWO of another ship might merely tell the other guy that you thought that his last choice of manoeuvres/actions was a bit odd. Whereas 'Falcon Code 99' may be translated into 'You are a complete wanker – you should not be allowed into the Ops Room of a rowing boat!'. Falcon Codes, then, were also very helpful for letting off steam.

While at Action Stations one day, we accidentally invented the game 'Catchphrase', although we never progressed it. We would spend the boring hours drawing in fluorescent chinagraph over the 'tables', and making others guess what we were getting at. 'H' (John Aitchison) and I would pit our wits for hours doing that.

The mess we were in was the 'Aft Seamens' Mess' – the whole arse-end of the ship in fact. There were all branches of sailor in there – gunners, Anti-sub, and RPs, and believe it or not we all got on brilliantly. We had a messdeck lawyer, who, if you needed to know anything, would be able to tell you. He could also play a mean hand of poker. We also had this large gun positioned immediately above our heads, which would give us a nice surprise when it was fired. It would also shake all the dust from the deckheads and all the goodies out of all our little, personal hiding places.

Coming from other ships, we all had previous skills and ideas, which meant we could play crib, uckers, nominations, chase the pisser – all sorts. We would sit up for hours playing while Duty watch, despite pleas and threats to 'get your heads down – NOW'. That only encouraged us to post lookouts who would tell us of the forthcoming of the Duty PO on his rounds (whom we could normally negotiate with or bung him a couple of cans to shut up), or the OOD on his, in which case we'd be turned in before he got to us then back out as soon as he'd gone.

The 'Tanky' in charge of the spud locker and other food stores around the ship was in our mess, 'H' again. He had keys to various places, and could be relied upon to provide cheese and pickled-onion snacks while playing these night games. No wonder we kept the air-conditioning on day and night whatever the weather. That and the spare crates of beer we'd hide around the mess for special occasions. We knew every square inch of our own messdeck, and could hide anything, anywhere, knowing it would not under any circumstances be found, not even during the most strenuous search. Handy to know, bearing in mind that Customs would always check us over coming back from foreigns.

The beer boat is zealously guarded. It does not actually exist, but can provide loans and end of commission 'runs'. It works like this – we always paid for our allowed three cans per day, but tradition was that you always paid a penny extra per can, which went into the 'boat'. When there was enough in there, we'd either have a 'free' day or save it for a mess run somewhere special. There was always plenty of dosh in there and this could be used for an informal 'sub' until payday. The catch was you paid it back at 10 per cent interest, which still went back to the kitty, so you all dipped in, in the long run. After a couple of months of paying in, we ran to enough to pay for a stereo cassette deck, amplifier and speakers, which we all had shares in, and would take it in turns to play our own music. Unless whatever was playing really annoyed someone, in which case the aforementioned tape would mysteriously disappear. As a result, those who were the biggest and made the most noise and fuss generally ensured the chosen music was either Led Zeppelin or Pink Floyd.

One night, when me and George were Duty watch, we were detailed as Duty hands, meaning if anything wanted doing we were on call immediately, usually to tighten (or more likely loosen) ropes or springs, or even put more out. After all, 'Windies Guardship' was there during the hurricane season, so if it 'blew up' at all, the Duty hands would be up in the middle of the night to put out the hurricane hawsers, just in case the other twelve ropes and wires securing us to the jetty broke. This night, we were actually piped to the gangway after pipedown. A rare occurrence indeed, as sometimes Duty hands were allowed to kip all night. Or do I mean that no pipes were ever made after pipedown unless it was a real panic job. We dressed hurriedly and mustered at the gangway, where we were told a stoker had come back on board drunk and had decided to hang himself. He had gone for'ard to the Buffer's store for the rope. Being a dipshit stoker, and not knowing the difference, he had selected 'ginger-string' to do the job, had strung it, tied it and jumped. Ginger-string is not very strong. In fact, it should be called thick, coloured cotton because it is that weak. The stoker had tried again, with the same result. Without further ado, me and George (both well in excess of 6 ft) found him, wrestled him gently to the deck and wrapped him in a Robinson's stretcher. This is a bamboo and leather affair designed to immobilize critically injured patients for airlift, but doubled as a straightjacket. The clanky took exception to this and told us so. Unfortunately, me and George took on a sudden hearing disability and quickly got the better of him. We did not make it easy for him. We then manhandled him through the ship, taking care not to drop him too frequently, nor did we make his head collide with the ship's bulkheads. We were then instructed to put him in the empty hangar to await the Duty MO. We threw him tenderly to the deck and exited the hangar. We walked back through the mortar well to the gangway – all of 10 yds. By the time we got there, the clanky had shed the stretcher and was coming at us. I seem to remember him trying to damage George's fist with his chin, and dropping to deck level for at least the third time in ten minutes. We restretchered him, a bit more securely this time, and he was transported in the back of the Duty ambulance to the nearby barracks at *Victory*. He earned himself several weeks in the holiday camp in the naval base for that little escapade.

On one of my frequent trips to *Dryad*, probably while P7R (sick enough to go shore based for a while), I had met a chap called Taff Moorson. He came from Hereford, where the heifers come from, so whenever he entered the club at *Dryad*, I'd bellow 'MMMOOOOrson', and he'd reply with something unrepeatable. While at Portland one weekend, I met him ashore, following which he 'came round' for a few beers and decided I ought to go back to his ship. Coincidentally, while doing the customary weekly war/exercises, we had been 'attacked' by FPBs based in Portland. These fast patrol boats would hide in coves along the coast, then fly out at us at a great rate, lock on with their radar, pretend to throw a few missiles or torpedoes at us then retreat.

It was therefore a great pleasure to get the call round returned by Moorson when I found out he was the Buffer on the *Cutlass*, one of the three FPBs that had attacked us. We had lots to drink and suddenly we were putting to sea. We slipped, and proceeded at a leisurely pace, within the confines of the breakwater. Everyone I looked at had the same vacant, apparently alcohol-induced stare as me – officers, the lot. Before too long this leisurely pace was deemed boring, so the speed was wound up. To flat out. That made it somewhere in excess of 45 knots, as the boats were only fitted with two of the three engines it should have had. Peculiarly, the speed of that thing cornering made it lean into the turn, rather than the outward fling all other vessels had. So, after crossing from one end of the breakwater to the other in a matter of moments, and having seen and felt this beast pirouette around on its own length, that too was getting boring. The smoke generators were set off. There we are, now, charging round Portland harbour with an ever-increasing lump of vile-smelling smoke growing from our arse end. Totally unforgettable!

As a member of the Tartar Rifles, we would this time be involved in the 'attempted takeover of Portlandia by insurgents', which then meant spending all day and most of the night with the booties and ourselves lurking around, setting up roadblocks and traps, looking for people hiding in the bushes. At which point we would give them a kicking and take them back to our base. As these 'baddies' were 'junior leaders' which we took to be junior NCOs from various Army regiments, we took it as points of honour to catch these people. We set flare traps etc. to find them. One night, we found two in civvies, a male and a female. They swore blind they were not 'the enemy', but we knew they'd deny anything like that. We gave them the smacking the head routine, then the body searches, then marched them at gunpoint back to base, where they were interrogated until they explained they were both on the hill for one reason, which had nothing to do with anything we were doing. We checked – they were right! We let them go, and red-faced they ran like hell back to HMS *Osprey*.

We also did live rifle and SMG firing at empty lube-oil drums thrown over the arse end. We shot them until they sank. If all else failed, the booties produced an anti-tank weapon (known as a 'Charlie Gustav'), which was as noisy as our own 4.5s. If we missed they didn't, and made the oil drums disintegrate. We'd also tie several drums together into a raft, strap a mast to it, and shoot the shit out of that too, not only with the above weapons, but also with Light Machine Guns, GPMG's, 9-mm pistols, shotguns, in fact anything we could lay our hands on which fired bullets!

CHAPTER 22

The Windies

It would be difficult to describe the feelings of the crew on 3 October 1974, as we finally left Portsmouth for the promised tour of the West Indies. Once more, they were mixed – sadness for the marrieds and courtings and absolute elation from us singles, on the way to a six-month holiday.

We sailed to the Azores and spent several hours refuelling at St Miguel, before lurking out into the Atlantic and straight into an electric storm with sheet lightning. I'd never seen one before, and spent hours on the darkened bridge watching. We then spent several weeks in Defence Watches, six hours on – six hours off. After some days, you get used to it, after a week, you start hallucinating, waking up wondering whether you should be on watch. Or if you have dropped off while on watch. After ten days, you start dreaming that you are on watch. You just go to ratshit after that, getting totally disorientated. While you are off-watch, you have to clean up the messdecks. The only thing you knew for sure was – if you were asleep – someone would shake you to tell you it was time to go on watch, and if you were on watch, the only thing that mattered was that your relief was on time and not under any circumstances adrift. Even by a matter of seconds. Whether you were going on or coming off, food was always available. Just to break the monotony, we'd try to get some fresh air, but generally we only wanted to shower then get our heads down coming off, and eat going on. Occasionally, as a bonus, we'd be stood down while on watch, meaning we could grab an extra hour (or more) sleep. More frequently, you ended up doing the RAS half asleep.

All naval personnel are put into 'watches', either port or starboard. These are broken into two – 'first part' and 'second part', creating four watches in all. This also gives Duty watches, taking place on a one-in-four basis while alongside, and every fourth watch while at sea. Thus, during normal sea watches, you'd 'do' every fourth watch, or two watches a day. The naval day is broken into watches. The first watch in any twenty-four-hour period – the Middle lasts from 2359 to 0400. Morning which lasts from 0400 until 0800. The Forenoon, which lasts from 0800 until 1200, while the

Afternoon, which goes from 1200 until 1600. Then it gets confusing: the First Dog is 1600 until 1800, the Last Dog from 1800 until 2000. Finally, the First takes you from 2000 until 2359. That makes seven watches in a day, which you rotate round over a four day period. This gives you, say the Forenoon, then the First. This is clearly a good set of watches, as not only does it get you out of turning to for the Forenoon, it also makes you miss the movie or the tombollocks or the party in the mess. Following the First, you'd get the Afternoon, again good, as it meant you knocked off working at 1130, and went to lunch at that time, meaning you got first divvies on anything good going, followed by a relaxing afternoon on watch. The drawback was your next watch – the dreaded Middle. This meant that whatever time you went to bed, you couldn't sleep, and even if you did you'd be rudely awoken at 2345, ready to be closed up by 2359. There you'd be, awake all night, drinking coffee, troughing vast amounts of nutty and stolen food, smoking yourself silly, then wonder why it was that when you went off at 0400 you couldn't sleep. You'd lie tossing and turning until Call the Hands went at 0700, at which point you'd be up and around again, totally shattered. You'd turn to for the Forenoon, then get a make and mend in the afternoon, which is traditional. After you've done the Middle, you get an m&m, normally time to get some sleep after lunch, if you can. There are several problems with this. First, you go off so deeply, you don't hear a thing, and when you get the 'shake' for the First Dog, you tend to go back off again. Or you can't get to sleep at all, due to your mates yapping on the other side of the screens. Or some bastard decides to have a big RAS, or worse – flying stations – in which case, you're required for Specials. Then you have to do the First Dog, after which you get what's left after everyone else has had supper. After that – you do the Morning – getting up at 0345. The snag here is that you slept so deeply during your m&m, you can't get off later on, so again you toss and turn until you get your shake. Doing the Morning is easy – bacon rolls, coffee, watching the sunrise, seeing all the sleepy people mooching round. Until 0800, breakfast, do 'cooks', turn to at 0900, generally after snatching 40 winks. The next one would be everyone's favourite – Last Dog and all night in. Total luxury! Get to watch the film, get 9-o-clockers, get a few cans and relax for the evening. What we would normally do, was switch Dogs, so after the m&m, you'd do the Last Dog giving you two extra hours kip. Then, finally, back to the Forenoon. Fortunately, if anyone generally wanted to do anything silly, like the RAS, it would normally be during the Forenoon.

The watch system, then, ensured a fair deal among us sailors. We would eagerly anticipate the Last Dog/all night in, but dread the Middle. Again, OK for us RPs in the warm, plenty of vittles, but for the upper deck sailors having to do lookout, it could get a bit beyond a joke. Remember the maxim I mentioned at the very start of this book? After a thirty minute stint on the bridge wing, at the top of Iceland, in a force nine, you would remember that. You could also tell who had what watch, by the tiredness on his face. It took a long time for us to get rumbled, but there were at least eight '2s' (RP2s, the same radar grade as me)on the RatRat, and we took one watch per day and a bit, meaning the only time to worry was after the hey-diddle-diddle, but we'd cover for each other then.

While alongside, it was traditional for the Duty watch (obviously they were the only ones left aboard) to clean the ship up for 'rounds' every night at 1930. While at sea, it would be Afternoon watchmen who did this chore. Each evening at 1930, the pipe would be 'Men under nourishment and stoppage of cheese and custard. Stand by for rounds' – it should have really been 'Men under punishment and stoppage of leave to muster – Stand by for rounds'. At this point, all the naughty boys who were not allowed ashore had to muster outside the Joss's office, to make sure they hadn't slid off anywhere, though it wouldn't have been the first time a MUP had got changed and slithered over the headrope for a few hours ashore.

It was also difficult to refuse to 'stand in' for an oppo, when you knew he was Duty and wanted to get ashore and you weren't Duty but didn't want to go ashore. So we'd frequently swap duties, either the full biz, or do a stand-in after rounds so you didn't have to clean up. The further proviso was that the one who now went ashore, should return with big-eats for the one left behind. We'd also swap weekend duties, giving us three-day Duty weekends, ready to swap for three weekends off afterwards.

We made it, into Bermadu (*sic*) – called 'The Island Paradise' – where we tied up at the naval base on Ireland Island, far away from Hamilton. To get there, we ran liberty boats (skippered by yours truly) which were MFVs. The trick was to take it across in daylight, remember the positions of every buoy and light in the area, then try to do it at night by heading for the correct one. Simple really. The easier way though, was to get a taxi right round the island. What we did find was a new disease – 'mopey-rash'. The local island moped hirers would appear on the jetty, urging us to rent a moped for our visit. We would take the mopey to a point on the island, engage in a 'session', then try to drive back to the ship while under the affluence of 'incahol', otherwise known as, 'I'm not as thunk as some drinkle peep, I am'. Generally, this could be achieved fairly safely, however, sailors' balance is in inverse proportion to their level of alcohol consumption and they fall off. This would normally be OK, but while in Hamilton, 'rig' was shorts and T-shirts, and bare skin does not fare well against tarmac. One chap was hospitalized for weeks – he scraped off most of his face and much of one side of his body too. We all laughed at his new appearance when he finally rejoined us, but learned the lesson.

There was much to do on Bermuda, including snorkelling in the clearest sea I had seen, up until then. We found a local hotel that would accept us, and swam daily. Or played footy or rugby against local sides. There was also a bar in the naval base HMS *Malabar*, and, if we were feeling idle, we then would stay there, singing. As the base was a restricted area, we would also play at being Barry Sheene, attempting to scramble on the mopeds we had hired. Not that it did any good – they had no real power. The favourite trick was to return to the ship on the moped, drive like hell down the road, along the jetty, across the jetty, off the jetty, separate from the moped – then swim back to the jetty, climb out and return on board with a big grin. Obviously this did not go down well with the hirers, but they must have been used to it and made some money, or they'd never have been there each time, would they?

What we found was that everyone there wore thin, nylon jackets with zip fronts and a hood built in to the collar. These had Bermuda logos on the breast pocket, and within hours I think everyone on board had one. Mine was white, and went well with the sweatshirt (with Bermuda on) and the Levis and desert boots everyone still wore. We wore the jackets for the next six months, until they fell off our backs and rotted away through too many dhobeys, then bought a new one when we returned.

After a week, we sailed to the West Indies proper, first port of call Tortola, in the Virgin Isles. A very quiet place, I remember it pouring down with rain for most of our visit. We were visited by a photographer, who took pictures of most people who wanted their photographs to appear in the papers back home. Of course, I had mine taken, something that was to change my life forever – it was the first picture of me that my wife saw!

We held (as we frequently did) a party for the local orphanage here, where we dressed as pirates and generally played around, while the kids gorged themselves on sandwiches and jelly. These parties were always very successful and well attended. We would be the first to volunteer to host these events, and I still have a photograph of me at the Tortola party, resplendent in ripped shirt, eyepatch and scars.

While there, a rumour went round that the ship was looking for volunteers for a work party in Antigua, our next stop. The rumour was aimed directly at us by our Ops Room officer as we scanned the ever-turning radar during user-checks, who hinted that there was a major banyan in the wind and that we should get our names down or we'd dip out. Unquestioningly, we ran to the list and registered for it, then ran round all our oppos to get them to register too. We were quickly mustered on the jetty with boots and puttees and SLRs for guard training – for that was what we were also volunteering for. In front of an appreciative local audience, we marched up and down, and presented and shouldered arms – a far cry from the cold, wet parade ground at *Raleigh*! At least the rain here was warm!

We went from there to San Juan, Puerto Rico, where the most memorable part was our entry into harbour. We observed these birds that would fly several hundred feet in the air, fold their wings and crashdive into the sea. We didn't recognize them at first but deduced from the size of their beaks that they were pelicans. A very entertaining 'entrance' for us.

From there we travelled to Antigua, with several days in St Johns, right next to the duty free bar on the jetty, where they sold bottles of Mount Gay (rum) for less than the price of two tins of Coke to mix with it. They sold the ice too, but as it wasn't a pub there were no glasses. I still have the very attractive souvenir one I bought on that first night. When we finally got off the jetty, in the biggest taxi I had ever been in, decorated inside and out with lights, we discovered the locals were very fond of saying 'No big ting', a phrase we picked up quickly, and something that was to also feature later in our tour.

Just before we arrived in Antigua there was a minor earthquake on the island, and we could see the cracks on the jetty. We visited a local school to tear down unsafe masonry in order that it could re-open. But eventually, RatRat sailed, leaving us behind. We picked up our chattels, put them carefully on the police bus and headed across the island to English Harbour, a naval dockyard and fortress dating back to the 1700s. It had been used by Nelson to sort out the French. It was steeped in history, and we took great delight in exploring not only it, but its historic past. The first thing we came across was an old ship's bell, incredibly from a much earlier *Tartar*, what a coincidence! The next thing was the local inn, The Admirals Inn which featured heavily in our itinerary for the week. Then we saw our 'lodgings', the old canvas/clothing store, roofless, but who cared!

We set up camp, sorted our gear out, then one by one slid off to the Admiral. This was populated by Yank tourists, rich ones, most of whom owned the gin palaces moored in the harbour – a different grippo every night. We also met Ethel. She was the manageress of the Admiral, we think, because she lived there. Nothing was too much trouble for Ethel, whether it was yet another round of drinks or food at strange hours. We passed a pleasant first evening there, then back to the store for some sleep. Well, that was the plan – unfortunately, the mosquito population had better ideas. Even we got little sleep for the constant buzzing. Next morning, we discovered the damage – everyone was covered from head to toe in mozzy bites. We really relished the thought of the next night. A strange thing – we only had one electric light in our quarters, which was constantly surrounded by moths and other large, winged things, which we would often refer to as 'flying dogs'. Hopefully, it wasn't those which bit us.

We rose early, drilling up and down the main road of the dockyard, working towards the Independence Day celebrations at the end of the week. So we put effort into it. After some hours, we retired for breakfast, then turned to, either clearing a path through to the fort, or digging out the decaying dock, or whatever else required doing. In exchange we would be brought more breakfast, generally toasted BLT sarnies, and beer. At any hour. At about lunchtime we would secure, change into clean(er) T-shirts and either swim off the back of the lodgings or adjourn to Ethel's. We would then stay until we fancied more food. Or perhaps we would once more tour the museum, wondering at the artefacts linked directly to Admiral Nelson.

This became the pattern for the week, broken by one day, when we crossed to St Johns and rehearsed the route we would march at the head of the procession from the police station to the sports ground. As we marched we were surrounded by Antiguans, all of whom seemed to want to shake our hand. We learned that we were allowed, rather than be shouted at by 'Guns', and we marched virtually all the way with rifles slung, being grinned at, patted, touched and encouraged. Most of the population was due to turn out for this finale, in uniform, as police, scouts, guides, first-aiders – any excuse for what was promising to be a wonderful display.

The bus we used to get around the island was always driven by the same driver, who was good for a laugh, so we entertained him with traditional naval songs there and back, no matter what time we went. By the end of the week, he was word perfect on many of our ruder ditties.

One day, one of the tasks was to clear a tennis court in a property overlooking the harbour. As the quickest way was with PE, we duly planted it, retired to a safe distance, hit the plunger and watched as lumps of concrete sailed gracefully up in the air, described perfect parabolas away from the epicentre, over the harbour, mostly into the waters, spattering the moored gin palaces below. We could only smile sweetly, confess and apologize for that one.

Another day, we were given the use of a powerboat for the afternoon, and we sailed across the harbour for a banyan. We shouted hello at a lady tending her garden, and she asked if we were from the naval party. We confessed, hoping 'concrete' wasn't going to be mentioned. She then asked us in for drinks, and told us she was an ex-WRNS officer. We drank there all afternoon, being waited on hand and foot by her servants.

After secure one afternoon, we went en masse to a nearby beach, complete with carry-outs, and were verbally abused by a Rastafarian living in a den near the roadside, claiming we would all suffer 'hellfire and eternal damnation'. We told him he ought to 'fuck off and mind your own business', then all ran like crazy back to the harbour, and safety. For he chased us with a rather large machete.

We would, of course, continue diligently to do the clearing up we were ostensibly there for. In between the drill every morning and the scratching every night. We found the best protection against mosquito bites was lots and lots of rum – taken internally, mixed with other strong liquor and flavourings. Well it worked for us . . .

By now we were in the habit of marching past the Admiral, at which point we would be instructed '–one–two–three "Good Morning Ethel"' at the absolute tops of our voices. Sometimes, Ethel's head would appear from the window, accompanied by a wan smile and a weary wave.

Towards the end of the week, it had been noted by Guns that I was taking loads of photographs, and after some discussion, I was persuaded to take the official camera, use official film and be the official photographer for the parade and march past. I agreed, but I really would have preferred to be on the parade rather than observing. Nevertheless, I put on my ice-cream suit along with the lads, and attended – snapping away like a maniac until both cameras ran out of films. It was a wonderful atmosphere throughout the whole proceedings.

That final night in English Harbour, while waiting for the *Tartar*, we put together all our remaining BWI (British West Indies) dollars, hired a local reggae/steel band, bought loads of food and booze, then invited all those people who had been so kind to us during our time there to attend. I have to admit the turnout was not what we had anticipated – we had expected a few, but word got out, and we subsequently couldn't move in our digs for bodies! Everyone, apparently, had a good time, and it was with great sadness we shouted our final 'Good Morning' to Ethel as we made our final journey in the dilapidated coach back to St Johns.

Next stop was Chaguaramus in Northern Trinidad for a mini refit. We did this in a civilian dockyard, moored opposite a large floating dock, in which ships were bottom-scraped before being repainted. This was done at such a furious rate, it seemed a new ship went through every other day (or two), and the noise was literally deafening as they did the scraping with shot-blasters throughout day and night.

Across the bay from the jetty was one of the very few beaches boasted by Trinidad, with the inevitable bar. We would either launch the canoe, and paddle that across, or we would dive off the ship, swim across the bay, dry off and drink, then walk back to the ship. Or we'd walk round to keep our dollars dry.

The canoe was the ship's, bought by the welfare committee. It was lashed under the seaboat, for most of its career, and anyone could use it. It came to pass that George and I took a liking to using it as a taxi between us and this bar, and we discovered the fastest way to achieve our objective was to carefully drop the canoe straight over the side, chuck the paddles in the sea, then jump in after it all. This meant we got wet, but BWI dollars were always acceptable wet or dry. Once in the oggin, we'd mount the canoe from the rear, slide up until one was in, then the other would follow. We'd recover the paddles, and hurtle across the bay to the bar . . . but I can't remember how we ever got it back, due to the absorption of too much beer and Mount Gay.

One afternoon, I started swimming around off the beach, complete with obligatory mask, snorkel and speargun, looking down, as you do, when something moved underneath me. It looked like eyes, but on investigation, it had a long tail, and was, in fact, a very, very large ray of some description. There is a scene in *Jaws* where the bathers burst from the sea in panic. I walked across the waves to get out, followed by the population of Trinidad. I'm sure the ray was scared to death by all this, but it was a while before anyone plucked up courage and went back in to see if it had gone away.

We also had a weekend banyan, taking the whaler several miles around the coast to a bay, setting up camp, then realizing we had loads of Mount Gay, but no mixers. Seawater isn't really recommended, but 'Carib' (the local gorgeous beer) boilermakers are. We spent a strange weekend there, as one of the first things I did was stub and break a toe. I hobbled everywhere for weeks afterwards. Potentially more rewarding, though, was being offered several thousand dollars by one of the locals for the whaler, (I was the co'x'n). But could only wonder what my excuse would be for losing it, bearing in mind that wherever I would need to lose it, the ship's divers would eventually go and take a look for it, with an official view to getting it back. With this in mind, but after much thought, I declined his offer.

In this tiny bay we were surrounded by the island's rich, who would 'powerboat' to this bay each weekend for recreation. Even though it was heavily populated by barracuda, which we drunkenly chased with our spearguns, we swam enthusiastically in the sea. We also heard strange noises, later identified as being local monkeys, and observed flashing lights in the evening, which had us wondering at the Mount Gay, until we realised it was fireflies! With them and the hummingbirds the place was full of wildlife.

One fine day, George and I went into town, and had our photographs taken in the passport office. We had dozens of copies made, which we collected some days later. We then placed an ad in *Melody Maker* for young ladies to write to bored sailors. We had thousands of replies, and ended up dishing them out by area to nearly all the unattached – and to some of the attached – ratings on board. This passed several hours, and resulted in me replying to one of the correspondents, who later became my wife after we had exchanged many, many letters and photographs.

We found a Seaman's Mission too, one that did real chips and proper cheese (not Spanish) omelettes, which we would eat while watching *Sesame Street*. The favoured local food in Trinidad, though, was Hot Roti, which was made from something we were never able to identify, but didn't taste like anything we knew. It was meaty, very hot, and went down well after a night out. As did the local chicken, cooked on street corners or in the small shops, which seemed to be open at all times of day and night. There was also goat curry, freely available, if you felt brave enough.

However, there was a drawback, the following days would prove that if the bottom hadn't fallen out of your world, the world would certainly fall out of your bottom.

We sailed from Trinidad to Tobago, and from there we sailed for Barbados for Christmas. I had never spent a Christmas away from home before, and never expected in my wildest dreams that I would ever go to Barbados. It was amazing to combine these two new experiences in one.

After attempting to water-ski off the back of our Dory in Tobago, I decided I didn't want to do that any more, so I aqualung-ed off the beach and was attracted by the conch shells littering the sandy sea bottom. I thought one would be nice as a souvenir. I dived down and picked up the conch, and as I did so, several thin, black fingers emerged from the open end, grabbing my fingers. I almost dumped in my trunks. I dropped the shell, instantly. However, I was not going to be put off that easily, and eventually the hermit crab in residence was forced to swim off to fight for another home. I still have that conch shell, and smile whenever I remember the surprise I got.

We moored opposite a cruise ship, put the Christmas tree on the top of the 965, then got away on two days' station leave. We headed into town, and once past there, we started knocking on hotel doors to see if they had room. We, was George and me. We felt like Joseph and Mary, but ended up in a self-catering apartment overlooking the swimming pool, the beach and the sea. We stocked up with some food, but didn't expect to eat it. We also laid on booze then invited the rest of the mess round for a party. We ate soft-boiled eggs and soldiers, washed down with Bacardi and Coke. The next day, we ventured as far as the pool, climbing out only to relieve ourselves. The pool, you see, had a bar in it, which you swam round while clutching your banana daiquiri.

We returned on Christmas Eve, and rose bright and early Christmas Day. The day started slowly, with breakfast, decorating the mess, then prezzy opening, lunch (served by the wardroom) and all kinds of abnormal, traditional naval things. It was a really excellent day. Oh yes, and there were extra beer rations, as well as the extra rum and Bacardi, which somehow appeared, having previously been carefully smuggled aboard. Another thing I remember is that whenever I was away from home, either for a birthday or at Christmas, I always received a huge fruit cake from Mum and Dad in Northampton, in a tin, nice and fresh, which we would all tuck in to.

At that time, there was a new item of wear, called a personalized T-shirt. Barbados sold them, and you could have anything you wanted printed on it, provided a) it was available and b) it wasn't offensive. I wore mine, with a cartoon dog, emblazoned with 'Whacker' on the front (my official Navy name – all 'Paynes' were called that), until it rotted away. Then I bought a new one. There was also a market inside the Customs House at the top of the harbour where we brought some terrific rabbits. However, we soon sailed from there, and that was the first stop we had made where it hadn't rained.

A ship's magazine is normally issued once or twice in a deployment. It contains information about the cruise, dates, events and some light reading. A 'letter home' published in it summed up one person's feelings:

My Dearest Flower

I thought you might like to hear how I was getting on, as it has been three months since I left. I hope you are not still waiting at Southsea to see us leave, as we slipped out at night. The Skipper said it made it easier for some of the officers that way.

We've been to some rotten places – Bermuda, San Juan, Tortola, Antigua and Trinidad. I hardly ever go ashore, as they are all so different to Pompey. They are all full of half-built houses, and everyone moves very slowly – except for the one who stole my wallet. And the taxi driver who almost ran me over. I tried to stop the thief, but one of my shoes had earlier gone through a window when I kicked a fag packet. Pity, they were your brother's shoes, the ones I borrowed to get married in. Anyway, it was difficult to run in just one platform shoe, and I lost all my money.

In Tortola, the Governor asked me up for a cocktail party. He was very nice, and I think his wife liked the joke about the male parrot with no legs holding on to his perch. Perhaps I shouldn't have told her in front of the Commodore, as I got a job change next day – I am now 'captain of the heads'. All of them.

My messmates are OK, but they go ashore too much for my liking, and come back smelling of rum. I prefer to stay on board and save up to buy you a present, and also to pay the repair bill to Mr Mopedman in Bermuda. The jetty there was very narrow, and it was difficult to decide what to do when it started to skid like that.

Your letters are a great comfort, but please resend number 53 (which didn't arrive), as my messmates want to know what happened to the daughter of the old witch at number 8.

I may not have time to write again before we get back on the 3rd of April, as we have to work very hard, however do not worry too much, as the Master-at-Arms says he is taking a personal interest in my welfare. Please imagine your Christmas Present this year – it is a diamond ring. Yours, Everloving,

Bill Barnacle.

. . . although I'm not sure he was being totally truthful.

We exercised frequently off Puerto Rico, doing gunnery shoots, and arrived in Roosevelt Roads, a rather large US naval base. We moored opposite our sister ship – the *Eskimo*, which had been there a couple of days. We either called round, or were called round for beers and to swap stories. We queried the unusual number of facial and other injuries they appeared to have sustained, and were told how they'd been to the PX the previous evening, but had been physically attacked by the resident non-white USN population. We were told even the rest of the USN (white) guys backed off, including even the shore patrol.

We went ashore that night – two ships' companies worth of liberty men, in several coaches, to investigate. We travelled in coaches because it was a very long way to walk. When we arrived at the PX (US forces Naafi stands for 'part exchange'), we started to chat to both the (white) US servicemen and *Eskimo*s there, and exchanged beers and pleasantries. Apart from the fact that one of our oppos was dancing with his bird, a large, different-coloured guy started verbally to abuse our mate, which was just what we had been waiting for. The result was like the Clint Eastwood *Dirty Harry* film, where everyone in the bar exploded into a fight, with the inevitable glasses being thrown, chairs being smashed on people and tables collapsing. In all, really good fun and just what we needed to let off some of the steam which had built up while we were at sea. After several minutes, the Yank shore patrol, accompanied by our own Duty SP, moved in, but stayed on the edge, not really wishing to get involved. While we were on top and to prevent further injuries to the locals, the SP moved in, arrested and carted off all the trouble-makers, escorted all of us back to our bus, grinned and 'disapprovingly' wagged their fingers and sent us back to the ships. The fight was never mentioned, and there was no more trouble any other time we ever went there.

In justification, there is an RN pecking order. At the bottom of the pile were waffoos of any description. Above them came middies, then tiffies, then pigs, then S&S (pen-pushers, stewards etc.). These were followed by greenies, then stokers, then flagwaggers, then us seamen. And among seamen: gunners, then 'TAS' and finally us RPs. So we looked down on every other branch. There was always considerable further rivalry between the various branches, and we would slag each other off, sometimes, going to Action Stations (fighting) to prove the point. This rivalry was only exceeded by inter-ship rivalry, where we would defend the honour of our ship and, therefore, our shipmates, no matter whether they were waffoos, stewards or whatever. This in turn would be elevated to inter-squadron fights, which were exceeded by inter-service spats. The only thing over this was that we'd have even fought with or alongside the crabs and the pongos against the services of other nations. Which was what happened here with the 'Mo' (*Eskimo*). There was only us very proud sailors to represent our nation – so we did!

To explain something else – all Pusser's ships are put into squadrons. Each ship's captain would normally be a commander, but the deputy squadron leader, and squadron leader would be skippered by a Captain, although they might carry a vice-admiral. There were many of these squadrons, and while we would all mostly act independently, occasionally we would muster as the squadron or part of. Then the squadron pecking order ran in terms of seniority of your skipper. It followed that the junior skipper therefore meant his ship was the gash-boat of the squadron, and had to 'pipe' first. The boss, known as 'Daddy-D', would have a large stripe painted round his funnel, so everyone knew he was more important than the other ships in his company. There would then be a mix of frigates – general purpose, anti-air, anti-sub – to form an effective mix of ships and skills. And whenever we met Daddy-D, if he was showing the black ring and flying the spotty flag, it meant only one thing – rounds, and a pep-talk. Oh lucky us!

We left Puerto Rico and mooched round the islands, looking for drug smugglers, gun runners or whatever. En route we stopped at Mustique one afternoon, where we were given permission to hold a banyan on the beach. We duly landed the whaler, full of sailors, beer and barbecue, and held an impromptu party, at which several personalities attended. One in particular (I hope that one day he reads this and remembers it, I have always held two grudges against him) was sitting on the jetty reading a book. We went across to him, and started talking to quite the most unresponsive person I have ever met, even for a 'major rock star'. When he did manage to grunt in response to a question, we got bored, decided to buy our own beer, said 'No big ting', and started to walk off. He asked 'What was that?'. Again, we said 'No big ting – it doesn't really matter'. And walked off. He refused to buy us a beer, first grudge, and then had the brass neck to release a record later on with a catchphrase that sounded suspiciously like our favourite saying – second grudge.

We were given the run of the beach and met other more famous people there, people who did talk to us. I went for a sailboard ride, fell off, and pierced my foot with sea-egg spines. You really, really know they're there when the sharp spines penetrate your skin to release poison that hurts like hell. One of the famous people, a model at that time, explained what to do to 'relieve' the pain, which I did, literally, behind a bush. The pain went almost immediately, although the spines can still be seen in my toe.

During our West Indian travails, there used to be a large gang, comprising me, George, Fart, Twizz, Eddie, Dick, Blackie and Dago, to name but a few, who'd always be ashore together. This would be handy if we got into trouble, and was more convenient for looking after the fallers down. It guaranteed we'd all get back safely. However, when getting brown on the nearest beach, it meant we could organize spontaneous sports events. Like volleyball. We'd play that with string stretched between trees. More than likely, we'd end up with tourists joining in, or playing against us. These games could last hours, until we got too dry or we became distracted by something else. Or we'd go into 'pyramid mode' – eight or nine in an inward facing circle for the base, five or six for the next level, three for the next, with the drunkest climbing to the top. More often than not we'd collapse before we got anyone to the top. Occasionally we'd do it, which would spark bigger and larger pyramids from the beach competition. Of course, we'd have this well practised and could do it easily when we had to. We would also make pyramids with all the beer cans we drained.

We also visited Martinique and looked at a volcano, we went to St Kitts where we drank our way through the drinks menu, including Yellow Bird, Coco Punch, Zombie and Liamuiga Cocktail – brilliant colours, superb tastes and no effect whatsoever the first time round the menu. So, we went through it again, then tried to walk back to the ship through and round the many sugar-cane fields. We forgot that the ship was moored in water so clear you could look over the side and see the bottom and that we had to catch the whaler back. Unfortunately, bad weather struck, and the RatRat had sailed without us in order to lay off safely. This meant we spent a night sleeping on the floor of a prison cell in the local police station, until we were roused the following morning by the ship's siren. Blearily we climbed aboard the whaler and returned, sailing without further ado.

It is hard describing what you feel when you try to return to the ship, only to find it isn't where you left it . . . Talking of 'Yellow Birds', it was, and probably still is, traditional, that if you were Windies Guardship, you had a large metal Yellow Bird bolted firmly to the funnel. This proclaimed your duty and was a constant source of questioning wherever the ship tied up. Many people tried to nick it, but, as far as I am aware, nobody ever managed to get it.

CHAPTER 23

The Royal Yacht

We stopped at Freeport, in the Bahamas, which is possibly the most gleamingly clean place we ever saw, then went on to Nassau, where we were forcibly ejected from the Sheraton for performing in their pool. Well, to be truthful, it was more for trying to create a pool to swim in – on the first floor of the hotel . . . with fire extinguishers. That and switching the 'Do Not Disturb' signs and 'cherry knocking' doors at two in the morning.

As usual, we parked opposite a cruise liner, but when this slipped away, it was replaced by HMY *Britannia*. Shortly after she arrived, she too was cleaned and burnished, from stem to stern, and within hours, throngs of locals began to gather on the jetty. Soon, the black car arrived and out sprang HM The Queen. We were now not only Windies Guardship but also Royal Guardship, and we were very proud to escort the yacht for the next few weeks. We were told what to do and more importantly what not to do – and also told what the increased punishments would be if we transgressed. It was drummed into us that from the time we picked up the yacht to the time we left, we were not only under close scrutiny 'from others', but under increased scrutiny from on board. We therefore must be extra smart, extra vigilant in our duties and, above all, extra sober.

Before we took over this prestigious duty, we had painted the RatRat from stem to stern, from masthead to waterline, and beyond with waterproof paint (yes, it does exist). We left Nassau after exploring the perfect beaches and buying loads of souvenirs. From there we escorted to Vera Cruz in Mexico. The yacht moored while we held off, but eventually we were signalled to moor well away from her. I was Duty watch that night, and got turned out early evening with a small fire in one of the generators, which was quickly extinguished. There were signals between the two ships, and I paraphrase:

RYB to *Tartar*: You are making black smoke. STOP making black smoke.
Tartar to RYB: Yes – sorry – we have a fire on board.

RYB to *Tartar*: That is all very well, but stop making black smoke.
Exit exasperated *Tartar* OOW.

Vera Cruz is classed as the gateway to Mexico, and when we arrived there was such a large crowd that the police arrived to disperse it. And they really do have Tijuana brass bands – everywhere. It seemed that all you had to do was order a drink, and they would break into tune. Either that, or the shoe-shine boys would appear. One chap had his shoes buffed to a brilliant shine – the best they'd ever seen, costing many pesos. It was only when he sobered up in the morning, that he remembered they were originally suede shoes.

I will state here, that while we always drank ourselves silly ashore, anywhere, as soon as we sailed, we turned into absolute professionals and would not touch any alcohol again until we reached the next port of call. Many sailors would only drink soft drinks at sea, me included. Unless, of course, it was a special occasion. However, here we discovered Tequila, which gives you a twenty-four to forty-eight-hour guaranteed hangover, which further liquid only exacerbates. We drank 'slammers', which taste disgusting for the first few then gradually improve. You start to dispense with the salt, then the lime, until you are drinking neat tequila. At the time, it is great, but I recall getting up one morning with the mother of all hangovers and falling asleep standing up leaning against the for'ard gun turret.

After several days of this self-inflicted abuse, where we got drunk 'under cover' to keep out of the way, we sailed. We held sea days and visited Cozumel, until the *Britannia* finally went her own way. One of my most prized photographs is of the traditional 'steam past' performed by us, with HM The Queen waving at us, as we cleared lower deck and did 'cheer ship', all in white suits, on an absolutely gleamingly grey – with contrasting highlights, bollards etc. – and gleaming 'Yellow Bird' *Tartar*.

The signal which reached us read: 'Thank you for your escort. I was much impressed by the admirable way in which you carried out your duties, by the smart appearance of your ship and by your steam past on Sunday. I have also heard excellent reports of your highly efficient contribution to the Sea Day. My husband and I send all onboard our best wishes. Elizabeth R.' We were exceedingly proud during that period of time – it really was a memorable honour. We also bought some wonderful rabbits, mostly onyx items, sombreros and ponchos.

Our cruise was rounded off with several days at Fort Lauderdale in Florida, where we ran trips to Disney World. These started at 0300, with a six-hour drive, and we spent the whole day there, queuing for rides, again and again (especially Space Mountain), before meeting Mr Michael Mouse. Of course, we went there in rig, so as to make sure we stood out. We had a brilliant but exhausting trip, buying back-scratchers, ear-hats, giant bears, small bears, sweatshirts and insulated mugs with our own pictures in, which (some of us) kept for years.

We also visited Sea World, and watched nutters wrestle alligators by sticking their (the alligators') heads under their (the keepers') chins. Scary, and potentially painful, especially if the keeper hasn't shaved first. They weren't little alligators either! There was also the shark feeding, though we'd done that before. Other than that, we spent our time in a club/bar called The Button On The Beach, where naturally we also enjoyed ourselves.

We sailed from Lauderdale, called in at Bermuda once more to refuel, then legged it home with all our rabbits. On the way back, after we finally left Bermuda, we conducted a 'Burial At Sea'. A local person had died and had always wanted to be buried at sea, so we sailed and obliged. The coffins are weighted down so they sink immediately, instead of bobbing around taking in water. All very dignified, we stood on the quarterdeck in our (now gleaming after all those washes) white suits as an honour guard.

On returning to the UK, we had steamed 26,736 miles, spent 1,908 hours under way, burning 4,680 tonnes of fuel. We had eaten 70,000 lbs of spuds, 4,030 lbs of sausages, enough to reach 2½ miles, 60,000 eggs, 7,616 lbs of sugar, 7,000 lbs of baked beans. We had drunk 60,000 tins of assorted beer, but only 36,000 cans of soft drinks and had bought or been issued with 1,065,000 cigarettes. As much as £750,000 of 'funny money' had been handled. We had seen 91 films, and the Wasp had flown 110½ hours, making 284 landings, flying 9,950 miles, with an estimated 2,685,900 rotor rotations. Not that we cared – we were six months older but had enjoyed new experiences far beyond our tender years. We had visited dozens of ports all round the West Indies, and been paid for the privilege, seeing things that most people can never even imagine. However, even after all that, Portsmouth was the same. The train (full of other Jacks going home for the weekend from their barrack jobs at *Vernon*, or *Excellent*, or wherever unaware of our exciting experiences, not caring what we had done) to Waterloo was the same one we'd used last year – still stank of fag smoke, still grubby. And Northampton, my family, my mates? – hadn't changed a bit.

CHAPTER 24

Off Fishing, but Not as You Know It

After a mini refit in Pompey, and more well-earned leave, we sailed to Chatham for Navy Days. Now this is an experience, volunteering to show the tourists round. We would offer, and sometimes succeed in getting people to come with us to see the 'Golden Rivet' in the engine room. This rivet is (obviously) made of gold, and is always the last rivet to be placed into any warship. That and the place amidships on Tribals, where the whole ship used to flex as it went through the seas. I can still picture the 'flap' slightly in front of the for'ard funnel, and see it moving while traversing high seas at speed.

The *Tartar* sailed up into the North Sea, into exercises protecting North Sea gas fields and rigs, and during that time we went as far as Scapa Flow. We all knew what had happened there, so when we had a 'first watch party' that night at anchor, we were most careful to not throw our empties overboard. We then traversed the North Sea to Velje in Denmark, and made a trip to Legoland. It was during this trip that I took a very impressive photograph of an oil rig, with flames from the gases being burned off leaping from the top. It made a wonderful photograph, which won me a competition. This was only run by the local WI from my home village, and was entered by my Mum, but it was nevertheless a terrific photograph.

It was announced there would be a wild-dog shoot when we stopped in the Orkneys, and that volunteers should muster on the quarterdeck for training, after drawing helves and gaiters from the gunners store and bagmeal from the galley. Bagmeals are like picnics, usually comprising a hard-boiled egg, several sandwiches and an apple or an orange. If anyone went to the Chief Supply Accountant (no point in merely going to the Duty chef, it had to be the Chief SA) for a bagmeal, the buzz would fly round that something was afoot. Why else would you need a bagmeal at sea? And the stornophone (radio) from the wireless office? By the time they mustered, we were there to watch and hear the booties read the rules. 'Do not hit the dogs on the head with the helve – it makes them mad. Go for their legs. Marine Gardener will now hide, and pretend to be a dog, he is hiding somewhere on the quarterdeck, and will jump out on you. You have to subdue him.' We stood on top of 'Y' gun to watch, as a young, gormless sailor crept round, looking left and right for the 'dog', fearlessly making threatening gestures with his tightly gripped helve. When Jock jumped out of a hatch at him, he reacted well, trying to down Jock, but as Jock was well over 6 ft 5 in tall, and hideously ugly (but a brilliant geezer) – he stood no chance. Jock chased him round, barking at him – us? – and we wet ourselves enough to nearly fall off the gun turret. By the time the first one caught on he was being wound up, it was time for the next one, fortunately waiting in the wings, not allowed to see his predecessor. We laughed until the tears ran down our trouser legs.

We also had a weekend in Le Havre, and we took the train to Paris, where we spent the day running between the best sights, up the Eiffel tower and the Arc De Triomphe etc., before getting the train back.

At one point, the ship sailed 'round the coast', exercised off Cape Wrath, crossed the top of Scotland, cruised through and stopped at several west-coast islands, including Tobermory, then at Douglas (Isle of Man), before a weekend jolly in Liverpool. We were so impressed there, we all took short weekends – straight home, on the first available train out. While off that coast, we found Rockall (which rhymes with what it is . . .) a small, but high rock several hundred miles out into the Atlantic. We located it on radar, and landed the Wasp on it with a flag, reclaiming our sovereignty over it.

We discovered an instant and miraculous cure for acne one fine day. We had G6 which had to be lit by hand allegedly and was prone to flashbacks. One clanky got too close to the flashback, losing his eyebrows and the front hair on his head, as well as several layers of skin from his mush. We took great delight in winding him up about that for weeks afterwards – but it really did get rid of his acne, temporarily at least, until his face grew back again.

At the end of September we were due to sail on Fishery Protection duties around the North coast of Norway. Before we sailed, I invested in a duvet and cover, which, in light of where we were going, proved to be a sound investment. Bearing in mind our mess beneath the quarterdeck was separated from the elements by just fractions of inches of steel, our after mess used to boil in hot climes, but freeze in cold ones. My quilt kept me warm while my mates wrapped themselves in more and more blankets. It also took me seconds to make up my bed daily, rather than the minutes for my oppos. I could therefore lie in bed longer in the mornings, which was the true reason for my buying it.

We sailed and went as far north as Spitzbergen (but didn't stop), and as far east as Murmansk. In between we stopped at Bergen, Tromso and Harstaad. We also called at Hammerfest, the most northerly town you can get to. Norway was beautiful, but expensive. We rounded Bear Island and got our 'Blue Nose' certificates for crossing into the Arctic Circle. It was cold towards the end of the tour, but nothing extreme. We were very fortunate some nights to see the extremely beautiful and fascinating aurora borealis.

In one occasion we sailed down a fjord from somewhere and as we hit the open sea, we were buffeted by severe winds. I was on watch in the gloom room, where we had a wind gauge and a tilt meter. The wind gauge went off the clock in one movement. Immediately, we tilted over and, most alarmingly, kept going and going. In the centre of the gloom room was a chair, a very comfortable one, and very high. It was just high enough to be able to use the PPI radar, and be able to reach various microphones, radar controls etc. Fit for a captain, when he was in the Ops Room. And fit for the i/c of the watch to sit with his feet on the display. So during steaming watches, the i/c of the watch would plant himself in the chair, and not leave it until relieved – perks of the job. As the ship kept tilting, and I swear it went beyond 45°, there was a crack and a crash as the deckbolts holding the chair (and me) parted company, depositing me on the floor. Except that the deck was rapidly becoming the bulkhead as the opposite bulkhead became the deckhead. There were all kinds of crashing noises from all over the ship, until suddenly, we started going upright again. There was untold damage, not to the ship, but to people in bunks who suddenly found themselves on the deck. That was a scary one. We thought we'd lost the top hamper (the air radar) that night – it was rumoured to detach itself if the ship tilted too far, but not that night. We continued past Murmansk and were eventually overflown by a Russian 'Bear' aircraft, which continued to scan us for several hours. We were further east then, than the Middle East.

In extremely rough weather, the ship would occasionally meet 'milestones', which were larger than average waves, met every mile (or so). These would literally shake the ship, and could cause storm damage (as per the *Zulu* on our way to Gib). The *Tartar* was a vicious cow in rough weather, but we found if you went right up in the bows, to the Buffer's store, and connected with a milestone, you would actually go weightless for some seconds as the bows first shot up, then dropped leaving you several feet off the deck. Of course, she would corkscrew at the same time, making it difficult to walk the Burma Road (the main drag below decks on a ship) without ricocheting from bulkhead to deckhead. But when she hit milestones and corkscrewed, that was where the fun would start. All top bunks had bars to stop the occupant from rolling over and out – hence the expression 'over and out', and had straps to tie yourself in. Again, you could set the angle of the bed to form a wedge in which you would attempt to settle and sleep. There also had to be grab handles above the bed on which you would swing yourself upwards and then across to your pit. At least – that was the theory. During one such storm, the LMA was piped to my mess while I was on watch – it transpired that one chap during the corkscrewing, had swung himself up, and was in the middle of the 'over' bit. He let go of the bars, the arse end corkscrewed and dropped, meaning his bed was no longer below where he was heading for. As there was nothing there to break his fall, he dropped straight back to the deck, causing him a painful landing. Hence the LMA's visit. Not that we took the piss, but it was a long time before he lived it down.

When you get out of 'roughers', you feel absolutely physically and mentally drained. While it was rough, you didn't know which way to walk, or which bulkhead to lean against – you just knew you'd get shaken off it. So you were therefore mentally alert trying to pre-empt the roll and work out which way to lean next. You were also performing physically trying to keep balanced. When we found flat sea, it took a long time to get used to having the ship on an even keel. If we went from roughers to alongside it felt worse – the earth really did feel like it was moving.

We returned from that little trip and I went on a Leading Seaman's course, which I passed, and was promoted straight away. Fancy that now, me and Admiral Lord Nelson both reaching the absolute zenith of our naval careers. We'd even been to some of the same places! The course was held in Portsmouth, and involved spending several weeks of looking even smarter than usual, performing seaman-like evolutions, and creating extempore rigs with pieces of wood and plenty of rope, as well as drilling the 'awkward squad' for hours on end, while learning everything there was to know about RASing etc. Oh yes, and Morse code and the 'men, machinery, material' lecture, showing why the best asset the RN had was its men, but that without the machinery or material they were useless, and every type of buoy, lighthouse, flashing light – you name it. I did come top of the board, though, after all that hard work, and gained a City and Guilds certificate for my troubles.

There used to be a pub over the road from the Seamanship School (which wasn't actually within the confines of the Navy base, although it was run from Whale Island), which was in the civilian yard and therefore had civvy sailors loading and unloading various cargoes from coastal steamers scarcely bigger than the whalers we would charge round in to practice man-overboard drills. I don't recall the pub's name, but we went there every lunchtime, illegally in Eights, drank two pints, ate thick ham with mustard, or cheese and onion, sarnies with extremely fresh bread and returned for an afternoon's lectures. It broke the day up. It also meant meeting more new mates, and learning more new expressions, especially from 'Tiddly' Rowe, a CPO there I already knew from *Dryad*, whose favourite insult was 'chimp'. We quickly picked up on that, and everyone we met ashore (and even up to today) was insultingly called 'chimp'. What with him and Mitch, our PO instructor, who actually taught me much more than I ever thought I'd learn in such a short period of time, I enjoyed myself immensely.

CHAPTER 25

Cod Wars

Christmas 1975 was spent at home, after which the Icelanders got all protective about their fishery limits, causing us to set sail to sort them out. At first it wasn't too bad – the Icelandic gunboats kept their distance, and it was all fairly civilized. As control ship, each night we would call all the trawlers by radio, and plot their positions. We built up a rapport with the skippers, and were able to have a chat and a laugh with them, remote from us as they were. It made a change to talk to trawlermen, and to be able to curse and swear with them, as normally we'd have to say only correct, authorized words. Hull trawlermen were the best to talk to – every other word started with 'F'.

Trawlers like the *Farnella* and her sisters, all ending with '–*ella*' – we got to know well, and would be concerned if one failed to answer. Normally, though, another trawler would come up and tell us where the missing boat was – that they'd gone to so and so to follow a shoal. If we got near, the trawlers would radio, offering fresh fish, we'd then have to work out where they were. We could, you see, see dozens of lights in all directions, and we had to be careful not to steam through their nets. They would normally easily guide us straight to them. I was off-watch one night, in the dining hall watching a movie, when the hatch to the upper deck opened, followed by an enormous crash as something fell down the ladder into the dining hall. This turned out to be the largest cod we had ever set eyes on. We had that in the galley PDQ, gutted and chopped into large portions, with chips at a very good price. The money raised was sent to our adopted charity, Chailey Heritage at Littlehampton, which we often visited from Pompey, taking the handicapped kids there out for the day, to the fair or harbour or wherever, or back to the ship for a party. We loved doing it – they thought it was great too.

By now, you may be thinking 'What do booties do on board warships?'. We frequently asked the same question. We knew that even though we trained as IS platoon, if any poo headed for the fans, the booties would be landed first, with us as backup. They did 'Boarding Party', that is, when we cruised the Windies we would frequently assist the US Coastguard in their efforts to stop the smuggling of illegal substances into the USA. If we were up the Gulf, we'd be on the lookout for gold runners. We actually found some one day. So, if we saw suspicious ships, yachts, boats, whatever, we would make them heave-to, then carry out a 'stop and search'. By that, I mean we'd throw the marines over the side, hoping they'd hit the waiting Gemini semi-inflatable dinghy. They'd then bomb away, board, search, find nothing and come back to us. We'd make them climb back up the jumping ladder, then hoist the Gemini back on its davit. Then we'd steam off looking for someone else to stop.

During these operations, we were, allegedly, entitled to use whatever force we deemed necessary in order to stop anyone. And if we were disobeyed, it was amazing what change of heart could be achieved by training the for'ard gun turret in the general direction of the target, even though it was unmanned and unloaded. We could quite easily plant a brick through a funnel or a bow.

There is a naval expression, 'anchor faced', which means the person you describe, is very pro-Navy, and who puts the RN first, and his mates second. It implies you should have an anchor tattooed on your forehead or face, to warn everybody. Bootnecks really are anchor faced. Now, I'm all for everyone pulling in the same direction, but marines take this to new highs. The Corps come first, second and last. They do everything they are told, and I MEAN everything. If you find a job you won't get anyone else to do – order up a bootie to do it. In the detachment we carried, there would be a first-aider, a bugler, a cook and a bunch of general purpose and weapon specialists. The bugler would normally be the runt of the detachment, the rest would be, well let's say you wouldn't pick a fight with them. They would, though, be there to get you out of hot spots ashore. Not that we normally needed help, but if we did . . .

So, when a similar crash happened some nights later, we ignored it. This time it was a marine who, having gone to collect some fish, had fallen out of the Gemini and into the Arctic Ocean. He survived it, being immediately thrown into a hot bath until he warmed up, but suffered exposure. We laughed at his misfortune, him being stupid enough to fall in, and all that, but we all knew how close to death he had come.

Almost nightly we were stopped and offered fish, and were very grateful for it. Eating cod that isn't aware it is dead is different from that which you get in the local chippy. Half an hour ago it was swimming about with its mates, and now you are eating it. Wonderful.

We had several weeks alongside, home, in Pompey, then went back to Icelandic waters. This time, the rules had changed – the Icelanders were getting stroppy. One of their so-called gunboats (actually converted trawlers with an Oerlikon fitted) had deliberately driven into the *Lowestoft*, removing most of the *Lowestoft*'s forecastle. It actually removed the front 20 ft or so, above the waterline, and we saw her in this state, so we knew it was true. That meant that after a considerable amount of Damage Control, she had to sail back to Rosyth at 4 knots – astern all the way. We Tartars weren't going to have any of that.

So, one night (while we were closed up at defence stations), we came off at 0600 having tracked most of our trawlers and one of the gunboats, *Baldur*, for most of our watch, breakfasted and got our nuts down. At 0700, the action scraction alarms went, up we blearily rose and went straight away to 'Riding off stations', where we had to position ourselves between the gunboat and the trawlers. It meant we had to get out of our pits and sit in the Burma Road, well away from the ship's side, and only one deck down.

We would ride off the gunboat's assault on our defenceless trawlers by getting between it and the trawler. Our Skipper was brilliant at this, and could make the gunboats look totally foolish. On this occasion, though, the *Baldur* thought he'd get in the way. The boss thought much differently. For about an hour we rode off its attacks, and we both sailed about gesturing and posturing – keeping the thing away, as ordered. The *Baldur* finally got close, and we warned her by radio that we were rigged with stabilizers, stretching '2 to 3 ft' out of both sides. It got closer, and our Jimmy did a running commentary on the situation over the ship's broadcast. He reported the impending collision so precisely that it was exactly on the third 'now' in 'standby now, now now' that the actual impact was felt and heard by us below decks. This impact reeled us, but our port stabilizer unfortunately pierced the *Baldur*'s hull, necessitating her extremely rapid return to Rekyavik. We laughed like buggers, especially when, while still closed up, we heard about ourselves on the BBC world news. The stabilizers actually extended up to 6 ft out . . . It was his fault – he started it.

Another day, we were shipwatching round the south-east corner of Iceland, and picked up a distress call from a trawler in the north, that he was getting trouble from another gunboat, the *Tyr*. We went flat out round there, banging our way through a very wet and snowy gale. However, on the way, the on-task Nimrod joined us for his routine patrol.

We tasked it to go and see what was going on, and heard the Nimrod raising the *Tyr* on HF radio. The Nimrod pilot informed the gunboat that, as an RAF Nimrod on patrol, he was equipped with all kinds of things, including Mk46 torpedoes and depth charges, and that if he, the *Tyr*, didn't go away immediately and quickly, he would drop something on him to enforce the issue. The gunboat retreated, and the Nimrod carried on with his allotted task – that of dropping bright yellow mail canisters to us. The pilot must have got confused about his payload that day – fancy confusing Mk46s with letters to the *Tartar!*

While we were up there, it was cold enough to grow icicles on the upper deck, and we also swept off snow. I don't know how the trawlermen cope. We also sailed through fields of growlers (icebergs), but never saw any really big ones. Yes, we chipped ice off the four-fives whenever we got a good build-up, and yes we grew snow everywhere else. The bridge lookouts were actually allowed inside the bridge up there, and not, as they usually were, stationed outside on the wings.

When we first enlisted, we were – to remind you – issued with two seamen's jerseys. These were thick and would keep out most draughts, but still itched like hell, even after dozens of washes, and through T-shirts. For this extremely cold weather, then, we would scrounge/nick/beg/borrow thick, white, polo-neck jerseys, known as 'sub-sweaters', on account of their being standard bubble-head (submariner's) issue. If you caught anyone else wearing your 'legally' acquired sweater, revenge was imminent. After several washes, the yellow colour would go, leaving a milky white sweater. They did not shrink or warp regardless of what you did to them. They were an impressive symbol – if you had one you gloated, if you aspired to one you schemed devious ways to get your hands on one. Sub-sweaters then were extremely warm, and when worn over several T-shirts and sets of Eights, but under your foul-weather gear, you felt that you could survive any weather hardships, especially the oceans north of the Arctic Circle . . . unless you fell in!

It was at about this time that the Admiralty decided we would all have two new woolly pullies, similar to those worn in the Army and Air Force, but ours were a deep, navy blue. They had epaulettes on each shoulder, ready to put our new rank/rate badges on. We wore them self-consciously at first, but gradually got used to them, and threw away those bloody awful issue itchy things from all those sunrises away at *Raleigh*. We also were issued with berets, not that we knew how to wear them – we needed lessons for that. We wore these even more self-consciously than the woollies, as we all looked really ridiculous. They did, though, stay on our heads better in roughers, and could be jammed into the pockets of our foulies, along with all the rest of the stuff we carried, so from that point of view they were an improvement. We still had to keep our two ice-cream hats, for divisions, for being on duty and for being trooped and appearing before the Skipper. The berets had a further use as a quick shoe/boot cleaner, before finding your own to actually stick on your head.

Officially, your 'length of service' was proportional to the number of 'badges'. Otherwise known as long-service and good-conduct stripes, these badges, although officially LSGC, were actually more accurately defined as four years undetected crime. You got one of these to sew on every four years up to a maximum of three, but they could be taken off you as part of any punishment, along with stoppage of leave/a fine. On the *Tartar* we counted the number of badges apportioned to just a handful of ratings and got a combined service record in excess of 100 years. Badges made you look like a silly old git – you would be called 'grand-dad' or worse if you had them. I ended up with two, but kept forgetting to sew the second one on.

A further indicator of length of service was judged by the colour of your Eights or by your collar. The more faded your Eights were, the longer you had served. You did, though, have to buy more Eights during your service, mainly when they got too ragged to wear and the sticky tape we used to repair holes with found nothing to grip. Your collar then was the best giveaway, you would only wear it two or three times, then get it down to the dhobey wallah for cleaning. So, while your Eights were the first indicator, your collar would always be the best barometer. This was unless you were one of those people who never got dirty, never smelled, and therefore who would go for two whole days or longer without a shower, and only get your gear washed when absolutely necessary. Most people took exceptional pride in their appearance. Berets just got filthier and filthier – to prove a point.

At some point during the Iceland troubles we called in at Newcastle upon Tyne. We had 'ship open to visitors' and toured the local brewery. Remembering that the previous evening we drank every bottle of 'brown' in the city, it isn't difficult to imagine the state we were in by the time we reached the brewery. We were taken round evil-smelling tuns, full of fermenting ale, and observed every aspect of the process – the bottle washing, filling, labelling. We were also shown 'the old boy at the end of the barrel line', and told, yes – told, that under no circumstances were we to laugh. This chap sat there, with a hammer in his hand and every barrel that went past him, he would hit, just once with the hammer, to ensure the cap on the end of the barrel was secure. That was his job. We controlled our laughter until we got away from him, then collapsed on the floor.

Lunch was plates of sandwiches, washed down with as much 'Newcy Brown' as we could scupper. They left us to get on with it all afternoon. I have no idea what time we left, but it was late and the staff there wanted to go home. George and I walked drunkenly back, and as we approached the ship, we saw TV crews on the gangway. They asked if we'd mind coming back around the corner while they filmed our return. 'Not at all' we said, obligingly. We had several 'takes' of us walking nonchalantly back along the gangway, before we decided to spice it up. The next take was me and George, arms linked, legs kicking like tiller girls. The gangway staff, OOD, DPO and film crew just cracked up, and we went below, sniggering wildly, for a siesta before that evenings 'run'.

George, being from the Newcastle area, took several of us 'up-homers' one night for a feed, then out to his local club. Once more we left our wallets in our pockets. We awoke on the floor next morning and attempted to get back to the ship, moored almost beneath the railway bridge. The trains were late or missing, and we ended up getting a fast-black back, which cost us a fortune. I know we were adrift, but didn't get 'in the shit' for it as we weren't the only ones affected by the trains.

We had a Chinese laundry on here who would wash and iron beautifully everything you sent in. Though they had some not very endearing habits, such as washing noisily – sometimes. They only rarely took showers, preferring to take bird-baths in the sink, throwing water everywhere with their flannels. Or while we would eat our meals, they'd sit with us, chomping noodles from bowls with their fingers. They would also catch 'shitfish', so called because no matter which port you stopped in, shitfish would always gather at the sewage outflows. The laundry crew would catch them and cook them in the galley. We often pointed this shitfish matter out, but they just laughed and rebaited their hooks for supper. Laundry crews were always conspicuous by their absence – occasionally they would go ashore, come back legless, and noisily play Mah-jong for the rest of the night, locked up in their laundry room.

No one was allowed in the laundry except them, not under any circumstances. They slept, ate, washed and ironed in there, apparently getting in and out through the top half of a door, which would be closed every evening, and at every Action Stations, at which time they'd continue dhobeying, while we did whatever exercise we were supposed to.

A minor digression on the subject of sewage outfalls, concerns a trophy alleged to be held on the Royal Yacht, of a certain painted, framed item, originally belonging to a certain person (not The Queen, but close, very, very close), which was extracted from one such outfall many Middles ago. Subsequently, according to the sources, a 'smasher' was fitted to the outfall, preventing further such incidents. An excellent black cat.

The laundry crew would always have your gear delivered back to your mess by evening, except the days they would walk round bemoaning 'No Stim, No Stim', indicating that they hadn't been able to do any washing that day. This lack of stim would normally be caused by the clanks' inability to do simple things such as connect to a shore steam line without making a mess of it, normally halfway through a shower, so the water would suddenly go ice cold. At that time, you'd scream and shout, telling everyone what an incompetent bunch of wankers stokers were. I was doing this happily one day, when the Duty tiffy stuck his gormless head round the bathroom door to see what the matter was. He got told in no uncertain terms and ran off. The Duty senior stoker then turned up to find out what his little chap was so upset about – we told him too. Pretty soon, miraculously, the water got hot again.

There are few things more precarious than standing in a shower, covered in soap, trying to keep your balance while the ship has the wheel and rudder hard over, and is turning to port, at 20 knots plus. This tended to throw you against the side of the shower, or even out of it. As did attempting to stand on one leg to wash the other, while ploughing through a force eight gale. To make life easier we would always wear flip-flops while off-watch. These could be dangerous at the best of times, due to ring-bolts and other metal lumps growing at various points from the deck. Normally, in shoes you would curse and walk away, but in flip-flops – you came to a grinding halt, collapse swearing on the floor holding your foot, then, finally, limp back to the mess. You could break toes wearing them. They made life more interesting and stopped your feet becoming too pongy after wearing the steaming bats all day.

One of the associated dangers of warship design is the hatches leading from one deck to another, or from one watertight compartment to the next. Hatches are surrounded by an edge that grows out of the deck many inches. These have to be crossed by lifting your leg over the rim. Normally not difficult, except after a night ashore, when the hatch rims seem to grow extra height. This causes you to not lift your leg high enough, resulting in a rapid shin-to-metal contact on the hatch coaming. Now this hurts, and produces bruising and gashes which last for weeks, as well as leaving scarring for years. I still have mine.

An apparently favourite game played by the Jimmy, as mentioned previously, was 'throw the dummy over the side to see how long the lifebuoy spook takes to see it'. This was normally done at scran time by anyone not thinking straight. You'd be sitting 'enjoying' supper, having queued and rabbited for the best part of half an hour, to ensure the absolute best selection of food and the finest table in the house, the tannoy would then blare: 'MANOVERBOARDMANOVERBOARDMANOVERBOARDPORTSIDEAWAY SEABOATSCREW', and you'd grab at your gobbling rods and plate before they joined the scrapyard at one side of the dining room. The OOW, you see, would immediately order the wheel to be put right over, then back again to the other side, to swing the arse end away, then line up the ship to come back for the dummy – totally 'forgetting' that we were enjoying supper. You'd then be holding on hard to your tray full of food with one hand, the table with the other and gripping the chairs or benches with your legs, hoping the bulkheads would go back to the proper place so you could continue eating, while the seaboat crew recovered the dummy.

A word about tiffies, who after midshipmen, are a very elementary life form. Tiffies join the Navy to see the world, but having attained higher educational qualifications at school, assume they are on a higher intellectual level than sailors. Tiffies leave training, having worked hard mending engines and oiling lamps or whatever, and are then promoted, rapidly, until suddenly they are chiefs with lots of oiling and mending qualifications, but thick as pigshit with no concept of other people's attitudes towards them or how the Navy works. They then sit in the chiefs' and POs' mess, with chiefs and PO's who have taken years of professional labour to attain their rates. All tiffs do, then, is piss people off, then occasionally get a complicated job to do, like mend a broken screw or nail, which tends to stretch their capabilities. It is rumoured that when anyone who is electrically minded and wants to join the RN goes for their initial interview, they are handed a screwdriver side on. If they take it by the handle, they obviously recognize what it is, and how to use it, and can therefore be enlisted as an electrician. If they hesitate, or take it by the pointed bit, they are automatically enlisted as tiffies.

Every night in the Navy, especially on active warships, there is the Duty watch. This involves 25 per cent of the ratings – a quarter of all the sailors, then supposedly a quarter of the stokers and greenies, who, because they are not under any jurisdiction except that of their respective chiefs, will normally be able to slide off somewhere. There would also be a Duty Leading Seaman, a Duty PO (any branch) a Duty CPO (any branch) and an Officer of the Day. If, then, anything went on, a situation could arise and escalate. However, guess who would be called out first, and guess how the problem would be resolved? I'll give you a clue, not the OOD, not the Chief, not the PO but the Duty Leading Seaman, which I now was.

Midshipmen? Now middies absolutely were the lowest form of animal life. If you were fortunate enough to have a mid on board, he would need to wear his shit-deflecting hat and shitproof trousers all the time. If the Duty LS had a spare job, he would try and convince the OOD that it would be a good bit of experience for the Mid. Generally the OOD would agree, and the Mid would be summoned in the middle of the night as well as me to oversee the slacking off (or tightening up) of the cable or wires. Of course, the Duty watch of sailors would think that terrific and play 'awkward bastards' to liven the Mid up. Eventually, the Mid would shout and lose his rag, at which point the Duty Leading Seaman would get back in and resolve it all.

Of course, each chief had his own job to do, for example, the Chief GI, who would be the senior gunnery rating aboard, would be in charge of all the seamen, but also in charge of Daily Orders, and anything along those lines. There would be a chief greeny who did nothing, a chief stoker who perpetually had dirty hands and sweated a lot, the Buffer, who was a chief of some seaman branch, a chief caterer who was usually a lardarsed idiot, the jossman who was chief cementhead, and other assorted good for nothing chiefs who we never did discover the purpose of.

There would also be various numbers of POs, from all departments. The seaman ones would be in charge of their own Parts of Ship: traditionally the gunner would have the fo'c'sle, the RP 'top' and the TAS the quarterdeck. The greenies all stuck together, either doing radio, weapons or general (light bulbs). The stokers – well, I don't know, but they always had grubby rags hanging out of their overalls.

Next level was Leading Hands, and there were loads of them. They'd be the ones that actually ensured the work got done by the ABs and below. The 'hookies' therefore caught the most grief, from above and below. If it wasn't right, it wasn't the AB for not doing it, but the hookie for not making sure it was done. If there was extra work to be done, it was hookie who dragged the watch out to get it done. More grief.

CHAPTER 26

Once More into the Med

Eventually we got back to Pompey from the 'Ice War' to a heroes' welcome, from our families at least. We had a few more weeks refitting and, having taken some leave, we sailed for Gibraltar, Biarritz and Casablanca. Not before we had a scare while alongside in Portsmouth. A fire was reported in a compartment, and the Duty watch and fire crews dived in to extinguish it. The Damage Control bods suddenly realized that the compartment was adjacent to the deep Seacat magazines, which were fully packed. It was decided to go to Emergency Stations even though we were alongside, and we spent many frightened minutes trying to be the nearest ones to the ship's side, just in case the anticipated explosion actually occurred. If it had happened, we'd have made a large hole in the dockyard, Pompey and Hampshire, and would not have had time to jump anyway. The Pompey Fire Brigade eventually arrived, and helped us put it out. That was close!

While we played in the Med, we came across the *Ark Royal*. She had a full complement of aircraft, and it befell us to do Helicopter Guardship, sailing off her arse end as she held flying stations. We were there just in case one of the pilots was dumb enough to make his jet fall into the water, when we would fish him out. Unlike the Yanks, who, if an aircraft went over the side they just waved (allegedly they had loads of spares, and weren't concerned about the odd one or two), we would have to drop dan-buoys and divers to note where the aircraft came to rest so it could be retrieved later. We didn't actually have to carry out this particular evolution.

When we did guardship, or when we ourselves went to Flying Stations, we would equip the seaboat with a crash-bag, and hang the boat over the side on the falls, engine running, just in case it was urgently required. You had to sit in the boat while it was dangling apparently perilously above the ocean as you smashed along at flying speed. Our crash-bag contained various indispensable pieces of equipment: maul, bolt-croppers, axe, flashlight, crowbar and strops to attempt to keep whatever had crashed afloat, so we had a good chance of getting the crew out, should they feel the desire to ditch. This was based on the assumption that we got there before it sank, and that we could reach into it to extract the crew. Perhaps it made them feel better, knowing we were on full alert, but in actual fact we'd have been as useful as tits on a fish.

We would sail within a few hundred yards of the *Ark*, watching the aircraft taking off. At early dawn, this was the most spectacular event – we'd see a shape trundle up to the launch cat, we'd hear the engines rev, then see the flames from the back of the aircraft. The roaring and flames would increase, then we'd see the flames shoot forward as the aircraft lunged towards the front of the flight deck. We'd then hear the extra roar and see the flame shoot into the sky, the afterburners gradually tailing off as the aircraft got away. We got to know the noise difference between the Phantom and my favourite, the Buccaneer. We'd track them on radar, listening to their controllers. When they came back, we'd watch with bated breath as several tons of metal travelling at well over 100 knots hurtled towards the immovable rear of the carrier. If all went well, the aircraft would skim the rear, drop the last few feet and be caught by the arrester wires. If not, a flare would sear into the sky and the pilot would slam the engines back to reheat in a desperate attempt to give himself enough power to get airborne again, without smashing into the deck or bridge. We would laugh and make rude gestures to those who got themselves into this position!

What with them and the Gannets which would not seem to need the arresters – they'd creep up behind the ship, and seemingly drop directly on to the pitching deck! It was shortly after this, that Rod Stewart released the song 'Sailing', a record forever and indelibly ingrained into my mind for two reasons. First, my future wife would watch the television series about the *Ark*, and associate the record with me. Second, we were with the ship while they filmed the series, and I can remember all those brilliant shots of the Buccs screaming off the flight deck under full throttle.

Nice was different, and we visited Monaco for one day, and I think St Tropez for another, hoping to get a look at BB. When we went to Casablanca, we took the coach to Marrakesh to see the man with the sherbet water in the goatskin bottle. Whilst there, we rode camels and watched the locals racing on horseback, waving scimitars. We stayed out of the way, but were mightily impressed. However, we weren't quite so impressed by the very large cockroaches (known as Bombay Runners – big enough to put your foot on, and watch it still move) and rats that cruised the jetty at night. We demanded firearms while on gangway duty, but had to make do with the inevitable catapult. Eventually, we returned home.

In actual fact, we didn't get rat-arsed every night. If there was a new fairly decent film showing, we'd go to see it. We'd only see good films, and I recall going to see *Tommy*, but especially remember *The Exorcist*. This one stands out in my 'list of runs ashore to never forget' because of George, who, on becoming bored during one of the quieter scenes, nudged me, giggled, leapt to his feet and screamed 'BOO', frightening to death the entire cinema audience. We then sat chuckling through the rest of the film much to the annoyance of those around us. Like I said, me and George had some brilliant escapades. Then there was the time when I (and he) thought he had appendicitis, so we called for an ambulance. What actually turned up was the crushers in their patrol 'tilly, who diagnosed George as having nothing more than too much scrumpy. At least we got a lift back to the dockyard, but promptly turned back round, back to the nosh shop for eats.

If you were disgruntled, D by P, or discharge by purchase (buying yourself out), was a handy way of getting out. You applied for D by P, and if you were given it, you'd be a civvy again within months. If your job was menial, you'd stand a better chance of getting it. Dick, my mate, was a trained Seacat Aimer, so had no chance at all. D by P ratings would walk round muttering phrases like 'ROMFT', but if they got their request, they'd immediately become RDP and consequently not interested in the RN any more. They'd immediately set up a calendar and fastidiously tick off each day that passed, telling everyone at every opportunity exactly how many days (and hours) they had left.

CHAPTER 27

But Windies Guardship Means You're Just on Standby – It Doesn't Mean You Actually Have to Go . . .

We were standby West Indies Guardship in the September, in Portsmouth, with just an outside chance of having to go, when we got the order to sail, so off we went. Before we went, I met Jan, who I had been writing to since placing the *Melody Maker* advert. We spent a day in London, lunched at the Tower Hotel, visited Madame Tussauds, saw the newest Pink Panther film, toured HMS *Belfast*, walked across Tower Bridge, had a meal in the West End and finally bade a sad farewell on King's Cross station. We saw each other every possible weekend after that, and decided to get engaged that Christmas. Only the Navy put paid to that. We were supposed to be back in time for Christmas, but things changed so quickly.

I lost count of the letters I sent to and received from Jan, and would be extremely sad (now I knew how the married men felt on the *Zulu*) if the mail was delayed, late, or I just didn't get a letter. If you haven't been in that position, you don't know what a depressing feeling it is. You look forward so much to getting near land and getting mail, and if yours isn't there the only consolation is to go and drink a bottle of Bacardi with a teeny drop of coke, and a few icebergs, and hope the letter will arrive tomorrow.

Once more we sailed to Bermuda, exercising all the way, so this time it took us weeks rather than days to get there. We moored on the town quay in Hamilton, where the liners normally went. No need for hired mopeys, just borrowed ones. We had all the floodlighting rigged along the side and looked extremely pretty. Everywhere there were tourists stomping up and down the jetty.

We moved on to Trinidad, again, then to Jamaica, where we were told not to go anywhere unless authorized. We ended up in coaches to the Jamaica Pegasus – actually being jeered at en route – and eating there, before returning sober to the ship. We went on a coach tour to Ocho Rios, and up the waterfall that featured in the '007' films, Dunn's River Falls. That was an experience not to be missed. The tumbling water, after the air temperature being in the 90s, was freezing cold. I don't know how far up we climbed, but it was totally exhilarating.

For whatever reason our tour was extended, and we stopped at Norfolk, Virginia for a mini refit, ironically on the day we should have been entering Pompey for Christmas. One of the first things we wanted repaired was our stabilisers, which had gone drastically wrong some time earlier, making every inch of the remaining journey extremely uncomfortable. We made our way through a snowstorm to the jetty, at which point a matey pronounced it to be the 'coldest day here for twenny yirs'. Boy, were we impressed!

I was Duty that first night, and we decided to phone the local 'Domino' pizza delivery service, ordering extra large pizzas each. I have never seen such enormous pizzas and we spent hours trying to eat them – they were gorgeous – then hours trying to get rid of what we clearly could not eat. The Duty watch fed well that night. The following day, we discovered we were moored at the end of the Tomcat landing strip, and that we would be constantly buzzed as they landed – deafening. There was a PX there, which was massive – bigger than most Tesco stores are nowadays. They sold everything and anything. We topped up with 10-oz tins of tobacco, which cost us peanuts compared to our own baccy. And sweatshirts, real US Navy ones, which we insisted for years stood for unserviceable. We discovered that Norfolk was home to the USN Atlantic Fleet, boasting 200 ships and 77,000 crew – larger than the Royal even then!

We taxied out of the base, to a bar full of real Hell's Angels. They took an instant liking to us before spending all evening swapping booze. Eventually, well after closing time, the leader offered to throw a party for us, and asked if I wanted to go with him to the 'all-nighter' to get some supplies. We left the bar, jumped into his open-topped limo, drove across the road, and bought bourbon, 7-Up, and more bourbon. Back to the car and then 100 yds, round the corner to his place. By then, my mates and his were waiting for us to begin. Now, I am assured that the correct way to swallow bourbon is to drink a mouthful from the bottle, swallow, then take a small sip of 7-Up. This, we found, was a cracking way to drink. Wine, our friendly Hell's Angel, also had a Harley D suspended from his ceiling!

We were most sad to leave there, although we dropped just a few hundred miles down the coast to Savannah (Georgia) to spend Christmas, and I was quartermaster when we arrived, so was on duty on the gangway, where we had a shore phone. The idea of that was for locals to ring to arrange to take a sailor out for the night or day. This had been publicized locally, as 'Take a Sailor Home for Christmas'. Yeh Yeh – we thought! However, I noticed this family hovering at the bottom of the gangway, so like a friendly ol' salt, I invited them onboard. One thing led to another, and I ended up feeding them beer and getting them lunch while supposedly being on the gangway. Eventually, they asked if I wanted to go home with them for Christmas. Bearing in mind this was 23 December, I was straight round to my DO (who was OOD), and asked if that would be all right. The OOD agreed, so I arranged a hurried 'sub' for my Christmas duties, threw gear in my grip and headed off the ship for the next four days. We started by going out for dinner, then back to their home for the night. We were up early the next day for a quick visit to the C130 base where he was a part-time aircraft loader.

Then we piled into his car and set off for where his family lived. We arrived early evening, after stopping at a shopping mall, where I was wise enough to buy a few pressies for my host. We reached the small wooden bungalow and were met by all his relatives. A whole table was filled with different food, while a second was filled with beer and wine. No glasses, just jamjars! They were refilled as soon as they were emptied. The evening passed in a whirl of country music, wine, food and more wine. Fairly late on, they decided it was present time and we all sat round, and try as I might, I could only think of my girlfriend at home. Until the pressies started coming my way, and more, and more, until everyone had heaps, including me. To say I was overwhelmed was an understatement – I hadn't expected to be grippo'd, never mind travelling several hundred miles up country, to be welcomed like a long-lost relative, fed, watered and then given all this! I had an absolutely fantastic time. The kids in the family had been given one of those TV table-tennis games, which I could beat everyone at (having had lots of practice), although the more jamjars got emptied, the worse my performance got!

Next morning we started with more filled jamjars, more delicious southern food and hospitality and then a dance later. By evening I was exhausted, but nevertheless was very sad to leave the following day to return to Savannah. That was most definitely the best Christmas I ever spent abroad. I cannot adequately describe how friendly the people were. I did try to contact them, but never managed to trace them. I always wished I could somehow return the favour.

When I returned to the ship, I found out that there had been so many offers taken up – that the ship had virtually become a 'Marie Celeste', we actually had to turn the citizens of Savannah away – there were no sailors left for them to grippo.

Next we sailed, then, to St Petersburg, on the Gulf coast of Florida, for New Year, where after we had held the usual open day (attracting over 8,000 visitors), we made another run to Disney World. Having got that out of our systems again (via Space Mountain etc.), we toured St Pete's, visiting the aquarium, where we hand-fed the porpoises, and climbing the life-size model of the *Bounty*, built for the film *Mutiny on the Bounty*. Then we got ourselves invited to the Scottish expats festivities at their club. They all donned Scottish dress and indulged in Scottish drinking habits (we fortunately also favoured whisky), as well as enjoying country dancing and haggis piping.

The New Year came and went, and so did we, but not without taking half the jetty with us when we sailed, which was rather embarrassing!

CHAPTER 28

And Round the Windies
We Go Again

First stop this year was Belize – now there's somewhere to avoid, from the open sewers to the mozzies, and the humidity to the warm rum. We anchored 2 miles off and caught liberty boats to Belize City. We were happy to leave there and go on to Nassau again. On this occasion we found the beach – the previous time of course we escorted the Royal Yacht out and had to be on our best behaviour. Next stop was Barbados, followed by Freeport again.

It must by now sound like all we ever did was eat, drink, and be merry, however, while alongside in Chaguaramus (Trinidad) one fine night, we left hurriedly in the direction of Barbados. We spent several days scanning the ocean floor with our sonar, looking for the remains of a Cuban DC8, which had blown up shortly after take-off. We found both the big sections of it.

Whenever we were anywhere near Puerto Rico we held gunnery or aircraft exercises lasting days or even weeks. We were deployed to Anguilla to land our booties if the situation there deteriorated further, and landed a fifth of the crew in Dominica to search for a lost Brit. He saw our Wasp before we found him though, so we considered that a success. A team of our guys climbed an extinct volcano on St Kitts, and landed a work party on Grand Turk. We searched for (but didn't find) a missing fisherman off Grand Turk, and laid buoys for others. We were always on the lookout for smugglers, poachers and gun runners, and would often 'stop and search' while backing up the US Coast Guard. Even then, we still exercised the seaboat, the firecrews, the Ops Room, the sonar – everything really. We did a live Seacat firing one day, against a PTA. That was always worth watching – it was a point of honour among the Seacat Aimers to totally take out the PTA. A near miss was good, but to totally wreck it, now that was something! Standing on the quarterdeck watching while the Seacat blasted away from the launcher was a rare sight. It was even rarer when it burnt out on the launcher without going anywhere . . .

On our final trip to Antigua, we visited English Harbour, but found no trace of Ethel, nor anyone who remembered her. We went horse riding up into the hills one drunken afternoon, when we should have known better and stopped on the beach. Bearing in mind I used to carry at least two cameras with me, everywhere – drunk, sober – it seemed like a good idea to ride it. The first problem was trying to get on the silly thing. Boarding a horse is difficult enough, but full of rum, carrying cameras, and with no steps up to it makes it impossible. After much falling and giggling, we cracked it and got aboard, spurring them into life with the usual horse-starting phrases. They stood still. We kicked our heels in – they stayed still. We swore at them – nothing worked. We were on the point of giving up, having shelled out good money, when the lead horse, with its owner, decided to start off. When it went, the rest followed without further instruction, one behind the other – obviously they'd done this before. No matter how much we kicked or swore, they all plodded along at the same pace, giving us ample opportunity to take photographs as they ambled up the hill behind the beach, along the hill, over the streams, then started back towards the beach. We rejoined the beach probably a mile from where we left it and were gaily meandering back towards the bar, when the lead horse started to run. I mean 'run', not 'trot'. The rest of the horses also started to run, with us saddled, drunkenly, and vainly trying to hang on to horse, cameras and stomach contents. The headlong dash along the beach through the surf was exhilarating, but it was with great relief that we got back to the bar and refilled with Carib and Mount Gay. My bum hurt for days afterwards, as did my shoulders and arms where I had been clutching my belongings and the crazy horse. I have not been on a horse since.

We left the Windies in late February, refuelled in the Azores, got embroiled in Atlantic winter gales (bear in mind we had been stamping round in shorts and sandals 'till then, and it was always a great shock to change from bare knees to Eights) and came back into Pompey early March, 17,700 miles the worse for wear.

CHAPTER 29

Back to Portland, Working this Time

I left the RatRat, very sadly, in the spring, but with so many memories. I got engaged on my return from the Windies, and was pleased to be drafted to HMS *Osprey*, a Naval Air Station, and headquarters of Flag Officer Sea Training, Portland. This was where all the exercises had been done so many times before.

Having struggled with all my kit from Weymouth station, and having joined *Osprey*, I was immediately asked if I'd like to 'live out', as accommodation in the base was at a premium. This meant living ashore in digs in Weymouth. Further, I was allocated to 'models', part of the FOST team. Ops Room crews would come to us for shore-based training similar to *Dryad*, but smaller. It was my job, along with my colleagues, to ensure the smooth running of the models and the situations we played out. Working there meant I was 'blue card'. Living in Weymouth and blue card, all in the same day.

I remember doing Navy Days there and standing on the square in the base, having just watched the Red Arrows. All the grockles were so busy waving bye-bye to them, they failed to notice the Vulcan bomber sweeping in. As it approached, quickly and extremely quietly, I slapped my hands over my ears just before it reached us. As it got in my overhead, the pilot pulled back the stick, and opened up the throttles. The roar that emerged was deafening. I was OK with my ears covered, but you should have heard the screaming from the public.

We would 'lunch' in *Osprey* dining hall, and devise various methods of winding-up the naval airmen. One wind-up was to sneeze, loudly, and instead of 'atishoo', shout 'waffooo'. One lunchtime, me and Jonesy, my oppo there, went for lunch and commenced demolishing our food. Halfway through, I forgot myself, sneezed, and shouted 'waffooo', then remembered where I was. We both cracked up laughing, much to their annoyance. We were still giggling when we left.

As I said before, waffoos were also known as 'chockheads', as in having heads shaped like chocks, put under aircraft wheels to stop them (the aircraft, not the chockheads) from falling overboard. In reciprocation, they would call us fishheads. Submariners were known as bubbleheads, or just 'dirty bastards', due to their habit of not bathing while at sea. If a black pig moored against you, they would be straight on board us, down to our showers and would stay there removing layers of grime from their stinking, milky white bodies. We (fishheads) would always be brown, due to the sun at least. On submariners, they popularized the 'submariner's bath'. Given that you have several minutes to get ashore instead of the nightly shower, you would empty most of the contents of a tin of talcum powder down your Y-fronts, and in your hair (if necessary), and go ashore smelling sweetly. Subsplashers in their black pigs would do this more frequently, building up the layers of talc. No wonder they stank. Us 'skimmers' had an easy life.

After several days of getting a slow, unreliable bus from Weymouth to *Osprey*, I acquired a bike, and commuted, forgetting that where I worked was up a large hill. I eventually could climb it without running out of oxygen, but it took a while. The days it rained there though, I'd be very dejected after pedalling across Chesil Beach getting more drenched by the second. When it rains on Chesil, it really rains, and there is no shelter.

The digs were owned by a good chap and his very nice wife – I couldn't find it today, even if I searched for a whole month. It was close to the beach and the town. The digs was mostly populated by the air personnel, and, curiously, we would go ashore together, or in my case (as I was by then saving to get married), watch telly or find other cheap things to do. The owners cooked breakfast, and four-course evening meals. Soup, main, pudding, then cheese and biscuits if you were still hungry. Sometimes, we'd go mackerel fishing, bring back the catch, and eat them either for that tea or next night's.

After my Leading Seaman's course, the Navy invented a new rule stating all leading hands had to go on a two week leadership course before being 'confirmed'. It was with reluctance that I caught a train to Plymouth.

We arrived at HMS *Raleigh*, and prepared ourselves for the first lecture of the course, the personal introductions (who am I, what do I like doing, what ship am I on, where have I been) and discovered that the following weekend would be taken up with an Exmoor yomp. Also we'd be doing

PT etc. every day, which would include a gentle run, as well as all the lectures. We were then told we had fifteen minutes to prepare a presentation on twelve uses for a dead dog. Or something. We therefore learned the art of thinking on our feet, among other things. We had to stretch our man management, and while I knew how to march gangs of bods about, no other leading hand's courses prepared their particular branches' leaders for that. They all worked from taskbooks, where as soon as their boss okayed it, they would be promoted. So there was I, standing at one end of the vast (even bigger than I remembered it from all those years ago) parade ground, marching men up and down the other end, shouting like a maniac to ensure they could hear me and turn, before they marched in to something (like a wall). Not to be outdone, all the other prospective leaders had to do this too.

Taskbooks, to explain, were books that contained various tasks which had to be completed before the holder could move up to his next qualification or advancement. Taskbooks were the beginning of the end as far as seamanship was concerned. When I joined, you had to prove you could perform various evolutions, such as rigging a jackstay, tying the ubiquitous monkey's fist, splicing nylon – whatever your PO told you to do. With a taskbook you had to demonstrate a 'working knowledge' of the jackstay and tie some bowlines/reef knots etc. As you did each one, you got it signed off by your immediate boss, and once you had all the necessary signatures, and you were old enough, you were promoted. So we had the laughable scenario where alleged able seamen were having to be told what to provide in order to set up for stern refuelling, or towing. Me? I would have had to have known that, or it would quite literally have been knocked into me.

As a matter of fact, naval tradition has unwritten rules that say if your juniors get on well with you, enough to be accepted, then you will go out of your way to, for instance, teach them how to make bell ropes, or how to splice wire or nylon properly, or how to make beermats – whatever. It follows then that these skills were only selectively passed down through the generations of matelots. You had to be taught how to do these things because there was no possibility you could learn these skills from any books. If you knew how to do these ornate things, you could make a small fortune ashore, in various hostelries. Or onboard, where the clankies and other branches would buy them to sell for themselves.

We had the lectures daily, and we also were obliged to give lectures, frequently, and contribute to debates (of our own choosing), with officers, etc., being drafted in to answer our questions. Not that they were phrased to wind anyone up, of course, especially not when we got the sky pilots in, and gave them grief. Also known as godbotherers, or sin-bosuns, the padres would be met with mixed interest on ships. Ostensibly there to maintain morale, they would glide around the messdecks drinking beer and talking crap. They were never addressed as 'Sir', having no rank, but we felt uneasy with them around.

Bearing in mind there were waffoos, stokers, greenies – all sorts – and with two seamen on this course, collectively we were given tasks to resolve on a daily basis. The old chestnut about being given planks of wood, rope etc. and how do you get across this chasm populated by crocodiles. Piece of cake to us sailors – we had done it all on our leading seaman's courses, but the rest had to think hard about it. We sailors were usually barred from contributing, but would be there more in a consulting role, i.e. tying the knots, checking any rigging. The hardest one was allocated to me, where we all had to get down from the top of an old fort and across a moat without leaving any equipment behind, not even the rope we used as a slide. I confess it took a while for me to work that out, but we did it eventually. The scariest bit was convincing the first person down the slide that it was safe.

We also had to solve the conundrum about the aircraft crashing in the desert – what do you take, or leave, do you stay or do you go. I had to do this again some years later on a course when I left the RN, and the course organizers gave me top marks for convincing everyone to 'go'. They also had to revamp their answer – they'd always advocated the 'stay' solution, but after I'd explained my reasoning, based on sound knowledge and fact, they changed it!

The middle weekend, then, was led up to by the daily exercise, and we set off for Exmoor for two days of eating compo and yomping between various tors and checkpoints, each attended by the umpires in Landrovers, just in case of emergencies. I recall it rained that weekend (but when doesn't it up there), and again it was with relief that we finally crossed off the last of the checkpoints and dragged our gear back to the trucks to return. But we were still expected to have all our gear ready for the first lecture the following morning.

Apparently I did all right on the course because as soon as I got back to *Osprey*, I was confirmed as a leading seaman, having only been 'acting' up until then. The problem with being shore based then was that we had to pay towards our accommodation. That got expensive for me, so I volunteered (stupid thing to do, really) to go back to sea early, specifying that I wanted a ship staying around the UK, based in Pompey or Chatham. I didn't think this was entirely unreasonable, after all, I was saving the Navy money going back to sea with my expertise.

CHAPTER 30

The Plymouth? *The Worst*
Ship I've Ever Been on

I was drafted to the Chatham-based HMS *Plymouth* at the end of 1977. I had never been to Chatham for more than three days before, so I looked forward to being based nearer my home. However, if there was one ship that came as a surprise to me it was the *Plymouth*. I have already said that if you couldn't take a joke, you shouldn't have joined. I admit it, I couldn't take this particular joke. The *Plymouth* was the worst ship I've ever been on.

It was a run-down, smelly, grubby, rusty, ancient frigate, which, when I joined, was languishing alongside a dark part of the dockyard. It didn't look impressive, though it was where the Argentine surrender was eventually signed after they were kicked off the Falklands some years later.

First night, I slept on an unmade bed in the after sailors' mess, constantly aware of the smell of fuel oil and sweat. After the cleanliness I had been used to on the *Tartar* this was disgusting. Next morning I went through my Joining Routine, while we sailed for Portland for a week, before sailing for the Med for three months.

The only thing I found different on here was that in our 'mess' (literally) we had an old colour TV. This had been commandeered from somewhere, and bore pride of place above our mess 'bar'. It had an aerial attached, which had to be positioned on the upper deck through the partially opened hatch leading to the quarterdeck, and most of the fun was setting it up well enough to get a clear(ish) picture. Eventually though we would be able to distinguish images, through trial and error and a lot of shouting along the chain of people from viewer to adjuster. Peculiarly, the mess members would all come to a standstill at *Crossroads* time, and watch intently as Amy Turtle went through her nauseating paces. I could never, ever stand watching crap like that, though it seemed to be a religion on the 'Gob' ('Plygob' = Plymouth). However, I must admit I gladly watched Kenny Everett and *The Magic Roundabout* – I laughed like a loon at these two. It transpired that it didn't matter where we tied up, we could usually get a picture on that ancient telly, even in the USA.

We were trialling IRBs (Inshore Rescue Boats) then, rigid hulled with inflatable sides (such as the RNLI use), driven by extremely powerful 40 hp engines. I was now happy-ish. We trialled against regular seaboats from other ships doing 'man-overboard' exercises, and found we could be dropped, collect the 'body', recovered and out of the water, while any opposition was still chugging towards their 'body'. This was because we could drop this beauty while doing up to 20 knots. We would start the outboards, drop ourselves on to a convenient wave, bang it into ahead and scream off into the distance. We would recover and hurtle back alongside the ship, still shifting rapidly, secure to the crane/hoist and be back on board ready for the next one.

I found this vessel was jack-proof. Whatever you did it was forgiving, such as spinning the wheel right round while touching 35 knots had no effect on the boat, but you got whiplash injuries. It would skip all waves and bounce any sea state. In effect, this was fun. Except for the one day when we anchored off Penzance, and the Skipper decided he'd go ashore for some reason. I drove the IRB into the tiny, walled harbour, with him scowling at me in the back. We went alongside and 'waited there' for him, only after an hour, we got bored and went separately to find him, via a couple of bars and pints. We got back before him, and he decided he'd drive the boat back. He revved the engine, slapped it into 'forward' and drove straight on to a mudbank in the harbour. He immediately vented his fury on me, asking if I'd checked the tides etc. before we left. 'Of course I did, I checked the chart with the Navigator, and he also reckoned plenty of water in the harbour', I replied, 'But we didn't know we'd be this long'. I carefully extracted it from the mudflat, got off the driving seat and sat down at the front. He got the message and drove the boat sedately back to the ship. The subject was never raised again, but he tried to get his own back on me.

We had more fun with the boat when we had to go and get rid of the remains of the *Eleni V*, which was doing a good job of sinking out in the North Sea. I recall we were in Lerwick at the time, either that or we had called in for fuel. Whatever, I was detailed to slip the *Plymouth* with my boat's crew. I was then to drive the boat out, play catch-up, and be recovered. We stood on the jetty, slipped the ship and watched her sail off, quickly. We stayed near the boat, but not exactly making any hurry to return. The reason, you see, was that the locals, who had come to see us off, brandished bottles of whisky in our direction. In view of prying binoculars from the bridge, we dropped into the boat and made 'engine starting movements'. Despite our best efforts, the engine would not start and it required several large slugs out of the proffered bottles to help us. As the ship disappeared round the headland, we began to get 'What is the problem?' messages on our radio, to which we replied 'Engine won't start – think it's flooded. We will try again shortly.' The only thing we flooded was our mouths, with single malt whisky. After some time, we started slurring into the radio, and decided we'd better go now before we got into real trouble. We had one (or two) last mouthfuls, kicked up the outboard with the first actual turn of the key, shouted our thanks, and took off at the maximum speed (as I said, about 35 knots) after the 'Plygob'. We very quickly caught it up, and having told them we were on the way, she was already doing 15 knots or so. I got the boat alongside right away, hooked up to the winch, and was back onboard before you could say 'whisky'. I got rocks for that too, but steadfastly blamed the engine. No one could prove anything different except my bowman, and he was also pissed . . .

The *Eleni V* was eventually sunk by us planting PE all round the visible front end. We therefore blew the bows off it and watched it sink, to join all the other hulks at the bottom of the North Sea. We had stopped in Rosyth to load the PE, and therefore actually sailed with several tons of it stacked on the flight deck. No smoking, or anything.

We were due to exercise with Hunters to strafe and bomb-splash targets towed by us at high speed. These targets were wood and metal rafts, towed well behind us, and were configured to throw a large plume of water high into the air. We asked for and were granted a volunteer to be splash-target cox'n. This person, as I remember, had an unhealthy preoccupation with his bits and was always to be found with his hand round them. He also had abnormal ears, thus he acquired the nickname 'Wingnut'. He also had an absence of brains and was as useful as that after which he was named. However, he temporarily let go of his own tackle, collected his bagmeal, radio, boots, gaiters (standard gear) and mustered on the quarterdeck ready for his training. The buzz had gone round well on this one – we lined the AX and the flight deck, wardroom were there too. The muppet listened attentively as the gunners told him how he was expected to report the fall of shot from the strafing back to the ship, who would then relay it to the attacking aircraft. He was shown how to use a rake marker, and sit on the splash target at the arse end as people ran towards him simulating shot. They would hit the deck in front, behind and to the side of him, which he would report back as 'left 100' or 'over 200' etc. We got bored after half an hour or so – this kiddy was particularly obtuse. We rigged two fire hoses and told him that if he got hit on the head, he was to shout 'Direct Hit', but that clearly if it was a direct hit – he would get wet. Now what kind of a moron would sit through this? Would anyone in his right mind actually volunteer to sit on three pieces of wood being towed at 20 knots or more as Hunters shot live ammunition at it? Armed only with a bagmeal and a radio? So as one chap ran down and smacked him on the head, he screamed 'Direct Hit', we opened the nozzles of the previously charged hoses to simulate the hit and nearly knocked him overboard. Straighfaced he was asked, 'OK, that was excellent – do you need another practice'? The dipshit replied that he would. Once more our trousers became extremely wet. It was a long time before he lived that down, and it still brings a smile to my face.

On the subject of names, all Smiths were known as 'Smudge', and Browns were 'Buster'. On here we had a Hardwick who was known as 'Softjob', but otherwise people were given names to match their profile, i.e., Wingnut above, Alligator, because of his twitch that made him appear to be biting things, whatever they reminded us of. Continuing in this vein, everyone from 'the west country' was called Jan (from Janner), it was assumed everyone from anywhere near Sunderland was in fact a 'monkey hanger' (guaranteed to get an instant fight) and that all Yorkshiremen were considered to be 'a cross between a Scotsman and a Pig' (also followed by a punch-up).

We eventually got to Gib, where we were to be Gib Guardship over Christmas. Lucky me – I got to be crew on the MFV which was to prowl the straits while the ship sat alongside. We were twenty-four about for that, and guess who was even lucky enough to be 'on' on Christmas Day? We'd sleep on the 'Gob', then walk through the yard to the MFV. We'd then spend twenty-four hours catnapping and prowling, cooking our own food, before going back on board, by which time we'd be ready to go ashore. It seemed it was a much-coveted duty, but I could be wrong. The rest of the crew were all good, as was the officer in charge. So the day we all strolled down towards the MFV and found a yacht crew clearly in distress, we had to assist didn't we? Fortunately, we had the bottle opener the chap needed, then tasted both his beer and the scotch. We finally got on the MFV slightly the worse for wear, and it was still only 0800.

On Christmas Eve we were 'off', and got totally legless along The Strip, before going to 'The Hole In The Wall' (is that still there?) down by the border. When we got back in the early hours, we slept until shaken, then blearily made our way to the fishing boat. I think we all virtually collapsed when we got there, and I certainly missed most of the day. All too soon we were back on the 'Gob', and sailed for Toulon for New Year. We celebrated twice, once for French time, then for UK time, but didn't really enjoy the visit too much.

We then sailed to Haifa, which has to rate alongside Norway as 'The Most Unfriendly Place I Have Ever Been'. We were rejected, ejected and couldn't wait to get to our next stop. We did, though, make a trip to Jerusalem and Bethlehem, which was very poignant considering the time of year, and there were so many beautiful sights and things to see. We were only there a short time, though, and we quickly returned to Haifa, sailing immediately, overnight, to Port Said. Having just had a bad experience, we weren't looking forward to this, but found to our astonishment that Port Said was brilliant. We started by inviting aboard the 'Gully Gully' man, a magician, who had entertained passing ships for years. We all mustered on the flight deck, and paid a couple of quid each for his performance. To my amazement, I was dragged by his assistant from the audience to help him. I suddenly found live chicks being extracted from all over my body, as well as playing cards – I really enjoyed that. Also, there were the bumboats alongside (lessons learned by me from Freetown all those years before) where we bought copious amounts of oranges and ate them all, turning our skin yellow in some cases. Then we found the ship's caterer had bought loads too, which we were then expected to eat, after our own. That was another good point about Navy food – wherever you went, you'd get local bread, local fizzy drinks, sometimes local veg, and always fresh, local fruit. If we got wind there was watermelon or strawberries, a queue would form at the galley door. We also had a fridge in our mess, where we'd put our tins of drink, and God help you if you were caught drinking someone else's freezing cold savings. This is also where we'd stash our nutty, in the fridge, to keep it cool, or in the ice section, which made Mars Bars chewier.

A trip was arranged to Cairo, which I immediately put my name down for. We left, driving down the Nile to Cairo, the most heavily populated place I have ever seen. We ate grilled chicken and meat in olive leaves, which was absolutely gorgeous. We went out to the Pyramids, which I did not realize were actually stepped, not smooth sided. We rode camels to the Sphinx and back, then climbed up and into the Great Pyramid. That was easily the spookiest, eeriest and most impressive thing I had ever seen or done, before or since. The atmosphere inside that pyramid was indescribable. We ascended a 45° tunnel to the sarcophagus chamber, and gazed round in creepy silence. It was difficult to imagine that you were so far inside that ancient structure. It makes the hairs stand on the back of my neck even thinking about it now.

We returned, and fed, again, then went back to the plateau later, for the *son et lumière*, which entailed sitting far enough away to see the Pyramids and Sphinx, alternately lit in different colours, while a running commentary detailed the history of the structures. This was followed by a floor show in a huge tent, with local dancing, including a belly dancer. Guess who she dragged out of the audience?

At some point Malta was a port of call, again – I always liked it there. This time we arranged the legendary Malta Dog Hunt, watching with incredulity as the latest batch of baby sailors volunteered to march up and down the jetty with gas masks and bagmeals. Strangely, the midshipmen were always volunteered for this. They always got the biggest laughs. The 'dog hunt' rates alongside getting people to volunteer for MUFF diving (Marine Underwater Fire Fighting) courses as a constant source of wind-ups.

Sliema harbour on Malta is a wonderful sight, all walled with fantastic buildings, and a trip into the town, steeped in centuries of history going back to the Knights of St John and the Moors was always high on the list of things to do in Malta. Oh yes, and going down to the world-famous 'Gut' was always worth an evening. The Gut is an area of the town that connects alleys and streets and is mostly full of bars, believe it or not, where it is possible to drink all night. It is comparable to a rabbit warren! We returned from the Gut one night to find the lift that took passengers from the top of the harbour wall to the bottom had stopped, so it was with trepidation that we descended the wall and lift slowly by ourselves, climbing carefully through all kinds of prohibited areas to get back to the base of the lift. From there, on the customs jetty, you would then hail a passing harbour boat for the trip back to the ship, which would normally be moored near HMS *St Angelo*. On no account though, were you allowed to fall overboard from the boat to escape paying the boatman – the harbour was literally filthy, we were told. These boats would always be painted in garish colours, with large eyes to scare off evil spirits, and each boatman spoke enough English to try to charge you extra, or sell you something you didn't need.

Returning to Chatham, we stopped at Bayonne in France, and while there, and quartermastering one day with a severe hangover, it was decided to sail in the afternoon. I was therefore the driver, sailing the ship out (as Special Sea Dutymen), obeying the orders relayed from the bridge. As I was not yet sober, I could anticipate severe problems, the biggest two of which were a) I was going to be sick and soon, b) I couldn't see straight. Nevertheless, I signed on in the wheelhouse, I recall, which had a porthole out on to the forecastle, through which some of my so-called mates grinned at me through the closed window. I don't know how I survived – but I did. When I was finally fallen out, I carried my bucket to the heads and cleaned it out, before collapsing on my pit, fully clothed, for a well-earned rest. I was fortunate to get away with that. It was a very narrow river, where any error on my part could have parked us in Bayonne town centre.

CHAPTER 31

Married Life Lasts Several Weeks, Then Off to Canada and North America

We reached Chatham in one piece, and I finally got married to my fiancée, enjoying several weekends together before I sailed once more, this time for Canada and the USA.

We exercised all the way out, with me made to now operate on the anti-submarine side. This ship didn't have air radar, my speciality, but we could turn our hands to anything. So there we were calculating probable submarine positions from their last known, so we could at least make a best guess as to where they'd pop up. We therefore had to be spot on with our calculations, or we could be miles out. If, however, we resumed contact, we'd be heartily congratulated on our Rel-Vel (relative velocity) skills, and earn the praise of the PWO and Captain.

We had light moments, me and Ben Cartwright. We would be the chief sodder-abouters, and we would therefore find ways to wind people up. One way was to award ourselves decorations made from paper, which we taped to our shirts. We then crossed swords with this lieutenant from Scotland – a really foul, bad-tempered, nasty bastard he was, promoted from the ranks, and out to make his mark by shouting to impress his superiors. He would want information from you 'immediately', and, even though we were both capable of very quickly assessing and calculating what he wanted, and giving him the answer 'immediately', there was no way he was going to get it 'immediately'. We gave him two reasons for this: a) we only just got the info to work out the answer, I'll have that in two minutes, sir (spelt C.U.R.); b) say please you Scots git. We could play him brilliantly. One day, we stuffed cotton wool into our ears and feigned ear infections, which meant that if he wanted something from us, he first had to attract our attention by getting in our line of sight. We would then raise a warning finger and point to our headsets, then at him to indicate we were getting a message over our ship-to-ship radio, then we'd take off our headset, and say 'What? Sorry, what Sir?'. At this point he'd be on the verge of apoplexy. His rantings would possibly impress the Captain, but cut no ice with me or Ben. When this 'officer' started raving at me one day, I took it all, then calmly announced that once again I had an ear infection, and that while it appeared that I could hear him, I was actually listening to other ships' radio traffic, and that I couldn't hear him then due to the cotton wool in my other ear. Also, just because I was looking in his direction while he shouted at me, it didn't automatically follow that I was looking at him, but at the callsign board behind him so I could work out the other ship in our group, who was attempting to relay vital information to me about their new submarine contact. He ranted more, while I tried to keep a straight face, put the headset back on, turned my back on him and started talking back into the radio. As PWO, he was more concerned about keeping 'the battle' going (therefore had to rely on me and Ben to give him all that very relevant information), than he was about calling our bluff there and then. That would have made him look even sillier in front the rest of the Ops Room crew.

So, hours later while I was off-watch, I was summoned to his cabin (cabin nine), along with the equally ineffective Ops Room PO, where this alleged officer, attempted to give me a dressing down. I stood and accepted all he had to say, queried whether I was supposed to ask him, who was in front of me to wait, or to hold off the person on the other end of the radio in another ship, miles away from us, who was hopefully giving us valuable data about the submarine contact that we were chasing. Would he prefer I was to miss that and give him another reason to shout at me? He accused me of being subversive and of undermining his authority. I was then threatened and finally ejected from the cabin. Next time I went on watch I had a new decoration – CTC9 (Called To Cabin Nine). Ben and I fell about after that, as did everyone else who knew about it. Pompous bastard. Like I said, I always got my own back, and shortly after that, I was put on the surface plot, which got me away from the prat lieutenant. I wonder what happened to him, nothing too nice I would hope.

I always liked the surface side, as I said before. I knew I was extremely good at my job, at playing with radar, and could work out the course, speed, closest point of approach, course to intercept and any relative velocity problem, either by eye, or shortly afterwards. It was therefore decided in someone's extreme wisdom to take me off Ops Room duties, except for exercises, and dedicate my skills to being quartermaster for a while. This, as previously described, included standing on the gangway checking the crew on and off and ensuring the ship's security. This happened day on, day off. The days off were the best . . .

We stopped at St Johns, Newfoundland (closed the day we were there), and Summerside, Prince Edward Island, our visit happily coinciding with their lobster carnival. Everywhere sold lobsters, and I've never eaten so many. Apart from that, we were invited to the Canadian Forces base for the evenings. These started out with indoor games – darts, pool etc. Then we progressed to 'chug-a-lug', or what we'd call boat races. This entailed sitting like a rowing eight, each with a glass of beer. On the command, the first would scupper his and put the (nearly) empty glass upside down on his head, which was the cue for the next in line, and so forth, until the last glass was empty, therefore the winner. This happened several times, with us winning each race. Soon we got bored, but the Canucks wanted to raise the stakes. We then started boat racing with 'Swamp Water'. This, we discovered afterwards, was made up from cherry brandy, gin, vodka, lemonade, orange squash and lemon squash, which gave it its title – a muddy drink. The kick from this came later, and drinking it was the easy part. We had several more races then, until the poor Canadians' legs started to malfunction, at which point we proclaimed ourselves the winners, permanently. I don't remember how we got back that night.

Halifax, Nova Scotia – the gathering place of many historic convoys – came and went, before we then found ourselves in Bridgeport in Connecticut. As quartermaster, still, I drove my first car, a loaned, left-hand-drive automatic, and came very, very close to parking it in the sea.

By now, a small gang had been established by four or five of us Leading Seamen, called 'The Crunch', one of whom, Mitch, had several endearing habits when drunk. One was to eat beer glasses. This would happen after he'd stuck his thumb in his mouth and blown down it, inflating his chest as he did so. Each time he did this, his shirt would rip, just like the 'Incredible Hulk'. This was a terrific party trick of his. Mitch was my best mate, and he'd often pull these tricks to impress, or to annoy. One night, he went ashore while I was QM, and we later got a call from the Bridgeport Police, saying they had Mitch in hospital. Allegedly, they had tried to remove him from somewhere, he hadn't wanted to go, and he stuck his thumb. The police panicked, and hit him with a nightstick, which only enraged Mitch. They continued to hit him until he went down, at which point they wrapped him up and took him to hospital. He was back next day, very sheepish, with several bandaged lumps round his head. For our part, we swapped badges, hats, all sorts of things with the police. Our group also included Kev Hexley (who would call everyone either a 'Growbag', or a 'Bucket' (of shit), plus Mac the Gunner, and THELMA. We got to be a tight group before getting split up yet again.

While we were there we hired a car, and six of us got in it at 04 dubs one morning (just after I came off the hey-diddle-diddle) and we drove to Niagara Falls, just for the day. Another very impressive, not to mention unforgettable sight (we did get around), although we had trouble at the border. We saw the falls from the American side, but wanted to see the view from the Canadian side, too. We asked the border police if we could, but they refused. We pointed out we'd been in Canada just three days earlier, we had passports and that we were English sailors. The guard agreed, and over we went. On returning several hours later, the guard had gone 'off' and his mate knew nothing about us. They had to make some urgent, panicky calls to several places before they finally acknowledged we were who we said we were, and let us back in to the USA. We hightailed it back towards Bridgeport, got lost, fell asleep, got stopped for speeding – fortunately, as we were going in totally the wrong direction – and finally returned to the ship minutes before we were due to be back on watch. We were exhausted and slept dressed as soon as we next came off-watch, and had to be shaken to get up for the next one!

The Sunday we were there we got the AMTRAK down to New York, New York, and spent a memorable day walking Fifth Avenue, trying to get to the Statue of Liberty from the Empire State Building. I'll rephrase that, we came out of the station, eventually, and immediately found the Empire State Building, which we entered, caught the lift to the top and exhausted our camera films on everything there was to see. Then came the death-drop lift back to the ground floor. Kev Hexley assured us he'd been here before and therefore knew the way to the ferry. Not only that, it wasn't too far. Accepting this, we set off, but by the time we'd been waylaid by record stores and bought an LP called *Bat Out Of Hell* by a chap called Meat Loaf a long time before it got popular, we found we were still heading the right way, but were still miles away. We got a taxi in the end. We crossed on the ferry to the Statue, queued for hours, got the lift halfway, walked the rest and eventually reached the top of the head, where again we marvelled at the view. Then we descended, dashed back to the station, and caught the train back to Bridgeport. Amazingly, when we sailed we actually drove round the bay and Island before returning to the UK.

A memorable part of returning to the UK after time away, is that of sailing up the (English) Channel. This isn't yer ordinary sailing up the Channel. This is sailing up the Channel flat out, overtaking everything on the basis that if you're going past it, it can't come back up your stern. What it does require is an excellent radar lookout, reporting all contacts that may come within a mile of you only. Normally, you see – you'd report everything, inside 10 miles, inside 5 – whatever the orders were. Channel – forget it – 1 mile circle only. We'd be responsible for the avoiding action, especially trying to miss the ferries travelling across the bows rather than towards/away from you. Bearing in mind we'd probably be kicking more than 25 knots, you can imagine how on the ball we'd need to be.

So it was a peculiar thing that we'd always have Channel night on the approach (I'm not just talking about the 'Plygob' here), where we'd all get totally shitfaced, if possible, on all those crates of beer we had stored up over the preceding months. Channel night, then, consisted of probably a 'Sods' Opera', or just sitting on the arse end throwing the empty beer cans into the towering wake off the back.

Sods' Operas were evenings of entertainment, shall we say, which would have been practised for days or weeks beforehand, and would be skits or sketches taking off whatever we felt like. These ranged from 'Chelsea Pensioners' to 'Mr Men', to songs, comedy acts, impersonations, magic shows, but it was all done very much tongue in cheek. Chelsea Pensioners was several people in a line, slouching on chairs. At the command 'Chelsea Pensioners – AteeeenSHUN', they would sit up straight, eventually, groaning. It would then go to 'Quick March', when the 'pensioners' would pretend to propel the (wheel)chairs with their hands. It would then go to 'Double March', at which point their little (old) arms would propel them at top speed. But it was the order 'HALT' which sent us into fits – the 'pensioners' would be trying to slow down the 'chairs' with their hands, but as they were at speed, they would be burning their hands from the friction of the turning wheels, and cursing and spitting on their hands. You need to see it!

'Mr Men' is 'bellies', with giant hats worn covering the arms, upper body and head. Each 'belly' then has a face painted on it. The belly gyrates, the hat wobbles – again, hilarious. 'Three Shits', is a demonstration of the toilet habits of the three services. First, Percy

Pongo, 'eft 'ight 'eft 'ight HALT About FACE, two three, trousers off two three, sit two three, strain two three, grunt two three, wipe bum two three etc. Next RAF, mince in, wipe toilet seat, delicately sit down, contort face, daintily wipe bum, apply talc, dress, mince off. Finally, Jack (pissed), stagger in, throw up, take dump, remove trousers and perform 'grand-slam' (puking while dumping), clean self up, grumbling all the time.

My favourite was: rating goes into sick bay, says 'Doc, I have a sore throat'. Doc says, 'Have a gargle from this beaker'. Rating does so, and leaves, feeling much better. Next rating goes into sick bay, says, 'Doc, I have a stomach ache'. Doc says, 'Have a good drink from this beaker'. Rating does so, and leaves, feeling much better. Next rating goes into sick bay, says, 'Doc, I'm having trouble passing water'. Doc says, 'Hmmmm – you probably have a "dose", I'll need to test you – piss into this beaker'. Again, you have to be there.

Sometimes we would 'skit' the Captain or the officers, or an event which pissed everyone off on the trip, knowing that there was nothing they or anyone else could do about it. We would let off all the steam we had built up over the previous months at sea in just a couple of hilarious hours. So that was Channel night, always a good evening, unless you had the Middle on the way through, but always something to look forward to.

The other gang on the 'Gob', was made up from ex-field gunners, and their acolytes. The field gun looks great on the TV, and it is very exciting live, but once the volunteers are accepted something happens to them – following the brain removal, charisma bypass and deliberately induced psychotic personality disorder, they become incapable of rational discussion. I'll rephrase that – they become incapable of talking about anything except field-gunning. It becomes boring after several seconds, but the ex-gunners don't notice you falling asleep and assume your head is nodding in agreement. The hangers-on are no better, and there were several of them on the 'Gob', much to our disgust. Field gunners were the worst at attempting to black-cat, however it must be said that they would say anything to get other people's attention. There is always someone stupid enough to believe what field gunners drone and drivel on about. The phrase 'strong of arm, thick of head' describes them accurately.

On most Navy ships there is a Bosun dinghy, occasionally thrown into the sea for (normally) the wardroom to play with. On the *Tartar* and the *Zulu* I had launched it on numerous occasions, recovered it as often, and had known that you would put the thing on a 'shot mat' to drag it to awkward places. The 'shot mat' is normally put by the guns to soften the impact of discharged shells hitting the metal deck, though they have other uses. So when I was asked to move the dinghy, I got all my lads together, lifted it on to the 'shotmat', and we manhandled it to where it needed to go. Somewhere in transit, a ringbolt went through the mat, and made a small hole in the side of the dinghy. This was not a major disaster – it would (on a sensible ship, with sensible shipwrights and sensible officers) have taken perhaps three minutes to mix up some fibreglass resin and apply it. Not that the *Plymouth* contained any of the above. Within minutes of me telling the shipwright of the accidental damage, which I fully expected him to either repair, or give me the makings to do it myself, I found myself once more in front of the OOD, then the Captain, on a charge of negligence. I pointed out that in all my previous years that was how I had achieved moving dinghies, once more I was sent away, with the Captain more red-faced from his shoutings. They were definitely out to get me on that ship.

CHAPTER 32

Dryad, *Again* . . .

Very happily, and finally, I left the *Plymouth* well behind me in Chatham, and started a short spell at *Dryad*, while waiting to get my real draft to HMS *Londonderry*. Many years later, I discovered the *Plymouth* moored at Plymouth as a tourist attraction, and while I tried to convince the then civilian crew that I could find my way round it blindfolded, he still wouldn't let me on for free. Perhaps he had heard it all before. I didn't feel too sad, I had had a bellyful of that ship.

I arrived at *Dryad* one weekday, and was told I was to be quartermaster there. I asked when my first watch was, and was told 'Sunday, Afternoon'. What am I supposed to do till then?' 'Go home if you want' was the reply. I did. I came back Sunday lunchtime, started my Afternoon watch, and within hours of being there a fire alarm lit up in an accommodation block. I piped for the Duty watch, rang the fire brigade and watched the action. Within minutes, the fire was out, the fire brigade arrived, walked round and went home again. I finished my Duty, and went sleepy-byes. Shortly after I finished the Morning on the Monday, and only moments after my tired eyes closed, I was ordered to report to the (retired) martinet, sorry, lieutenant, who allegedly ran *Dryad*. He demanded to know who I was and what I was doing, and moreover – how had I known what to do when the fire was reported. I responded that I had tried to find out what my duties were, but had been told to go home, and that when I had reported there, no one had been at all interested. I also pointed out that it didn't take a moron to work out the alarms, or what to do, or how to do it. We never saw eye to eye after that.

Having spent many hours patrolling *Dryad* on previous visits, it was now my turn to direct the patrols, and woe betide them if I didn't get my coffee – frequently. One day, while we were at a high state of alertness, an officer entering the base got stroppy with the main gate sentry (controlled by me), demanding to be given admittance. I think he had forgotten his ID card, or something. Whatever, he got angrier, and the main gate sentry then radioed me to ask what he should do. We clearly had our orders to not give entrance to anyone without an ID card.

I suggested the sentry make the officer get out of his car while the sentry examined it, minutely, including using the provided mirror-on-a-stick to check beneath the car body, as well as the boot which had to be emptied, and the bonnet, which meant searching the engine compartment and making the officer explain each wire in it. After nearly twenty minutes, the officer was really, really fuming, at which point we finally let him in. I got a further bollocking from the martinet over that one, but us ratings thought it put us ahead – at least the officer didn't try that one on again and he remembered his ID card the next time.

Mitchell from the *Plymouth* was drafted to *Dryad* at the same time, so we continued our friendship, also teaming up with another man, Hall. Eventually, all three of us would end up on the 'Derry, and we grew as thick as the proverbial thieves while waiting ashore. Hall was also married, and as Jan and I lived in Hitchin, which was miles away, we'd go to his house on occasions, to play with his Scalextric (honest!). We would, though, divert past his local to fill up, then take some carry-outs back with us.

CHAPTER 33

HMS Londonderry

I was eventually taken off QM, after months of weeks on, days off, which really did wonders for my married life, and assigned to 'models' at *Dryad*, with the standard blue card. Now I could get home at weekends, if only I could afford to.

Models there were fun, we learned all about the shiny, brand-new, very expensive, computer-assisted radar installed on the 'Derry, and how to use it. It was nearly as good as me at working out courses and speeds. We were assigned to 'staff', which meant listening on the radio between models, recording it all, highlighting idiot bits, then picking holes in whoever it was at the post-exercise debrief.

Time passed quickly, and we left Portsmouth for Rosyth once more, but not before the whole of the 'Derry Ops Room crew and the officers had been to *Dryad* for a week of training. We therefore left for Rosyth en masse, but split up for weekends on the way. This first weekend, Mitch, Hall, me and a couple of others had arranged to get the overnight train from King's Cross, which called at Stevenage, where I got on. The lads had the compartments organized, and the beer, but when we stopped at Peterborough, Mitch and I ran to the nearest hotel for refills. At about midnight, then, we decided to try to get some sleep and crashed out, one on each seat, one in each luggage rack. This was our norm for the overnighter to Edinburgh. However, wise to what happens throughout the night – the continual stopping, the continual door opening and slamming and 'Move over please', we set our 'anti-disturb' traps. This took the form of two tins of vegetable soup, tipped one outside the compartment and one just inside. I don't need to describe what it looked like and, needless to say, we were never disturbed.

The 'Derry was of the same class and therefore the same age as the *Plymouth*, but without armament. She was now a trial ship, testing a new propulsion system (different-shaped propellers), and trialling new radar, which explained the aftermast, much higher than the foremast. And the hutch beneath it, with computers and boffins ensconced inside. For my part, I was detailed for upper deck duties, Leading Hand of the Watch On Deck and i/c of the fo'c's'le, both jobs I thoroughly enjoyed.

Also LHWOD's were Mitch, Hally and Shiner. We would have boat drills every time we went to sea, and as LHWOD it was our job to drive the boat. The first time I took it away, I got back alongside, where Shiner, Hall and Mitch were lining the flight deck, arms behind their backs. To my question 'What the fuck are you doing', came a display of score cards, like they do with ice-skaters, giving me my 'score' (up to a maximum of '5' each) for performing the recovery. I nearly fell out of the whaler laughing. We carried on that tradition, no matter who took the boat away after that. It was deemed that all leading hands should do it, so stewards, cooks, stokers, whoever, all lined up to take the boat away (remember, you dropped the boat into the sea onto a wave, then had to rebuild the disengaging gear before being hoisted again), and getting their score afterwards. It was terrific fun, with lots of laughs on what was a very relaxed ship.

We also did upper deck duties – I was i/c of the fo'c's'le as I said, Shiner was Quarterdeck. One day, both watches (of seamen) had to put up the awnings to make sure they fitted, and went up correctly. Foolishly, the Jimmy announced they didn't look right without the wind to billow them out. Solemnly, Shiner lined every sailor up with his respective nose inches away from the awning, and commanded 'On the count of three – blow. One, Two, Three – BLOW'. We did, and then fell on the floor laughing – even the Jimmy saw the funny side of that one. Not that the Jimmy needed any effort to wind anyone up.

We were still in the Cold War then, and while we were stamping round the North Sea one day, we were approached by an AGI, a Russian 'trawler' bristling with EW gear, determined to take a good snoop. As I said, we were unarmed, unless you counted the 'spud locker', but looked very impressive, with large masts. With great presence of mind, the Jimmy instructed us to drape canvas over the seaboat oar stowage (all in full view of the AGI remember), then put the 'DANGER, LAUNCHER MAY TRAIN WITHOUT WARNING' signs (left over from when we had teeth) on the stowages. The AGI obviously felt it had a scoop here, and made several passes with cameras going at full steam while we sat still for them. I wonder what they made of it? Or whether they knew we were winding them up? Or that we had a new and secret propulsion system.

It was nice to get back to Rosyth, to recall old runs and old stamping grounds, though at the drop of a hat we'd volunteer for all sorts of courses in the south, just to get the weekends at each end of it. I went on one to maintain the ship's onboard liferafts, with their automatic pressure releases, and the ship's stock of lifejackets. It also meant learning how to board rafts and repair them, which was extremely useful for me, and especially useful for the RN, who by then knew I was nearing the end of my twelve-year contract, which I was not likely to renew. It did, though, guarantee two weekends at home – one at each end of the course.

In my duties as LH of the fo'c's'le, I was in charge of it, but second to the officer, whose name I forget. One of the highlights of my job was that I was allowed to work the cable without anyone standing behind me saying 'not like that' or 'you're not allowed to do that – you're only a rating'. This came about one day when the officer was late getting there, and I had to get the anchors (hooks) ready to drop, as all ships did at special sea duty stations, just in case of emergencies. I requested permission to work the cable, and was told yes. I got the anchors ready to go, capstans steaming – the lot. I was greatly pleased with myself. The officer (therefore 'the bridge') would subsequently allow me to do it without interference. A further job, when getting alongside, was passing heaving lines and attaching mooring ropes to them, which were dragged ashore. We'd then tighten these up before securing them. The trick was in knowing when to pay out and when to take in. Assuming that the wire cables (springs) would take the strain of a 2,500-ton warship stretching it, it was then my job to gauge the strain by attempting to depress the spring with my foot, listening for it singing, assessing how much more strain it could take before parting and killing most of the handlers. I got good at that, and never damaged anybody. Also, the headropes, made from nylon, would crack alarmingly as pressure came on, worrying the hell out of anyone nearby. I'd nonchalantly kick the rope again, deciding when to give and when to take in on the capstan, winching and inching the ship nearer to the jetty to allow securing as directed by the bridge. I used to love doing that. I was also greatly elated by being allowed and trusted to do it.

We also used to set up for all evolutions such as RASing. On a normal ship it needed at least a chief petty officer, but the 'Derry had four extremely capable leading seamen, any of whom could at the drop of a hat do any of the jobs normally only done by the aforementioned chiefs. We had a Buffer, a petty officer, but he knew he could let us get on with it, and did. It ran extremely well, and we always did it professionally, and correctly and never, ever fouled up or took advantage. Then there were all the other tasks, such as the constant painting and repainting, cleaning, washing, deck scrubbing, and the hosing-down contests between 'parts of ship'. We would hand out make and mends like sweets, which, it seemed to us only encouraged our juniors to work harder, and we wondered why it had never been tried before. It made sense to us – put the time in, get the time off, at home, because they were RAs.

We actually had a banyan one Sunday at Rosyth. A gang of us took the seaboat away, with some crates of ale we 'found', a couple of loaves, and two cooked legs of lamb nicked from the galley while the chefs' backs were turned. We motored to just past the Rail Bridge, got near the shore, threw the anchor over the side and sat in the sun all afternoon, fishing, yarning and emptying tins until just before we were too drunk to drive it back.

Apart from the sudden training courses we used to volunteer for, we discovered that the RN was holding a fleet-wide tug-of-war contest. Several of us put a team together, and commenced training. This involved many things, among them running daily from the ship to the gym at *Cochrane*, often being dive-bombed by a rogue shite-hawk that lived on a building and which seemed to hate humans. We got him, though it took us a while. We'd then exercise vigorously and run back to the ship. We'd also pit our strength against many more people than the eight of us, always winning (well, nearly). Just to ensure more weight 'redistribution', we scrounged NBCD suits made from clear polythene. We discovered that while wearing them we would sweat heavily, therefore – lose weight – more properly 'redistribute' our surplus bits of relaxed muscle (fat) into proper muscle. That was the theory at least. Then we'd get changed, go ashore, drink copious amounts of 'heavy', and eat haggis suppers or Chinese take-aways. Eventually, when the big day came, the Scottish Command teams all met at *Cochrane*, where we pulled every bit of competition right away. We were therefore Scottish Command Champions, with the medals to prove it. As the PTI was in our mess, and all the other leading hands, he convinced the powers that be to feed us special diets on top of all the above mentioned. We therefore got steaks on demand, which was great, while it lasted!

As champions there we were then able to compete at the next level, i.e., the whole of the Navy. With great anticipation we set off for Portsmouth again on the train, with the obvious weekend en route. We then reached the playing fields at *Dryad*, where the events were to be held. We got through the first round, then went ashore to celebrate that. We went to Sid's place, and imbibed the old wine mixture, then found our way back via Dot's, then to bed. When we crawled out the following morning, Mitch and me were summoned to the Regulating Office, where we were interrogated about an alleged incident the previous evening. Apparently, a Reliant Robin, innocently parked within the base gave the owner a surprise when he inspected it – it had miraculously overturned itself during the night. Imagine that, trying to blame me and Mitch for it.

Whatever, it must have affected our performance in the tugawug, as we were knocked out in the second round. The week's jolly in Pompey was therefore cut short, and we returned to Rosyth with our tails between our legs. Well, until we got on the train, and all mustered at the buffet.

We used to the Daily Orders on an old typewriter, then print them out on an old Gestetner, before distributing them around all messes, offices etc. We had a strange habit, though, of slipping naughty bits into the orders, vertically. For instance, a separator line might be all FFFFFF across the page, which looked quite attractive, but if the next line was UUUU and the next was CCC, then KKK, then OOOOOO, followed by two lines of FFFF – you begin to see what I mean. On a Friday, the lines would spell POETS (Piss Off Early Tomorrow's Saturday), FOREST (Fuck Off Reasonably Early Saturday Tomorrow) or FUFUFFFH (Fed Up, Fucked Up, Far From Fucking Home). Funnily, while most of the junior ratings saw through it, no one else ever did, or if they did they never told us.

Eventually, we sailed from Rosyth back down south, back to Pompey at last, but via Hull where we had a quick weekend. During this weekend, we, as usual, challenged local teams to play us at rugby, so it was with hangovers that we turned up to play, I think, a local police team. Mitch and me used to play 4 and 5. We changed, groggily, then mooched out on to the pitch, almost ready to play. Mitch still had one trick up his sleeve. He waited until both teams were gathered for the 'riot act', walked over to the ref, indicated a hideous Neanderthal throwback on second row of the opposing side, and in full earshot of everyone, including the caveman, said, 'Before I play against that – I want to hear it talking first'. We collapsed laughing, the caveman got stroppy and we ended up playing 'dodge the fist' in all the scrums. That was a dirty game. By full time, though, we were all best of friends and celebrated as only rugby playing matelots know how. At least, we didn't get nicked while we were there.

We recommissioned in Portsmouth, and entertained our wives and girlfriends in our cramped quarters. One thing about recommissioning, or any other major event in the ship's calendar, was that the food was outstanding. Especially when all the leading hands were billeted together on the 'Derry, including the cooks and stewards. That day, we were waited on and got the best food (after the wardroom).

My last few months were taken up with my EVT (extra vocational training) course, which everyone leaving the forces gets. I had expressed a desire to get involved with computers, having seen how powerful they were, and applied for a six-week course in Wandsworth, which I knew I had no chance of getting on. There had been a cancellation shortly before I applied, and I found to my amazement that I was placed on it. Unfortunately, this meant that I had to live at home for six weeks (with my wife – remember her?)! I commuted from Hitchin to Wandsworth daily, while the Navy paid for my travel, oh and they also paid me much, much extra to live at home. I couldn't believe my luck. I even met an old mate from the *Tartar* on the course, so we spent six weeks doing lectures and site visits, with the obligatory pub visit each and every lunchtime, with a special one on the Friday, prior to sliding off home early. I will point out that when I left for the course my regulation haircut was longer than normal, due to having avoided the on-board cementhead. After the course, I deliberately went back to the 'Derry with my hair even longer, solely to wind up that same cementhead. My hair survived slightly longer than it took the top of his head to blow off.

ROMFT is a word every tar will be familiar with – it is the word that appears on the guitar of one of the members of, I think, 'The Spinners'. I wonder if he knows what it means? ROMFT is the expression used by a disgruntled jack after, for instance, he has had to get up at 4 in the morning to check the mooring ropes, after some panicky, junior officer of the day has decided, wrongly, that the wires need slacking off. This evolution usually takes place three hours after he last got you out to tighten them. Or when he is roused for Action Stations minutes after he has finally got his head down. ROMFT stands for 'Roll On My Fucking Time'. It has been quoted for years, and obviously means 'please let me out of the Navy, soon'. ROMFT ratings are created as soon as they see an end to their naval career, say after their D-By-P (discharge by purchase) has been granted or when they are within months (or even years) of the end of their contracted service. ROMFT ratings usually begin to suffer from chronically severe RDP (run-down period), and run down, quickly. I always maintained that when (no, not 'if', but, categorically 'when') I went outside, I would sweep roads rather than re-enlist. 'You'll be back', or 'You'll sign on again within a year' was the favourite wind-up for those too far away from their own discharge, and, yes, more than a little jealous. I swore vehemently they'd never see me again. Sorry fellas, I miss you all, some more than others, but I was right, I had the last laugh.

CHAPTER 34

My Final Farewell to Arms

It is not possible to describe my feelings during my last few naval days, apart from a growing elation. Summing up this large part of my life, career and personal development would cover attributes such as pride in oneself and the Royal Navy: absolute professionalism – being able to do anything with any equipment at the drop of a hat under any conditions or circumstances; the ability and eventually the willingness to do anything for one's mates, but not necessarily for anyone else; and the comradeship that totally ignored anyone else from any other walk of life, ship, or organization. These qualities would apply through thick and thin, hell and high water. And the dedication we all had to see a job through, whether we had volunteered, or been volunteered. We used to say 'the quicker you stop moanin', and get it done, the faster you get back to bed'.

Finally, you would always know that although your best oppo had just called you all the bastards under the sun, and a few more choice names besides, and had then threatened you either with physical violence or a chair, all because you'd just given him a whitewash at uckers and then accused him of not being able to take a joke, but you'd know that minutes later he'd be crying like a baby on your shoulder because he'd just got a 'Dear John' ('. . . I don't love you anymore . . .') or worse. And that ten minutes after that, you'd be poncing a tenner off him to go ashore, finally asking him to 'stand in' for you, while you went ashore and pissed his money against some wall, ensuring you always had enough to bring him some big-eats back, even if it was by then cold, and that you shook him at three in the morning, unable to comprehend why he was now telling you to 'Fuck off 'n getcher head down, yer pissed'. Now that is comradeship, that is what mates are for and that is what the Navy is all about.

However, my day finally came, and I left the 'Derry and my mates, who all fell in, piped me over the side and saluted me as I left for the short fast-black journey from the dockyard to the dispersal section of HMS *Nelson*. I handed in all my gear (over a three-day period), gave back my ID card (but renewed my passport, just in case I needed it in the future), had an exit medical, assured them I didn't need the dentist, and left the base with just my grip filled with my remaining personal possessions and civvies. I was thinking about not having to shepherd pissed matelots any more, not staying awake half the night on a cold gangway, not having to get up at oh-six-dubs to weigh anchor then RAS. Now I was going into a normal job, to a normal life with my wife, who I had hardly seen since we married, and looking forward to getting up at sensible times. Strangely, the hardest thing I had to adapt to, was getting out of the habit of going into a pub and getting as pissed as I could as cheaply as possible in the shortest space of time. It took years to break out of the habit of knocking a pint back in two or three hits.

I strode – no not marched – strode out of the gates of *Nelson*, turned left, ambled in a very leisurely manner up the road, past all my old haunts, take-aways and food stalls, en route to Portsmouth Town station, and without looking back, I boarded the train, with my final, free, Navy issue one-way ticket to Hitchin. While I was on that final free train ride, I left behind all those memories, all those escapades, all those mates, all those experiences, all those runs ashore and all those buzzes.

However, although I was Jack, and really didn't give a shit about anyone or anything at the time, I get the shivers down my back every time I hear the naval hymn ('For Those In Peril On The Sea'), and even now the tears roll copiously down my face whenever I hear the Last Post or think about Poppy Day.

You see, although I was safely installed in 'civvy street' by then, I lost mates on the *Sheffield* and *Coventry* and *Amazon*, and I'll never forget, nor will I forgive Argentina for that, but I'll always remember my mates. The peace treaty was signed on the *Plymouth*, if you remember, and a bomb actually went right through where I used to sleep.

Two final things. First, the answer to the question about what runs from for'ard to aft on the port side and vice versa was pennant numbers, and the ship's nameplate. There you are, naval expert, and you didn't know that!

And the second thing – a final sea story. You know when you and your kids screamed 'Oggy Oggy Oggy' whenever Devonport did their field-gun run at the Royal Tournament? Well, I have to tell you that phrase comes at the end of the filthiest (lyric wise) song we ever used to sing, containing subject matter ranging from camels' orifices to tramps, paint to people from Cornwall, and Aladdin and his famous magic lamp to Indian currency. I leave it to your imagination. And if you don't believe that, you can always ask your mate's uncle, and if he doesn't know, then you know he really was making it up all that time, don't you.

Glossary

Aggie Weston's	The Royal Sailor's Rest. Originally created by (Dame) Agnes Weston as a temperance hostel for ratings, and usually abbreviated to 'Aggie's'.
AX	The quarterdeck. If the fo'c's'le is FX, then the quarterdeck, at the opposite end of the ship and known in Tudor times as the Aftercastle, is the AX.
Bends	Knots.
Bins	Abbreviation for binoculars.
Black cat	Sea story.
Black pig	Submarine.
Booties	Bootnecks, or Royal Marines.
Budgie	Helicopter, *see also* Parrot.
Buffer	The Chief Bosun's Mate, a senior petty officer or chief petty officer. In charge of all seamanship operations on the Upper Deck.
Burbs	Short for Burberry or any raincoat.
Burma Road	A passageway running from fore to aft below decks.
BWH	Both Watches (of the) Hands.
CDF	Common-sense (work it out).
Clanky	Any marine engineer; more specifically, a former stoker who has trained to become a mechanician – a half-price 'tiffy' (see below).
Closed up	Closed up at Action Stations means all ready to defend the ship.
Cockies	Cockroaches.
Compo	Ration pack.
Crabfats, or Crabs	Members of the Royal Air Force. The colour of the RAF uniform, introduced in 1918, is supposed to be similar to the colour of the ointment (known as crabfat) issued to the troops in the trenches, which was applied to deal with body lice or crabs.
Crash out	To sleep; to wash by hand.
Daddy-D	Captain D, the Captain commanding a destroyer squadron (or a frigate squadron.)
Desert wellies	Suede ankle boots, as worn by the Eighth Army in the Second World War.
DF	Duty Free, as in booze, cigarettes, but mostly the former; Direction Finding, as in HFDF, or Huffduff,

	High Frequency Direction Finding, or SHFDF, Shuffduff, Super. Note, 'duff' means defective.
DI	Drill Instructor.
Divisions	A parade, with all the ship's company mustered by divisions.
Double, to	To run, at double-quick time.
DQs	Detention Quarters – the Navy's own prison, until recently in Portsmouth.
Dubs	As in 04 dubs – Oh-four-double-O means 4 a.m.
Fanny	A large mess utensil – the derivation is from 'Fanny Adams', but it's a long way round!
Fast black	A taxi cab.
FES (Fez)	Far East Station, usually referred to as Fez.
Fo'c'sles	Pointed ends of ships.
FPB	Fast Patrol Boat.
G6	Gas turbine power plant.
Gemini	An inflatable, semi-rigid dinghy used as a seaboat.
Gizzit	A contraction of 'Give us it'.
Greeny	Any electrical engineer.
Grippo	A generous person who pays for all your 'entertainment', usually a local or Navy fan.
Guzz	Plymouth – there are as many explanations for this name as there are pubs in the city.
Hey-diddle-diddle	Rhyming slang for the Middle (watch).
Hitches	Complex knots.
'Ho'	The Navy's executive order to stand at attention. From being 'A-tten-shun', the 'shun' rising to a squeak (which would carry), it became 'A-tten-hun', then 'hun', then 'ho'.
IS	Internal Security.
Jack-proof	If it can't be bust by the average matelot, it must be good.
Jackstay	The line sent across between two ships alongside, about 150 ft apart, along which men and equipment can be transferred.
Jimmy	The First Lieutenant (aka Jimmy the One).
Joss/Jossman	The Master at Arms, or one of the regulating petty officers, the ship's police, not the best-loved ratings on board.
Liberty boat	Used to get you from ship to shore, and back, for leave.
Liberty men	Anyone who can go ashore for leave.
Make and Break (M&M)	Nothing to do with electrics – slang for 'make and mend', originally meaning a sailor's free time to 'make and mend clothes' and now any free time. You got/get an m&m if you had stood the Middle watch the previous night.

MFV	Motor Fishing Vessel – a small naval tender, based on the design of a small fishing boat.
Mod Plod	The MOD Police service, who provided security in the dockyards.
NBCD	Nuclear, Biological, Chemical Defence.
Nutty	Any chocolate, from 'Fruit and Nut'.
Oggy	Tiddy-oggy, or Cornish pasty.
Oppo	Particular friend, from opposite number – the chap in the opposite watch, who had the same duties as you.
Ovies	Overalls.
P7R	A medical category, meaning temporarily unfit for service at sea.
Parrot	Short for Paraffin Parrot, or helicopter.
PE	Plastic Explosive.
POS	Part of Ship.
PTA	Pilotless Target Aircraft.
Pusser	The Navy.
PWO	Principal Warfare Officer – the officer running 'the battle' in the ship's Operations Room, in the absence of the Captain.
RA	Ration Allowance – if you were RA, it meant that you were living at home and in receipt of RA, rather than being victualled on board.
Rabbit	Formerly, a piece of dockyard material unlawfully 'borrowed' for one's own purposes – by extension, a rabbit-job came to mean a semi-official job done by the dockyard for one's greater comfort/efficiency on board; in turn, this was extended to mean any present taken home for one's family and friends. Also used as a verb, 'to go rabbiting' – shopping for presents or going on the scrounge.
RAS	Properly, an acronym for Replenishment At Sea, but by extension, to not steal, but permanently acquire what wasn't yours in the first place.
RatRat	Endearing term for HMS *Tartar*.
RDP	Run-Down Period – the period towards the end of a commission, or of one's engagement, when a couldn't-care-less attitude tended to develop.
RFA	Royal Fleet Auxiliary.
ROMFT	Roll On My F(lipping) Twelve. In the days when one signed on for a standard twelve-year engagement, this was a cry frequently heard when one had 'had' the Andrew up to here!
RP	Radar Plotter.
R & R	Rest and Recreation.

Scribes	A writer rating – masters of clerical and accounting procedures – until they got your pay wrong one payday!
SNLR	Services No Longer Required.
Still, the	The alert made on a bosun's call.
Tea-boat	Non-floating – the tea-boat was the contents of a corner of the Ops Room, or wherever, where tea, coffee or kye were on the brew permanently.
Tiffies	Artificers – the Navy's skilled technicians.
Trooped	Charged with an offence.
Troughing	Eating, greedily.
Waffoos	Fleet Air Arm personnel, originally WAFU – Wet And F— Useless.
Weekly war	A pretend war in which many ships and aircraft operated together over a period of days to 'fight' hostile forces from other units.
Windies, The	The West Indies.
Windy Burbs	Short windproof jacket, *see* Burbs.
WOD	Watch on Deck.

Index